MAYA RUINS IN CENTRAL AMERICA IN COLOR

Illustration 1. Maya area

Maya Ruins
in Central America
in Color

Tikal, Copán, and Quiriguá

William M. Ferguson and John Q. Royce

Foreword by Linda Schele

The University of New Mexico Press / Albuquerque

Library of Congress Cataloging in Publication Data

Ferguson, William M.
  Maya ruins in Central America in color.

Bibliography: p.
  Includes index.
  1. Mayas—Antiquities.   2. Indians of Central
America—Antiquities.   3. Central America—Antiquities.
I. Royce, John Q.   II. Title.
F1435.F39   1984   972.8′01   83-14750
ISBN 0-8263-0688-8

Contents

Foreword

I first met Bill Ferguson and John Royce in 1976
when, at the recommendation of Dr. Michael
Coe, they asked me to share with them what I
knew of Palenque's art and architecture. I agreed
to help them in their first book, *Maya Ruins of
Mexico in Color,* and began a lasting friendship
with and respect for them. At the time of their
first venture, neither of them knew much about
the Maya, except that they were deeply im-
pressed by the remaining art of this American
culture and that they wanted to spend their time
and personal resources in sharing the Maya with
other people. They began to gather material to
produce a book on the Maya which would feature aerial photography, but unlike the authors
of many other popular, large-format books, and
even many scholarly books, they were determined to include the latest understanding of the

Maya, rather than to parrot ideas that had been
fossilized in the literature since the early nineteenth century. In this context, they contacted
me and other scholars in the field to join our
expertise and opinions with the photography
and maps of their own efforts.

In the time since our cooperative work on the
first book, Bill Ferguson and John Royce have
become regular attendants at major conferences,
and in 1979–80, Bill Ferguson spent a year as a
special student at the Universities of Texas at
Austin and San Antonio, where he took courses
with Jacinto Quirarte, Clemency Coggins, and
myself. Now Bill Ferguson and John Royce have
embarked on this new labor, which follows the
format of the first book, with the addition of
much more detail in iconography and hieroglyphic writing. As with the previous publi-

cation, the authors have been in intensive consultation with the professional archaeologists who have done major work at each of the sites included. As a result, this book—like the last—offers information and insights not previously published.

Both this book and the authors' last book fulfill an important function in the world of Precolumbian studies because they provide a vehicle for public and popular access to a period of history and glorious art in the past of the Americas of which we as a people have little or no consciousness. In the best of all possible worlds, books for popular audiences should be written by the scholars who work on the Maya, but in the real world, these scholars do not have time to produce such books; and a great many of us simply do not have the skill nor the desire to write in understandable and simple language. By spending their time and funds and by consulting with us, Bill Ferguson and John Royce not only give the general public access to the history of the Maya, but they provide a voice to professionals, such as myself, that likely would not be heard in any other media. I congratulate them on their accomplishment and sincerely hope that such cooperative efforts between the professionals and the lay admirers of the Maya will continue in the future. It is important for modern people to become conscious in a much more profound way that the history of the Americas did not begin in 1492.

    —Linda Schele
       University of Texas at Austin

Preface

Maya Ruins in Central America in Color includes the ancient classic Maya centers of Tikal, Copán, and Quiriguá. Of the many other Maya sites in Central America, none can compare with the tropical beauty, architectural grandeur, and the historical and artistic importance of the carved stelae and hieroglphic inscriptions found at each of these sites.

During the halcyon days of the Classic Maya (A.D. 250 to 900), Tikal, Copán, and Quiriguá were great centers for religious ceremony, and political and commercial activity; they were also the seat of residence and power for the kings and nobles of the Maya. Now each site has been partially restored and the ruins made into a national park, each containing a plethora of buildings and monuments.

Tikal thrusts its massive temple roof combs above the lush jungle of northeast Guatemala. It was the largest of the Petén lowland Maya cities. Located in the low mountain country of northwest Honduras, Copán bears the appellation "Athens of the Classic Maya cities" because of its magnificent sculpture. The Quiriguá ruins are nestled in an island of primeval forest in the midst of a sea of banana plants, located just off the main highway near Puerto Barrios, Guatemala.

The ancient Maya Indians developed the most advanced civilization in the New World. They refined and embellished the cultural achievements of the Olmec and of others who preceded them, to produce one of the world's great "neolithic" cultures.

With no beast of burden and no industrial wheel, the Maya workmen built their huge platforms, buildings, pyramids, and temples using rubble fill borne on their backs, a basketful at a time. Artisans dressed the stone and carved the reliefs and inscriptions without metal tools. These Classic Maya also produced a written language—the most sophisticated one in the New World; a calendar of incredible accuracy and complexity; a vigesimal (base 20) numeration system, which included the zero—a concept undiscovered by the ancient Greeks or Romans; and inscriptions in stone and painted ceramics of grace and beauty.

The noble families of the Maya created a life-style for themselves, the accoutrements of which were unexcelled anywhere in the world (with the possible exception of Byzantium or Imperial Cathay) between the fall of Rome and Charlemagne. A part of this life-style was their cruel and sanguinary practices (by our standards) of ritual torture and human sacrifice and excruciatingly painful self-inflicted bloodletting.

All of the significant buildings and monuments discussed in this book have been photographed in color and described in detail. Many of the photographs are aerial views, which bring into perspective the interrelationship of the structures within the site and the intrinsic beauty of the setting. The 275 color photographs were chosen for their emphasis on architectural and iconographic detail. For the most part, the stelae are portraits of rulers, most of whom have been identified. Much of the symbolism that appears on these stone shafts and altars has been interpreted. This book contains more than eighty drawings of inscriptions and monuments of Tikal, Copán, and Quiriguá, with the iconography identified—much of which has never before been published.

This volume is composed of a series of descriptions and essays, any one of which is substantially complete within itself, with illustrations, photographs, and text forming a unit. One can read it from start to finish, or use it as a reference. The introduction provides a general background of the Classic Maya of the lowlands (the area north and east of the mountains from Honduras to Mexico). The material discussed includes the results of research carried out through 1983; much of it represents breakthroughs in the understanding of the Maya. This book is a follow-up volume to *Maya Ruins of Mexico in Color* (1977); the format is similar, but new material is presented.

While we are not anthropologists, we have attempted to keep abreast of the discipline. In this work, we have endeavored to convert the erudite professional books and papers into layman's language without destroying the thrust and sense of the material. In addition to this research, we were given personal instruction, assistance, and guidance by a number of Mayanists. To each of them we express our appreciation.

Linda Schele of the University of Texas at Austin reviewed the work in progress several times and read the manuscript. Without her help this volume would not have been possible. It was Linda Schele's willingness to share her profound knowledge of the Maya—particularly the iconography and epigraphy—that enabled us to present much of the information about the religious beliefs of the Maya. Christopher Jones and Claude Baudez were of great assistance in the preparation of the Tikal and Copán material. In addition, we wish to acknowledge with thanks the assistance given us by Arthur Miller, David A. Freidel, William R. Coe, Clemency Coggins, Jacinto Quirarte, Marvin Cohodas, Francis Robicsek, Nicholas Hellmuth, Wendy Ashmore, Peter D. Harrison, David H. Kelley, George Stuart, Merle Greene Robertson, and last but certainly not least, Andrea Stone and Dorie J. Reents.

Unless otherwise noted, the photographs and drawings are our own. We also extend our special thanks to Lisa Ferguson, niece of one of the authors, for her drawings of stelae. These drawings were made from photographs by the authors with some additions and corrections by Linda Schele. We also thank Michael D. Coe, whose assistance made our first book possible and without which we could not have done this one.

—William M. Ferguson
—John Q. Royce
    Wellington, Kansas
    1984

x

MAYA RUINS IN CENTRAL AMERICA IN COLOR

Introduction

An Introduction to the Classic Maya

As an introduction to the ancient Maya, we have prepared a series of short discussions of Maya culture. These two dozen sections are designed to give the reader a background for understanding the people who created the magnificent art and architecture pictured in the *Maya Ruins in Central America in Color*. These summaries are based on the work of respected authorities on the Maya.

The authors are not academicians; this book is not designed as a text book, but rather as a guide for the traveler, art lover, and the Maya aficionado. Various theories and viewpoints concerning Maya civilization are presented, not only to acquaint the reader with the history of the Maya, but to illustrate the complexity of issues of concern to scholars on Maya studies. There is much disagreement among Mayanists, and the "truth" may never be known. While this text has been written with a minimum of footnoting, the authors have elected to follow the consensus of Maya scholars where possible, and have relied heavily on Dr. Linda Schele.

Maya Antecedents

The ancestors of the Maya and all other American Indians came to the Western Hemisphere from Asia. As hunters and gatherers, the forebearers of the Indians came in waves out of Asia beginning near the end of the Wisconsin ice age that ended about ten thousand years ago. These nomadic Asiatics pressed eastward across the land bridge, which (because the water trapped in the great glaciers of the ice age had lowered the level of the world's oceans) then connected Siberia with Alaska and followed the ice-free corridors south across what is now Canada into mid-North America, Central, and South America. It is not possible to determine the precise time that the peopling of the New World occurred, but it is now believed that the period of migrations were from about 16,000 to 11,000 B.C. However, there is some evidence to indicate that man arrived in the Western Hemisphere as early as 35,000 years ago (Adams 1977b: 59).

Los Tapiales in the highlands of Guatemala is the earliest site so far discovered. Recently new discoveries by Richard S. MacNeish, S. Jeffrey K. Wilkerson, and Antoinette Nelken-Turner in 1980 suggested that the Maya forebearers may have lived in the Belize area as early as 9000 B.C. MacNeish says the oldest sites indicate that these ancient Indians lived from about 9000 B.C. to 7500 B.C. as nomadic hunters of big game. By 4200 B.C., they settled along the coast of Belize and developed a fishing culture. Then, as the population increased, these people migrated inland and established a sedentary farming culture, planting corn, beans, and squash.

The 1978 excavations in the Puuc area, near the Uxmal ruins in Yucatán, Mexico, revealed occupancy in the Loltún cave going back to 2000 B.C.

The earliest remains from the Maya lowlands have been found near the Pasión River that date about 1000 B.C. Xe (prounounced "shay") and Eb pottery discovered in several areas indicate that during these times the Petén, in the lowlands, was occupied by people in scattered farming communities.

Cuello, in northern Belize, is the site excavated by Norman Hammond indicating continuous occupation from about 2500 B.C. These people, Hammond says, were culturally Maya and were the earliest known direct antecedents of the Classic Maya. The Cuello evidence has modified the earlier concept that the Classic Maya culture was a composite of earlier cultures that stemmed principally from the Gulf Coast Olmecs.

The Olmec civilization (1200–900 B.C.) certainly influenced the later Maya culture, but probably not directly.

Michael Coe says the Izapian civilization occupies the middle ground between the Olmec and the Maya. The Izapa site is located on the Pacific coast in southwestern Mexico near the Guatemalan border. The Maya stela-altar complex, some of the Maya deities, and Classic Maya costume details probably were transmitted through Izapa.

In addition to Izapa, Abaj Takalik, Ocós, and El Baúl, located on the Pacific slopes of Guatemala, are sites that inherited Olmec cultural attributes and, after development and modification, passed them along to the Maya. These attributes include stela art, calendrics, the bar-and-dot numbering system, and, possibly, language. Much of the pyramid-plaza architectural technique which later flowered in Maya Classic times were developed in the Cuello area of Belize.

The extent to which these cultural attributes were distributed throughout the Maya area by cultural contacts or by the actual incursion of people may never be known. It is known, however, that by the beginning of Middle Preclassic times (1000 B.C.), the Maya area from Yucatán, Mexico, to Honduras was occupied by people who were the antecedents of the Classic Maya.

The geographic region occupied by the ancient Maya can be divided into three general areas: the Pacific Coast and Guatemalan highlands, the central Maya lowlands, and the northern Yucatán peninsula.

The Pacific Coast and Guatemalan highlands was an important area during the Preclassic development of Maya civilization (300 B.C.–A.D. 250) and was one of the areas that felt the influence of Olmec culture. In addition, the cultural impact from Teotihuacán (in the Valley of Mexico) during the Early Classic period seems to have caused these highland Maya to develop independently of the culture of the central Maya lowlands.

The central Maya lowlands included the rain forest of western Honduras, the Guatemalan department of Petén, Belize, and the Mexican states

Illustration 2.   Major topographical features and cultural areas.

3

of Quintana Roo, Campeche, Tabasco, and Chiapas. Among Maya sites in this area that have been excavated are Copán, Quiriguá, Tikal, Uaxactún, Mirador, Yaxchilán, Piedras Negras, Xunántunich, Altun Há, and Palenque. The principal elements that distinguish the Classic Maya—temples with corbeled vaulting, hieroglyphic writing, and the Maya Long Count calendar—were developed in the central Maya lowlands.

Recent excavations of early sites, including Mirador, Cerros, and Lamanaí, have shown that this area was populated with major cities in Preclassic times and that much Early Classic iconography developed at these sites.

The third geographic region of the ancient Maya was in the northern Yucatán peninsula. Major excavated sites include Edzná, Chichén Itzá, Dzibilchaltún, Mayapán, and the Puuc sites of Uxmal, Kabah, Sayil, Xlapak, and Labná.

By the beginning of the Classic period (A.D. 250), the Maya occupied a large part of Mesoamerica: present-day Guatemala (except portions of its Pacific coastal strip); Belize; the western portion of Honduras; northern El Salvador; and the Mexican states of Yucatán, Campeche, Quintana Roo, Tabasco (except for an area on the west), and the major part of Chiapas.

The Olmec Connection

During the nineteenth century, it was argued that Classic Maya civilization could not have been indigenous—that it must have been subject to some outside influences. Numerous theories, some of which are still in vogue today, were postulated to show that the civilization was the result of a foreign incursion. The lost tribes of Israel, the Phoenicians, the Egyptians, the Japanese, and even extraterrestrials have been named as the source of Classic Maya culture. Compelling evidence exists for none of these theories, but some evidence suggests that the Classic Maya of the lowlands were influenced by a number of earlier Mesoamerican cultures, including the Olmec, and the peoples of Izapa, Teotihuacán, Belize, and the Guatemalan highlands.

The Olmec, creators of the huge stone heads wearing football helmet-like headdresses, were Mesoamerica's first civilization. The Olmec had two great bursts of development—the San Lorenzo phase (1200–900 B.C.) and the La Venta phase (900–400 B.C.). This culture, centered south of the Tuxtla Mountains near Minatitlan, Veracruz, Mexico, was the primary contributor to the development of Maya civilization.

Most Mayanists trace the developmental connection between Olmec and Maya through the cultural intermediary of Izapa—a site well worth visiting because of the monuments still in place—on the Pacific coast of Mexico near Tapachula, on the Guatemalan border. Izapan cultural development continued at the highland Guatemala site of Kaminaljuyú.

Among Classic Maya cultural characteristics traceable to the Olmec is the manifest power of individual leaders as illustrated in Olmec art. The great stone heads of the Olmec portrayed individual chiefs, whereas the Maya represented their rulers on upright stone slabs, or stelae. Another aspect of this cultural trait is the representation of the capture and public humiliation of captives. Other Maya traits apparently derived from the Olmec are the presence of elaborate headdresses, the ball game, the bloodletting ceremony, or autosacrifice, ceremonial incense, ceremonial bars of office, and the bar-and-dot numeration system. Many Mayanists feel the Maya language also came from the Olmec.

Among the most impressive cultural achievements of the Maya were the calendar and the glyphic writing system, which were probably refined from a system developed by the successors to the Olmec prior to the Maya Classic period, which began about A.D. 250. Olmec concern for monumentality in architecture was further developed by Maya architects who incorporated additional innovations, such as the corbeled vault and extensive use of plaster floor and wall covering. Thus, while a distinctive Maya civilization was developing, the debt to its predecessors is undeniable.

Maya History

Maya history can be divided into three periods: Preclassic or Formative (2500 B.C.–A.D. 250); Classic, which is the period covered by this book (A.D. 250–900); and Postclassic (A.D. 900–1540).

The Preclassic can be divided into Early Preclassic (2500–1000 B.C.), Middle Preclassic (1000–300 B.C.), Late Preclassic (300 B.C.–A.D. 50), and Protoclassic (A.D. 50–250).

The earliest people in Mesoamerica were nomadic hunters and gatherers who lived on game animals, seeds, fruits, and nuts. Beginning about 5000 B.C., these nomadic people began to domesticate corn and somewhat later beans and squash. By 2500 B.C. they learned to make pottery. The people no longer had to move about following game; they could raise and store food. They gradually became farmers.

Until Norman Hammond's work at Cuello in northern Belize, there were no known Maya sites in the lowlands earlier than 900 B.C. At Cuello the radiocarbon dates show continuous occupation from 2500 B.C., thus pushing back the beginnings of the Maya Preclassic and showing a continuity of Maya development from then until the arrival of the Spaniards in the early 1500s, for a total of four thousand years. Today some two million Maya Indians live in Yucatán and Chiapas in Mexico, Guatemala, and Belize. These modern Maya have cultural attributes and language that are directly traceable to the ancient Maya.

The Cuello excavations revealed a continuous development during Preclassic times. Corn was genetically improved from finger-size ears to high-yielding varieties. Jade was imported. Sandstone manos and metates were brought in from the Maya Mountains a hundred miles to the south. Formal burials in graves were cut into the bedrock, with jewelry and pottery interred with the deceased.

Ceremonial structures were constructed at Cuello prior to 2000 B.C. Platforms topped with timber-framed buildings set around a plastered courtyard built in Early Preclassic times were the architectural forerunners of the great pyramid-temple complexes of Classic times. Also the excavations suggest that Early Preclassic Cuello may have had elite residences built adjacent to the ceremonial areas, suggesting that a governing elite, or at least a ranked society, was in place prior to 1000 B.C.

Buildings on oval-ended platforms with poles supporting a thatched roof were erected at Cuello as early as 2000 B.C. in a manner very similar to houses built by the Maya today. Single door, oval-shaped, thatched-roofed Maya houses were constructed as early as 1600 B.C.

The pottery of Cuello is of the Early Preclassic Swazey complex. Hammond reports that even the earliest layers at Cuello (2500 B.C.) reveal technically sophisticated pottery (Hammond 1982a: 114).

The excavations at Cuello demonstrate that by the end of the Early Preclassic (1000 B.C.) the pyramid-plaza ceremonial architecture, the design of Maya houses, food staples, good pottery, a governing hierarchy, and trade in luxury and utilitarian goods all were well established and central to the later Classic Maya culture.

Mamon, the pottery style of the Middle Preclassic, has been found throughout the Maya area from Dzibilchaltún in northern Yucatán to Kaminaljuyú in the Guatemala highlands, and is evidence that there was heavy population growth after 1000 B.C. of people linked together by a common Maya culture. As part of this expanding population, numerous Maya sites were first settled during this time, including Tikal, Uaxactún, Altar de Sacrificios, and Seibal in the Maya lowlands and Kaminaljuyú in the highlands.

Hammond's excavations at Cuello demonstrate that even in these early times, the Maya had a propensity to build over or rebuild their public monuments—a characteristic that followed the Maya through the Classic period. In about 650 B.C., the Cuello central courtyard was reconstucted and expanded, and a rectangular limestone masonry building was built and covered with plaster. This is the oldest known Maya masonry building.

Some evidence indicates that, as a part of a later remodeling of the Cuello ceremonial center, old structures were ritually destroyed, or their sanctity was destroyed, and the rubble made a platform for the new structures.

Human sacrifice accompanied the new construction. More than twenty skeletons showing torture and sacrifice were found in a mass burial dating from about 400 B.C. The old platform and structures were destroyed, and the new temple precinct was consecrated by the ritual of human sacrifice. The new platforms were several feet high and more than forty feet long. They were topped with temples of timber and thatch.

The Middle Preclassic era of the developing Maya civilization is marked by trade in jade and obsidian and a cultural interaction between Maya sites and other areas of Mesoamerica. Plazas surrounded by pyramids and temples were built in a style that was followed in the Classic period.

By 300 B.C. Maya Indians were living in more or less organized societies from Yucatán to Honduras. They had a class society with permanent leaders. It can be said that basic Maya social organization dates from this time. Yet to come was the Long Count calendar, hieroglyphic writing, and the corbel-vaulted masonry.

The characteristic pottery of the Late Preclassic lowlands is called Chicanel. It is a plain slipped ware and is usually red with a waxy finish. The amounts and location of Chicanel pottery have been the yardstick for estimating the population increase that took place during Late Preclassic times after 300 B.C.

Not only was there a population increase at existing sites, but centers of population became more numerous. Villages changed into cities as plazas lined by pyramids and temples were erected.

One of the hallmarks of Maya architecture developed during the Late Preclassic: corbel-vaulted masonry. The vault was not a true arch, but rather was created by rows of loaf-shaped stones, or corbels, set with each row extending inward until the rows of corbels met at the top of the vault with a capstone cover. The vault corbels were stabilized and held in place by a rubble fill. The earliest known vaulting was utilized in burial chambers at Tikal.

These burial chambers and the grave furnishings that were interred with the deceased, such as jade, jewelry, and ceramics, indicate a developing elite class.

During the Late Preclassic in the Guatemala highlands at Kaminaljuyú, the opulence of the nobles suggests that they held great economic and political power. The numerous massive buildings and fine burials indicate a fully developed and stratified society. The dead were buried in temple pyramids, the tallest of which

reached sixty feet. The deceased nobles were enshrouded in finery and buried with hundreds of artifacts. Many burials also included sacrificed children and adults.

The artists of Kaminaljuyú created carved stelae, generally in the Izapian style. These stelae were the precursors of Classic Maya sculpture. The monuments of Kaminaljuyú also displayed the beginnings of glyphic writing.

The Late Preclassic period of the lowlands also showed a cultural efflorescence that has been called the Chicanel culture. Here, too, the burials indicate a rich nobility.

After 250 B.C. the massive cut-stone temple-pyramid construction began in the Tikal North Acropolis and with the great 5C-54 (Lost World) pyramid with its four stairways and huge masks. The Late Preclassic structure, E-VII Sub, at Uaxactún, just to the north of Tikal, with its magnificent masks and apron moldings, is an archaeological jewel of the times.

Recent discoveries at Cerros in northern Belize by David Freidel and others show that a general flourishing of culture in the Maya lowlands occurred between 50 B.C. and A.D. 100. At Cerros during this period there was a massive surge in the construction of ceremonial structures. The Cerros Maya built a large complex consisting of a planned open plaza with adjacent pyramids and public buildings. Prior to this burst of building, since 350 B.C., Cerros had been only a small fishing and trading village, but it had a Maya-like public plaza with a pyramid. This small pyramid was the model for the great Structure 4 pyramid that was built later.

The massive rebuilding program was a part of the general cultural explosion which was occurring at other urban centers in the lowlands. The special significance of Cerros to Mayanists is that it flowered in the Late Preclassic times and that its monumental building was not remodeled in later times because the site was abandoned about A.D. 100. The Cerros rulers ordered the ritual destruction of the sanctuary area before the city was abandoned. They left Cerros probably because it was no longer economically tenable as a result of the growth and development of Maya urban centers inland.

Owing to the abandonment, the excavated site

reveals the status of Maya culture in the Late Preclassic period and demonstrates that many of the elements of the Maya Classic culture were in place even before Protoclassic times.

Surrounding the Cerros center, the Maya built a canal, which was approximately four thousand feet long, twenty feet wide, and six feet deep, that enclosed about ninety acres of the urban center. The canal was a part of the raised-field system of agriculture, consisting of irrigation ditches and drained fields.

The city center included two ball courts and a pyramid-plaza group. Pyramid 29B faces west and the huge Structure 4 faces east. The pyramids of Cerros displayed stuccoed and painted images. Excavation of Structure 5C revealed four masks which represent the sun and Venus and possibly one of the Palenque Triad of Gods. At Cerros, as at Cuello, the private houses were very similar to the houses of the modern Maya.

Cerros is located on a peninsula extending northward into Chetumal Bay. In its heyday it was a trading port for chert tools, salt, obsidian, and jade. The local pottery shows the influence of other Maya centers including Tikal and El Mirador in the Petén, Becán in Quintana Roo, Mexico, and perhaps Kaminaljuyú in the Guatemala highlands.

Cerros traded with other Maya centers and was influenced by them. Cerros was not unique as an urban center and therefore portrays the status of Maya civilization in Late Preclassic times. The excavation at Cerros has demonstrated that by A.D. 100, Maya civilization was already well advanced.

By the beginning of the Protoclassic period, about A.D. 50, Maya pyramid-plaza architecture and ball courts were already developed. Vaulted and pyramid tombs and stelae were in use and demonstrated the existence of a ruling elite. Trade, cultural exchange, and probably a common language existed within the Maya area.

The three aspects of Maya culture that Mayanists formerly utilized to mark the shift from Preclassic to Classic times—vaulted stone construction, monumental inscriptions, and polychrome pottery—all are now known to have appeared in the Protoclassic.

Previously it was thought that much of the cultural change that took place in the Classic period came as a result of physical intrusion by non-Mayan Mesoamerican peoples into the Maya area. Now it appears that the evolution of culture was a local and indigenous phenomenon. The recent discoveries indicate a development of Maya culture by Maya people beginning in Early Preclassic times and continuing to the Classic period.

Why did some of the sites that flourished during Preclassic times fail and others continue to thrive in Classic times? Tikal, for example, became a great Classic center while Cerros was largely abandoned. El Mirador in the lowlands and Dzibilchaltún in Yucatán became relatively unimportant during the Classic period, although they were major sites in the Preclassic. Hammond suggests it was warfare and conquest between Maya centers—warfare precipitated by the increase in population which necessitated an expansion of territory. Becan, in southern Yucatán, and Muralla de Leon, east of Tikal, were fortified Preclassic sites and are perhaps evidence of the imperialism of the larger centers.

The unrest that came with expanding population probably resulted in a refinement of the social organization, creating a ruling class with a firm control of food production, the military, and the commerce of the center. This kind of social organization was necessary for either offensive or defensive war. The Maya centers that developed this kind of leadership survived; the others failed.

Classic Period

The "Golden Age" of the Maya refers to the Classic period (A.D. 250–900). In the New World, the term *Classic* is an adoption of the term used to refer to the zenith of ancient Greek and Roman cultures, and carries with it the connotation of the full flowering of one of the New World's most striking Precolumbian cultures. For a 600-year period—from the beginning of the collapse of the western Roman Empire through the rise of the Byzantine civilization and Christianity, the birth of Mohammed and Islam to the age of Charlemagne—Classic Maya civilization burgeoned, waned, and died.

The subdivisions of the Classic period are not precise and vary from site to site, but they follow a general pattern. At Tikal in the Petén, the periods are: Early Classic (A.D. 250–475), which ended with the death of Stormy Sky; Middle Classic (A.D. 475–681), beginning with Kan Chitam (Kan Boar) and continuing until the reign of Ah Cacaw; and Late Classic (Florescent) (A.D. 681–810). The Terminal Classic extends from A.D. 810 to 900. Classic Period activities had virtually ceased, but Tikal remained inhabited.

At Copán, the Classic period divisions are Early Classic (A.D. 550–650) and Late Classic (A.D. 650–800); at Quiriguá, the periods are similar, with the Late Classic extending to perhaps A.D. 850.

No sharp division separates the Preclassic and the Classic periods. Early in the Classic occurred an expansion and perfection of architecture, art styles, and the introduction of the stela as a major vehicle for public aggrandizement of rulers. Corbeled vaulting was fully developed, monuments with hieroglyphic texts were being erected at many Maya centers, and Maya art was developing its characteristic features.

Between A.D. 550 and 600, Maya lowland ritual activities decreased noticeably, particularly in the carving of stelae bearing the Initial Series (Long Count), which had been going on for some three hundred years. This period of relative inactivity, called the Classic Maya "hiatus," was followed by another three hundred years of activity. The cause of the hiatus is the subject of almost as much debate as is the cause of the collapse of the Classic Maya culture; however, many scholars now doubt its existence except as a local phenomenon. Some scholars have suggested that the collapse of Teotihuacán in the Mexican highlands created a disruption in the Maya culture of Kaminaljuyú and in the Maya lowlands. Other theories include a breakdown of the system caused by ecological adjustments, sociopolitical divisiveness, and population pressures similar to those causing the final collapse three hundred years later (Willey 1974: 417).

The Late Classic period embraced the greatest era of sculpture, hieroglyphic writing, ceramic art, and building for the lowland Maya. The production of fine painted pottery, moldmade figures, and lapidary work prospered; the study of astronomy and mathematics flourished; and the number of ceremonial centers and stelae increased greatly.

Classic Maya Collapse

As Culbert has observed, "The Classic Maya of the southern lowlands suffered one of the world's greatest demographic disasters" (1974: 109). He estimates the loss may have been a million people in a single century. It has been suggested that these people probably did not die, but that they simply moved on, perhaps north to Yucatán.

Beginning at 10.0.0.0.0 in the Maya Long Count (equivalent to A.D. 830), the collapse spread throughout the lowlands. Why? No one knows, but the possible reasons are numerous. A single catastrophic cause, such as earthquake, climate change, hurricane, or epidemic has little support. The final contributing factor may have been pressure from peoples outside the area, who were able to cut the trade routes and overcome the Maya made weak by overpopulation, overexpansion, and a failure of leadership.

As Michael Coe puts it:

> Almost the only fact surely known about the downfall of the Classic Maya civilization is that it really happened. All the rest is pure conjecture. The sad story can clearly be read in the failure of centre after centre to put up commemorative stelae following the opening of Baktun 10 of Maya history, in the first half of the ninth century of our era. The katun ending date 10.3.0.0.0 (A.D. 889) was celebrated by inscriptions at only three sites. And the very last Long Count date to be recorded anywhere was the katun ending 10.4.0.0.0, incised on a jade from a site in southern Quintana Roo. Thus, by the beginning of the tenth century the Classic Maya civilization had been extinguished in the Central Area, and we may be sure that most of its great centres were by then deserted, abandoned to the encroachments of the waiting forests (M. Coe 1980: 118).

We know that by the end of the Classic period, foreigners had moved into Seibal, located near Tikal, but Tikal shows no evidence of having been invaded. Infiltration into the Palenque area and Yucatán occurred, yet a foreign invasion and overthrow of the Classic Maya sites there seems not to have happened. Christopher Jones proposes the concept that Tikal was a mercantile center, which collapsed when its extensive trade routes were superceded, and that other Classic Maya sites may have suffered in the same way.

At the beginning of the Late Classic, the Maya elite of the lowlands shared similar training and common beliefs with respect to government, the status of the nobility, and religious ritual. Evidence exists that power in many of the lowland sites was shared by a few families. The Sky family is referred to on stelae throughout the lowlands.

During this period times were good. The agricultural system was providing an abundance of food, and trade flourished. The increase in population brought greater urbanization. With the urbanization and the probable resultant competition between the cites came more and grander public buildings and perhaps more resplendent rituals. The rich became richer, and the poor became poorer. Then, when outside pressures began to build in the late eighth century A.D., the entire system began to fall apart.

The ruling elite were either unable or unwilling to salvage their culture. The Classic Maya state was not monolithic. Rather, it was a group of cities, each with its own ruling nobles. Although evidence shows that the noble families of the Maya cities were related, it also reveals a destructive competition based upon factionalism, perhaps in a similar fashion to the Classic Greek city states (Bove 1981).

This factionalism between Maya cities may have triggered a series of revolts by the commoners, which resulted in a breakdown of the entire economy because of the destruction of the governing elite. Once the government was destroyed, maintaining the system of intensive agriculture or long-distance trade upon which the large population depended was no longer possible (Hamblin and Pitcher, 1980).

Ancient Egypt and Rome, and the collapse of the French monarchy at the time of the French Revolution provide historical analogies to this scenario.

Mayanists generally agree that the collapse had no single cause, but they do not agree on the factors contributing to the collapse. It has been suggested that the lifespan of a civiliation is similar to man's: it is born, grows to maturity, reaches old age, and then dies. The Maya culture flourished for at least nineteen hundred years, from the beginning of the Middle Preclassic period (1000 B.C.) to the end of the Classic (A.D. 900).

Postclassic Period

In the north, Maya civilization continued during the Postclassic period, which J. Eric S. Thompson (1966: 310) calls the Mexican period (A.D. 925–1200), and the period of Mexican Absorption (A.D. 1200–1540). In the Mexican period, Mexicanized groups conquered Chichén Itzá, introducing highland Mexican architectural features, art, and the worship of Quetzalcoatl (Kukulcán in Maya) and other Mexican gods. The use of metal, the making of plumbate pottery, and the use of turquoise were important features. The fall of Chichén Itzá signaled the end of the period.

The period of Mexican Absorption was marked by the formation of the League of Mayapán in Yucatán and the dominance of the Quiché in the Guatemala highlands. Ruling groups abandoned their Mexican culture and gradually returned to the old Maya ways in speech and religion. The architecture and the arts were less refined than during the Classic period. After revolts against Mayapán and the Quiché, the Maya were governed by small independent chieftains, who continually warred among themselves. The cultural decline continued until Maya civilization was cut short by the Spanish Conquest in 1525 and 1541. Today, some two million Maya Indians live in the Guatemalan highlands, Chiapas, and Yucatán, Mexico. They still retain a distinctive culture and speak Mayan languages which stem from the ancient Maya tongue.

Discoveries made during the 1970s and 1980s have changed our perception of the Postclassic Maya. Recent archaeological research at Flores,

Tayasal, and Topoxte in Guatemala; at Santa Rita Corozal, Altun Há, and Lamanaí in Belize; and at Tulum, Tancah, and Cozumel on the east coast of Yucatán indicates that these Postclassic Maya sites shared a common cultural base, while maintaining great individual differences in artifacts, architecture, and urban planning.

In the Guatemala highlands, the Postclassic Maya were ruled by dynasties of Mexican origin. They were Mexicanized in somewhat the same way as the Maya of Postclassic Chichén Itzá. The ruins of the cities of Zacaleu, Utatlán, Iximché, and Mixco Viejo built in defensive hilltop positions along the spine of the Guatemala Mountains give testimony to the greatness of their Postclassic civilization. These centers were viable until they were destroyed by the conquistador Pedro de Alvarado in 1524.

In the Petén in Postclassic times the island cities of Topoxte in Lake Yaxhá resembled the fortified towns of the highlands. Nearby Tayasal on Lake Petén Itza was not conquered by the Spaniards until 1697.

The Maya Postclassic, which extends for more than six hundred years from A.D. 900 to the time of the Spanish conquest in the 1500s, evolved in its own distinctive way from the Maya Classic. Raised platforms with rubble-core construction and pyramids with corbeled roofs were important features of Classic architecture. Postclassic construction employed low platforms and post-and-lintel techniques in permanent construction—colonnaded halls found at Chichén Itzá and Mayapán are Postclassic architectural types. Settlement patterns of Postclassic sites show a greater concern for defense and a tendency to build on or near bodies of water. Despite these distinctions between the Classic and Postclassic periods, some similarities existed as well. Evidence shows extensive trade in obsidian, manos and metates, jade, turquoise, honey, salt, textiles, feathers, and cacao in both periods. The Postclassic Maya produced a distinctive style of mural painting and ceramic art from that of the Classic Maya, and although it was different, it was not necessarily inferior (Chase 1981: 25).

Thus, as recent research indicates, Postclassic Maya culture was not one of decline and decadence. Rather, it may be characterized as related

10

Illustration 3.   Maya Postclassic sites.

to, but distinctive from, the Classic. As the civilization of the Byzantine Eastern Roman Empire differed from the Roman Empire which it followed, so too did Postclassic Maya culture differ from its Classic predecessor.

Physical Appearance

As far as can be determined, the ancient Maya had copper-brown complexions with straight black or dark brown hair. They were short in stature: the men probably were no more than five feet one inch tall on the average, and the women were smaller. They had rather long arms and small hands and feet (Morley 1956: 23). Pacal, ruler of Palenque, however, was much taller—five feet, eight inches. In the Maya Classic period, sloped foreheads and large noses were considered attractive, and parents deformed the skulls of young children by fastening boards around their foreheads. Adults of both sexes were often tatooed and scarified and had their front teeth filed. Bishop Diego de Landa (1524–79), whose writings are a principal source of our knowledge of Maya culture, said of the women:

> They are not white but of a yellowish brown color, caused more by the sun and by their constant bathing than from nature. . . . They had a custom of filing their teeth leaving them like the teeth of a saw, and this they considered elegant. . . . They pierced their ears in order to put in earrings like their husbands (Tozzer 1941: 125–26).

Illustrations 4 and 5 show the Maya concept of the handsome male as portrayed at various Maya sites. Ideal features included an artificially deformed head with sloping forehead, almond-shaped eyes, a large nose, a drooping lower lip, and a slightly receding chin.

Agriculture

The civilization of the New World was founded on the cultivation of maize or Indian corn (*Zea mays*). The domestication of corn, says Michael Coe, was "the most important discovery ever attained by the American Indians. For this plant created and fed native New World civilization" (1968: 32). This corn, along with beans, squash, breadnut (or *ramon*), fish, and meat formed the basis of the Mesoamerican diet.

In Early Preclassic times, Maya agriculture probably included techniques very similar to those currently employed by the descendants of the Maya living in Yucatán. The method is called swidden or slash-and-burn agriculture. It involves cutting the trees and underbrush in a section of the forest, burning the dried trees and brush, then planting and harvesting. Corn was the primary crop (Ill. 6), with squash and beans generally planted in the same field, as well as pumpkins, chili peppers, tomatoes, yucca, and sweet potatoes. The basic tools were the sharp planting stick (*xul*) and the stone axe (*baat*). When the corn was ripe, the heads were bent over so that the husks would shed the rain, and the corn would keep until harvested. The milpa (cornfield), if continuously planted, produced less and less corn each year; after a few years it would

Illustration 4. Present-day Lacondón Maya (Stela 1, Bonampak). From *Third Palenque Round Table*, vol. 5, p. 44.

Illustration 5. Beautiful Ancient Maya from Palenque. From J. Eric S. Thompson, *The Rise and Fall of Maya Civilization*, p. 60.

become necessary to abandon one milpa and clear and burn another field.

Swidden agriculture could not have supported the number of people that lived in the area inhabited by the ancient Maya.

Mayanists now have concluded that a substantial portion of the lowland Maya area was swampy, and in these areas the Maya constructed a system of raised fields.

After an expedition to Guatemala early in 1980, Richard E. W. Adams, Walter E. Brown, Jr., and T. Patrick Culbert reported that an airborne radar survey made in 1977 and 1978 revealing a network of ancient canals had been confirmed by investigations on the ground. Narrow ditches about ten feet wide and two feet deep constructed in grid systems covered more than 2,500 square kilometers (about 965 square miles) of Petén and Belize jungle.

The airborne radar also revealed that the great cities of the Maya were located on the edges of the largest swamps because the swamps were the principal food-producing areas. These new revelations not only explain the location of the large cities but give a rational reason for their being there. As Richard E. W. Adams observes, "The raised field systems and canals clearly indicate agricultural support for millions, not just thousands. The numbers are astounding, but correlate with settlement pattern data. Some 300 reported cities are known for the whole Maya area, including small centers as well as the largest. Tikal alone is estimated to have held at least 50,000 people" (Adams 1982: 28).

Mayanists now conclude that the raised-field method of food production was an integral factor in the development of Maya civilization. The nobles provided the management for the construction of the grids, the planting and harvesting of the crops, and the distribution of the produce. As David Freidel stated in a Public Broadcasting System Odyssey documentary, *Maya Lords of the Jungle:*

> This allows us to view the Maya as having a much more sophisticated and powerful political economy than we previously supposed. We never really have understood what the Maya needed civilization for in the jungle. If they were slash-and-burn agriculturalists, what do you need some overburden of elites for? What do you need your priests for? Certainly not to tell them when to plant. Any farmer worth his twenty-five years of experience since he was five years old, knows when to plant and when not to plant and when to burn. He doesn't need somebody dressed up in fancy jades to tell him when to do that. We never really understood the practical consequences of a social hierarchy among the Maya. Intensive agriculture gives us a brand

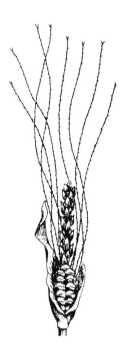

Illustration 6.   Original corn plant. From Michael D. Coe, *American's First Civilization,* p. 32.

new lead into exploring why the Maya were civilized in the first place.

Maya civilization was probably similar to European medieval feudalism, with the nobles owning or controlling the land and the production of food. For the Maya, the water lily and the fish symbolized the intensive farming of the raised fields. The symbol of the fish nibbling on the water-lily bloom is relatively common as an element of Maya royal dress. As such, it was a symbol of power, representing a prime source of food and sustinence. The fish and water lily were together symbols of abundance, wealth, and power.

The Maya "fish and water lily" symbolism found on the dress of the Maya kings may be similar to the crook and flail of the ancient Egyptian pharoahs or to the hammer and sickle of the twentieth century. Each manifests the symbolic underpinnings of the society.

Commoner Food, Housing, and Clothing

The basic food, maize, was prepared by boiling or soaking it in lime water. The wet maize was then ground on a metate (a stone slab) with a mano (a round grinding stone), and the resulting paste was mixed with water to make *pozole*, which was used either as a liquid or as a cake now known as a tortilla. Then, as now, the tortilla was cooked on a flat pottery griddle and eaten with beans or chili.

The Classic Maya raised dogs for food and domesticated the turkey and ducks. The Yucatán Maya were also beekeepers. In addition, they ate the flesh of deer, wild boars, birds, fish, iguanas, rabbits, turtles, and insects. Intoxicating beverages were made with a honey base.

Bishop Landa described the diet of the Mayas in the sixteenth century thus:

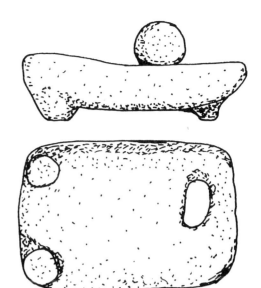

Illustration 7. Mano (roller) and metate (receptacle) for grinding grain into meal.

> Their principal subsistence is maize of which they make various foods and drinks, and even drinking it as they do, it serves them both as food and drink. The Indian women put the maize to soak one night before in lime and water, and in the morning it is soft and half-cooked. . . .; and they grind it upon stones, and they give to workmen and travelers and sailors large balls and loads of the half-ground maize and this lasts for several months merely becoming sour. And of that they take a lump which they mix in a vase made of the shell of the fruit, which grows on a tree by which God provided them with vessels. And they drink this nutriment and eat the rest, and it is a savory food and of great sustaining power. From the maize which is the finest ground they extract a milk and thicken it on the fire, and make a sort of porridge for the morning. And they drink it hot and over that which remains from the morning's meal they throw water so as to drink it during the day; for they are not accustomed to drink water alone. They also parch the maize and grind it, and mix it with water, thus making a very refreshing drink, throwing in a little Indian pepper or cacao.
>
> They make of ground maize and cacao a kind of foaming drink which is very savory, and with which they celebrate their feasts. And they get from the cacao a grease which resembles butter, and from this and maize they make another beverage which is very refreshing and savory.
>
> They make good and healthful bread of different kinds, except that it is bad to eat when it is cold, and so the Indian women take a great deal of trouble making it twice a day. . . .
>
> They prepare stews of vegetables and flesh of deer and of wild and tame birds of which there are great numbers, and of fish of which there are large numbers.
>
> In the morning they take their warm drink with pepper, as has been said, and in the daytime they drink the other cool drinks and eat their stews at night. And if there is no meat they make sauces of pepper and vegetables. . . . They eat a good deal when they have it and if not they endure hunger very patiently and get along with very little; and after eating

Illustration 8.   Maya hut, Yucatán, Mexico.

they wash their hands and mouths
(Tozzer 1941: 89–91).

As Morley suggests "The Maya thatched hut,
with its sharply pitched roof of two slopes, was
the prototype of the corbel arched stone buildings" (Morley 1956: 310). The thatched hut of the
common people has remained substantially unchanged for more than thirty-five hundred years.
The earliest known Maya house has been found
at Cuello, built around 1600 B.C. The standard
method of construction was to build rectangular
seven-foot-high walls of saplings daubed with
mud or undressed stone. The houses were about
twenty-two feet long and twelve feet wide, usually with rounded ends. The roof was a thatch
of palm leaves worked upon a framework of
poles supported by four corner posts. Usually
the house had but one door and no windows.

Bishop Landa tells us that Maya clothing at
the time of the Conquest

was a band of the width of a hand,
which served them for drawers and
breeches. They wound it several times
around the waist, so that one end fell
in front and one end behind, and
these ends the women made with a
great deal of care and feather-work.
They wore large square *mantas* and
tied them over their shoulders. They
wore sandals of hemp or of the dry
untanned skin of the deer, and they
wore no other garments (Tozzer 1941:
89).

Tools

Maya technology was neolithic. While a few
metal ornaments have been found which may
date to the Classic period, and that is by no
means certain, the use of metal for tools during
that period was unknown. In Postclassic times,
metal was used primarily for ornaments; few

Illustrations 9 and 10. Old Sun God, Lord of the Night, carrying a jaguar bundle with a tumpline. The weight was borne by the head, neck, and back, leaving the hands free.

metal tools have been found in archaeological contexts. All building stones were cut and dressed, and the sculpture was executed with stone tools. The plumb line was used, and levels and squaring devices probably existed. There were no wheeled vehicles, and no animals were used for pulling or carrying. The Maya no doubt had ropes and must have used logs for rollers. Construction of the pyramids and of rubble-filled buildings was accomplished by manpower alone, probably with the tumpline or headband. Illustrations 9 and 10 depict the Old Sun God carrying a burden supported by a tumpline.

Stone tools were made of flint, obsidian, granite, limestone, and quartzite. The percussion-flaked flint core was probably the general utility tool for masonry work and stone dressing. Other stones were hafted for use as chisels or axes. In addition, flint and obsidian tools were used for scraping, polishing, and plastering. The tools required to work jade probably included hammerstones, grinding stones, rasps, and solid drills. Saws of wood and hollow drills of reed or birdbone were used with abrasives. Incising was probably done with jade or flint tools.

New Evidence Relating to the Life-Style of the Classic Maya Lords

The most exciting recent development in the study of Precolumbian civilization is new evi-

dence that enables us to portray the Maya lords and nobles as living, breathing people. No longer do we need to refer to persons portrayed on stelae or lintels as ancient priests or deities. No longer are we required to visualize the inhabitants of Tikal, Copán, Quiriguá, and other Maya centers as ghosts or shadows, who somehow built and used the massive "ceremonial centers." We now know that the ceremonial centers were sites occupied by real people engaged in politics, commerce, and warfare. They were Indians of high culture with manifold abilities, who exhibited also human frailties.

Sources of Information Concerning the Classic Maya

An abundance of information is available about the ancient civilizations that preceded what we call Western civilization. The Egyptian, the Classic Greek, and the Roman eras are almost as well known to us as the life and times of George Washington. We know about their history, literature, art, living conditions, and manners, in large measure because scholars can read and translate the historical materials that have been preserved. Much, of course, has been lost over the centuries, but enough has been preserved to allow a legion of scholars to re-create the ancient past with almost as much detail as we recall the events of yesterday.

With the ancient Maya, the situation is quite different. Beginning with the conquest of the New World, the Spaniards followed a deliberate policy of destroying the Indian cultures because they were considered to be heathen. Bishop Landa recorded:

> We found a large number of books of these characters and, as they contained nothing in which there were not to be seen superstition and lies of the devil, we burned them all which they regretted to an amazing degree and which caused them much affliction (Tozzer 1941: 169).

In addition, the deciphering of the existing hieroglyphs has been a tedious and slow-moving process. Until very recently, our knowledge of their hieroglyphic writing was limited to dates and other calendric data. However, in 1960, Tatiana Proskouriakoff demonstrated the existence of historical data in the inscriptions; since then the understanding of Maya history has grown enormously. Not only have the names of rulers been identified, but also major events, such as births, heir designations, accessions, wars, and capture, are known. Even detailed genealogies have been recovered from the Classic inscriptions.

Although Linda Schele, Christopher Jones, David Kelley, and others have recently made great strides in the total understanding of the written language of the Maya, much still remains to be done. The grammar of the system is not thoroughly understood, and often the original language values of the signs are difficult to reconstruct. Perhaps the most thoroughly studied inscriptions are those of Palenque. Some of the complexity and literary tradition of Palenque has been recovered by the team of Linda Schele, Floyd Lounsbury, Peter Mathews, and David Kelley.

The sources of written information about the ancient Maya are sculpture (stelae, bas-reliefs, and incised panels), mural paintings (such as those found at Uaxactún, Bonampak, Chichén Itzá, and Tulúm), the four extant books of the Maya (the Dresden Codex, the Madrid Codex,

the Paris Codex, and the Grolier Codex), and some painted vases. These original sources, plus some post-Conquest sources—Bishop Diego de Landa's *Relacion de las Cosas de Yucatán,* the *Popol Vuh,* and the *Book of the Chilam Balam of Chumayel*—written in the sixteenth century are the basic sources of information concerning the Classic Maya.

During the last several years, a considerable number of painted pots and vases, which were buried with Maya nobles of the Classic period, have come to light; some are originals, and many are fakes. These funerary vessels from Maya graves have added considerably to the fund of knowledge about the Maya in much the same way that grave inscriptions have added to our knowledge of the ancient Egyptians. Although Michael Coe considers these painted vases to represent only underworld scenes, they give us an insight into the court life of the Maya. Regrettably, though, many of them have become available through the terribly destructive and illegal excavations of looters, whose efforts are spurred by the insatiable demands of the international art market.

Three booklets by Michael Coe (see Ill. 13) catalogue in rollout form a number of Classic Maya vases, as does *Maya Ceramic Vases from the Classic Period* and *The Maya Book of the Dead, The Ceramic Codex* by Robicsek and Hales.

The vases and pots are painted with a great variety of scenes portraying deities, bicephalic serpents, and zoomorphic simian, reptilian, and feline creatures, all of which the Maya considered to populate the underworld. Many of the vases, however, depict Maya lords and ladies, nobles, captives, and a retinue of slaves or servants. These palace scenes give us an insight into the life-style and dress of the ancient Maya nobility.

These vases, coupled with a constantly expanding knowledge of glyphs and an understanding of the iconography that appears in the sculpture, have brought the elite Maya to life. The Classic Maya, we now know, had much in common with the people of other civilizations. The leaders fulfilled political duties, practiced war and sacrifice, and formed allegiances through

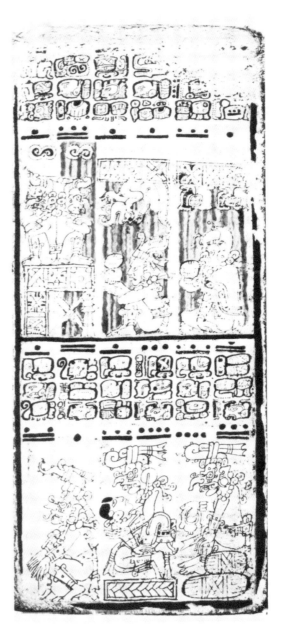

Illustration 11. The Dresden Codex. From J. Eric
S. Thompson, *A Commentary on the Dresden Codex,*
pp. 67, 68.

17

Illustration 12.   Hummingbird Vase from Burial 196, Tikal. Two Underworld Court scenes with an anthropomorphic hummingbird with a Nicte flower on its beak. The text is a variant of the primary standard indicating God G-9 plus "bacab" and may possibly refer to the missing 28th ruler of Tikal.

marriage. At times they were brutal and engaged in activities we would consider debaucheries. They believed in their gods and propitiated them with bloody sacrifices committed upon themselves, as well as upon captives. They took great pains to ensure continuity of rule and smooth inheritance to the throne. They were buried in sumptuous tombs and were honored by their descendants.

The contents of Maya burials also have assisted, in great measure, in determining the identity of rulers. Often artifacts in a burial revealed the person's identity, when he became king, how long he ruled, where he came from, and who his predecessors and successors were. Items buried with the lord may identify trade items and interregional contacts the city had with other Maya cities.

The Maya lord is generally shown seated on a raised dais or throne, with his legs crossed in tailor fashion. The throne sometimes has gathered draperies at the top and sides and is often covered. Women or servants stand deferentially to his rear. Jars and bowls of food and drink are sometimes shown. Some vases show the lord being entertained by dwarfs, monkeys, musicians, or dancers; sometimes he is shown with young or voluptuous women. Often he is depicted receiving gifts or in conference with or receiving obeisance from other lords and officials. Some vases show his captains before him, exhibiting captives.

The Bonampak murals, covering the interiors of three adjoining rooms of a single structure, depict three events in the lives of Maya nobility. The first room shows a ceremony involving the

designation of a young lord as heir by his father. The paintings show nobles in preparation for and during the ceremony, adorned in full regalia. The center-room walls depict the nobles in military regalia. In the third room, the ruler and his family are shown dressed in the white cotton robes of women preparing to perform the ritual bloodletting ceremony of self-sacrifice.

The nobles had servants and retainers to perform every personal service; the Bonampak murals show servants dressing the lords. In the bloodletting scene, a servant is on his knees, holding the lancet used to draw blood, and awaiting the lord's need.

The evidence indicates the Maya elite, nearly twelve hundred years ago, lived a sumptuous life comparable to the life of royalty anywhere at any time.

Illustration 13.   Rollout of a vase showing God L
and his nubile attendants. From Michael D. Coe,
Maya Scribe, p. 92.

Illustration 14. Bonampak lords, being dressed for
a ceremonial occasion.

Illustration 15. Lord seated cross-legged. Maya
lords were generally portrayed in this pose. From
Michael D. Coe, *Maya Scribe and His World*, p. 65.

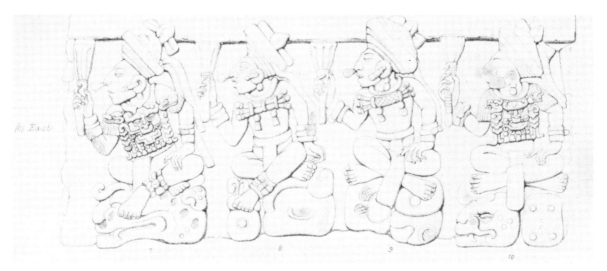

Illustration 16. Lords of Copán portrayed on Altar
Q (east side). Drawing by A. P. Maudslay, *Biologia
Centrali-Americana*, Illustration 92.

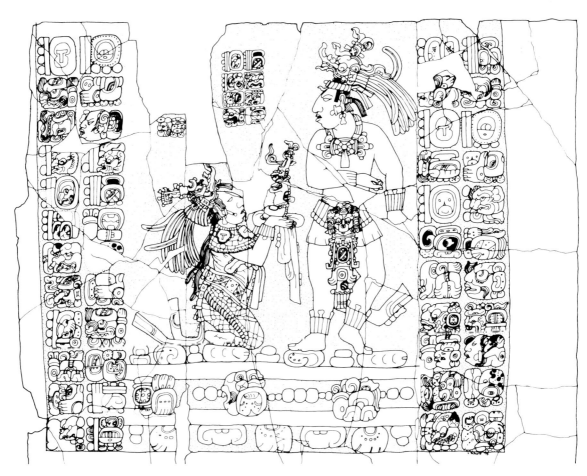

Illustration 17. Elite dress, Palenque. From
Ferguson and Royce, *Maya Ruins of Mexico in Color*,
p. 58. Drawing by Linda Schele.

Elite Dress: Figures of the ancient Maya elite—usually the rulers—appear on stelae, altars, sculptured panel reliefs, lintels of stone and wood, and ceramic vessels. These sources document how the lords dressed, and show that some items of dress were more or less standard throughout the Classic Maya area.

Lowland Guatemala, Belize, and Honduras have a hot climate, and the Maya dressed accordingly. Except on ceremonial occasions, the men wore only loincloths and the women cotton dresses, sometimes with breasts bare.

The loincloth, a basic item of apparel for Maya peasant and lord alike, was made of cloth, probably cotton. It was worn wrapped once or twice around the waist, then between the legs, with a flap in front. In their most formal pose, the lords are shown with sandals; in informal attire, they are depicted barefooted.

The lords are often portrayed wearing a kilt-like skirt of jaguar skin or cotton cloth, and anklets and wristlets of jade and shell in addition to the headdress, earplugs, and jewelry. They are also shown with capes made of skin, cloth, and feathers and, on some occasions, with a full robe. Body paint of red, black, or white is common.

The elite women wore strapless full-length gowns; sometimes they are shown wearing asymmetrical off-one-shoulder calf-length gowns; at other times they are shown bare-breasted with skirts. The women, too, generally wore headdresses, earplugs, wristlets, and beads. Generally, they, too, are shown barefooted. The elite women sometimes are shown wearing full-length robes or high-necked dresses gathered at the neck or open. The huipil worn by Maya women today appears in the same form as shown on vases painted a thousand years ago. Often a cape and skirt of netlike material is worn over a cotton undergarment, with the skirt tied at the waist with a belt.

Medicine and Surgery: Both the highland and lowland Maya believed an entrance to the underworld, Xibalba, existed somewhere in the Alta Verapaz region, where the highlands meet the lowlands at a place of the crossing of four roads. According to Coe, they believed that "the diseases that affected men came from this hole in

Illustration 18. Maya women wearing *huipiles,* Acanceh, Yucatán, Mexico.

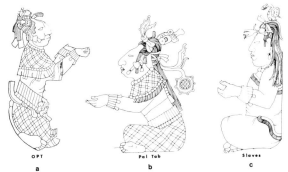

Illustration 19. Maya elite female dress. From *Segunda Mesa Redonda de Palenque,* p. 45. Drawings by Linda Schele.

the form of evil beings, whom the Maya curer had to send back to hell by incantation" (Coe 1973: 12).

Priests conducted the "medical" cure by incantation; the first task was to determine the cause of the illness. It was often determined to have been sent by an enemy, or caused by evil winds or the failure to conduct a ritual ceremony properly.

However, the Maya did have medical literature involving medicinal plants. The literature that survived the Spanish Conquest probably had its roots in the ancient Maya past. A number of Maya medical texts deal with treatment of illnesses with herbs; many herbs used by the ancients are listed in the United States Pharmacopoeia.

Surgery was a developed art. Evidence shows that the ancient Maya, like the ancient Egyptians, cut out sections of bone from the skull of living persons. The operation, called trepanning, was performed on rulers or elite persons. Some patients lived through the operation, as indicated by the discoveries of skulls with the replaced bone healed or partially healed. We can assume the high status of the patient because the skulls found also showed the cosmetic insertion of jade or green stone into the faces of the teeth.

Cannibalism: Nicholas Hellmuth and Christopher Jones, both of whom participated in University of Pennsylvania fieldwork at Tikal, believe that evidence shows the general practice of cannibalism around the time of the collapse. Human bones and ashes from cooking fires discarded from living areas indicates that human flesh was eaten, not solely in connection with religious rites (which is not unusual in early societies), but as a supplement to the diet.

Music: Scenes depicted on Maya vases indicate that music was an integral part of the Maya world. Musical instruments used by the Classic Maya include horns, trumpets, flutes, several varieties of drums, tom toms, various kinds of rattles, and carapaces. Illustration 20 shows a quintet of drum, rattle, trumpets and flutes accompanying the sacrifice of disembowelment. An enema ritual vase depicts a musical aggregation composed of a carapace (turtle back), rattles, and a tom tom. The formal heirship ceremony displayed on the Bonampak murals employed an orchestra composed of trumpets, carapaces, drums, flutes, and rattles.

Enema Ritual: During the 1970s, more than one hundred vases from Classic Maya tombs in the Petén and other areas were found which portray what is believed to be a hallucinogenic or intoxicating enema ritual. In some instances, the male figure is shown inserting a syringe into his rectum; in others, the service is performed by his female companion, or a specially costumed male attendant. The paraphernalia used in connection with the activity included a large jar with a neck and flaring rim. Nicholas Hellmuth suggests that "the shape, not size, is the distinguishing characteristic. Enema jugs have a neck much narrower than the rim top" (Hellmuth 1981: 1).

The enema syringe is generally depicted as a bulb, which was probably a deer bladder or a bulb of native rubber, and a bone tube. The liquid from the enema jug was sucked into the bulb for injection.

Hellmuth's research indicates that the ritual often involved the wearing of a special vomit bib and a special headdress. The ritual was preceded by drinking of stimulants, eating little "cookies," smoking potent native cigars, and, on some occasions, music and dancing. According to Hellmuth, these were "highly involved Maya rituals which involved a total chemical assault on every sense from a wide variety of stimulants administered in sequence" (Hellmuth 1981: paragraph 10).

The vase shown in Illustration 21 is from a private collection. It depicts a scene of ritual enema-taking and drunkenness. The figure on the left is dipping out intoxicating liquid from a vase, probably to drink. The vase is bound up in a manner suggesting overland transport. The female on the right holds an enormous enema syringe and is administering the intoxicant to the supine and surely drunken figure who, from the so-called speech scrolls above him, appears to be singing or crying out. Over him and on either side of the speech scrolls are two birds, which seem to combine the features of vultures and quetzals. Between the two standing figures is a large backrack used for carrying burdens. Its cargo may be two additional vases.

The use of drugs was widespread in Precolumbian Mesoamerica and South America. Nearly one hundred hallucinogenic plants used by the Indians are indigenous to the New World. These include the hallucinogenic mushroom, which is depicted in sculpture at Kaminaljuyú, a site with close connections to Tikal, Quiriguá, and Copán. Others are peyote, the water lily, tobacco, and morning glory seeds. The *Bufo marinus* toad was a potential source of a hallucinogenic drug as well.

Which of these hallucinogens were utilized by the Maya or for what purpose is impossible to determine, but the vases suggest that drugs were used in the enemas. Michael Coe concludes that most, if not all, of these vases represent under-

Illustration 20. Vase showing musical
accompaniment to human sacrifice. From Michael
D. Coe, *Maya Scribe*, p. 76.

Illustration 21. Vase depicting the Maya enema
ritual. Rollout photograph © Justin Kerr, 1981.

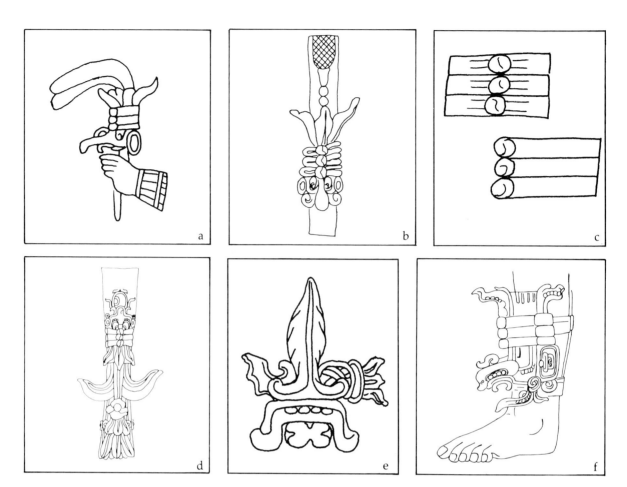

Illustration 22. (a) Yaxchilán, Lintel 14, bloodletting instrument personified as a deity. From *Primera Mesa Redonda de Palenque,* vol. 2, p. 70. Drawing by David Joralemon. (b) Penis perforator (personified) worn by a Copán lord (Stela A). From *Primera Mesa Redonda de Palenque,* vol. 2, p. 70. Drawing by David Joralemon. (c) Three-knot bloodletting motif (two views). (d) Personified perforator (Stela D, Copán). From *Primera Mesa Redonda de Palenque,* vol. 2, p. 70. Drawing by David Joralemon. (e) Quadripartite Badge, bloodletting stingray spine in center (Stela H, Copán). (f) Deity personified bloodletting anklets (Stela 26, Tikal). From *Primera Mesa Redonda de Palenque,* vol. 2, p. 70. Drawing by David Joralemon.

world scenes and indicate a connection between the enema and death, or the commemoration of the dead. The enema ritual, as well as autosacrificial rites, probably had important religious significance and were an integral part of Maya religious and ritual life. But the vases may also indicate that, in addition to the ritual use of drugs, the elite Maya took the enema simply to experience the effect of the drugs.

Classic Maya Sacrifice and Bloodletting

The Classic Maya elite practiced ritual blood sacrifice for the purpose of making offerings to the gods. Rituals included cutting ears, cheeks, tongues, and male genitals. In the sixteenth century, Bishop Landa recorded Maya male participation in the rite (Tozzer 1941: 114): "Holes were made in the virile member of each one obliquely from side to side and through the holes which they had thus made, they passed the greatest quantity of thread that they could, and all of them being thus fastened and strung together, they anointed the idol with the blood which flowed from all these parts."

Maya painted vases depict penis piercing and the passing of cord through the tongue. Lintel 17 from Structure 21 at Yaxchilán shows a double self-sacrifice. The lord holds a perforator and prepares to draw blood from his genitals, while the ornately dressed lady pulls a cord through her tongue. The lord's blood drips onto strips of bark paper, which together with the blood-soaked cord, will be presented as an offering to the gods.

Numerous stelae and vases depict the ceremonial instrument used to draw blood from the penis. David Joralemon has made an exhaustive study of the iconography of the blood-letting instrument. He concludes that the Mayas deified the instrument itself. The penis perforator instrument of self-sacrifice has a handle showing a jawless long-lipped deity head with large eyes. The most important identifying feature of this personified lancet and its associated complex is the stack of knots tied around its forehead. Bloodletting iconography is found on stelae, wall sculpture, and funerary vases throughout the Classic Maya area. An integral part of the bloodletting iconography, according to Schele, is the "three-knot" motif, which appears as part of the lord's regalia on stelae at Copán, Tikal, and other Classic Maya sites.

The "Quadripartite Badge" includes a bloodletting symbol—the stingray spine. The badge, as shown in Illustration 22e, is composed of four basic elements: the stingray spine in the center, the crossed bands on one side, a shell on the other, and the kin sign at the base.

There are two kinds of bloodletting—the self-imposed bloodletting sacrifice by the lord and the bloodletting or sacrifice of a captive.

Linda Schele has noted that iconography connected with the bloodletting ceremony includes non-Maya motifs on the costumes of the participants. The headdresses have Teotihuacán short-cropped feathers and year signs that the Maya seem to have borrowed at a very early time. They carry square shields with bangles along the bottom and representations of Tlaloc (usually

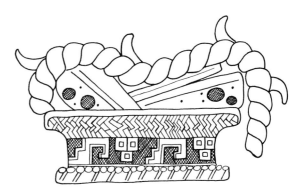

Illustration 23. Dish containing blood-soaked papers and a thorned rope used in connection with ritual blood sacrifice. Drawing by D. J. Reents (after Graham, 1977).

thought to be a Teotihuacán god), spear throwers (atlatls), and darts. This kind of paraphernalia was originally thought to indicate that Mexicans were being portrayed, but Schele observes that the great majority of these representations are associated with the bloodletting ceremony. She suggests that early in the Classic period this complex of "non-Maya" symbols became associated with sacrifice, and thereafter it became Maya in meaning and function. This Tlaloc complex is associated with sacrifice and bloodletting in other Mesoamerican cultures as well as the Maya, and may have included iconography shared by other peoples during the Classic period.

The intense pain occasioned by the bloodletting ritual produced hallucinatory visions represented on the stelae by a serpent monster rising out of the plate containing blood soaked ritual items. These bloodletting tools included the rope with thorns that had been pulled through the tongue and papers used to catch blood from incisions in the penis or ear.

Ceremonial events precipitated sacrifice and bloodletting: birth, heir designation, accession, anniversaries, period-endings, and ancestor worship. These ceremonies occasioned both self-imposed bloodletting and captive sacrifice. Schele believes that captive sacrifice and bloodletting were two separate ceremonies that could both occur on the same occasion. Captive sacrifice required capturing victims, and indications are

Illustration 24.   Sacrifice of captives. From
Thompson, *Rise and Fall of Maya Civilization,* p. 101.

that the higher the rank of the captive to be
sacrificed, the more efficacious would be the ritual in relation to the gods.

A central purpose of the human sacrifices appears to have been production of blood to propitiate the gods on occasions important to the
rulers. The murals at Bonampak depict sacrifice
in connection with designating heirship of the
child shown in the two throne scenes. Accession
to power by the king and death of the king were

occasions for sacrifice. At Tikal and Palenque,
the graves of lords have been found containing
sacrificial victims. At Tikal and Uaxactún, dedication of buildings involved human sacrifice.

The Classic Maya employed several means of
ritual sacrificial homicide. The most popular
method, as evidenced by the sculpture and
painted vases, was decapitation. Beheadings were
accomplished with a hafted flint axe, but death
was probably preceded by ritual torture de-

signed to draw as much blood as possible and to cause maximum pain.

Another method of ritual sacrifice was heart excision. According to Bishop Landa:

> The Chacs seized the poor victim and placed him very quickly on his back upon that stone, and all four held him by the legs and arms, so that they divided him in the middle. At this point came the executioner, the *Nacom,* with a knife of stone, and struck him with great skill and cruelty a blow between the ribs of his left side under the nipple, and he at once plunged his hand in there and seized the heart like a raging tiger and snatched it out alive and, having placed it upon a plate, he gave it to the priest, who went very quickly and anointed the face of the idols with that fresh blood (Tozzer 1941: 119).

Ritual sacrificial execution was also accomplished by binding the victim to a vertical rack and killing him with arrows or spears, or by disembowelment. Disembowelment and other forms of ritual sacrifice involved torture accompanied by music. Vase 33 of the Grolier Club Collection (M. Coe 1973: 76) shows the sacrifice being accompanied by a quintet playing end-flutes, an upright drum, rattles, and trumpets.

The Classic Maya rulers were, by our standards, a cruel and bloodthirsty lot, who believed in the necessity of human blood to ensure the approval of the gods for their activities, particularly with respect to the wielding and transfer of power. In the myth of the *Popol Vuh,* man is enjoined by the gods, who created him to nourish the gods by shedding his blood. All indications are that the Maya took this mandate seriously and copiously shed blood to propitiate the gods.

Ball Game

The ball game was an integral part of Classic Maya culture. The game was played all over ancient Mesoamerica, although the method and object of play varied from area to area and was

Illustration 25.   Vase showing decapitation. From Michael D. Coe, *Maya Scribe,* p. 92.

Illustration 26.   Graffiti from Tikal showing execution by arrows. From Thompson, *Rise and Fall of Maya Civilization,* p. 10.

modified by time. Nearly every known Maya site has one or more ball courts.

The myth of the Hero Twins, Hunahpú and Xbalanqué, which is a part of the Postclassic *Popol Vuh,* has the ball game as its core. It was their ball game that precipitated the call to Xibalba (the underworld) by Hun-Camé and Vucub-Camé to play ball with the lords of the underworld. Clemency Coggins suggests that the game was as ancient as it was ubiquitous and may have come from northern South America as early as 1000 B.C.

The game was played on a rectangular court. Since the sixteenth century, it has been called a *palangana*—a Spanish word for bowl or basin.

The architecture of the courts varied somewhat, but essentially the rectangular playing area was flanked by two parallel range structures, some open ended and some I-shaped with closed ends.

The game was played by the Classic Maya with a large solid rubber ball. It was either a two-man or a team game with a number of players on each side. Generally, each player wore one knee guard and a hip protector of a durable, lightweight material such as wood or leather. Illustration 234 is a drawing of a Copán ball player. General knowledge of the game indicates that the ball could not be advanced with the use of a player's hands, although rules may have permitted directing it to the hip with the hands, palms up. So far as is known, the stone ball game paraphernalia found in the Veracruz area (stone yokes, *hachas*, and *palmas*) were not used by the Classic Maya.

Vases and other ceramic vessels with painted scenes recovered from Classic Maya tombs indicate the ball was struck with the hip while the player was down on one knee. One can well imagine that a huge solid rubber ball, larger in size than a basketball, would require substantial padding to protect the player from injury.

In his *Historia General De Las Cosas De Nueva España* written shortly after the Conquest, Sahagún describes the game played in the sixteenth century in his chapter on how rulers took their pleasure. Although it was a different game played with another variety of ball, the description resembles the game played by the Classic Maya eight hundred years earlier.

> They played ball. There were his ball-catchers and his ball-players. They wagered [in this game] all [manner of] costly goods—gold, golden necklaces, green stone, fine turquoise, slaves, precious capes, valuable breech clouts, cultivated fields, houses, leather leg bands, gold bracelets, arm bands of quetzal feathers, duck feather capes, bales of cacao—[these] were wagered there in the game called *tlachtli*.
>
> On the two sides, on either hand, it was limited by walls, very well made, in that the walls and floor were

smoothed. And there, in the very center of the ball court, was a line, drawn upon the ground. And on the walls were two stone, ball court rings. He who played caused [the ball] to enter there; he caused it to go in. Then he won all the costly goods, and he won everything from all who watched there in the ball court. His equipment was the rubber ball, the leather gloves, girdles, and leather hip guards. . . .

> The ruler, when he beheld and knew that the common folk and vassals were very fretful, then commanded that the ball game be played, in order to animate the people and divert them. He commanded the majordomos to take out the rubber ball, and the girdles, and the leather hip guards, and the leather gloves with which the ruler's ball players were dressed and arrayed. And things were arranged on the ball court; there was sprinkling, there was sanding, there was sweeping.
>
> And all which the ruler was to wager in the game—the valued capes, the duck feather capes, the costly breech clouts, the green stone lip plugs, the golden ear plugs, the green stone necklaces, the golden necklaces, the wrist bands with large, precious, green stones upon them, and all the precious capes and bedding—the majordomos brought out and placed in the ball court. And those who were to challenge and play ball against the ruler then matched all his costly goods. And all the poor folk placed [for] the ruler, each one, old capes like those which the vassals wore. And if they won from the ruler, then the majordomos brought out others and laid out all the costly goods which they had won of the ruler, and also they gave to the vassals all which they had won of the ruler (Sahagún 1956: 29, 58).

The purpose of the game was probably ceremonial. In the Mexicanized Maya area of Chichén

Illustration 27.   Ball Court B, Copán (located southwest of the park).

Itzá, sacrifice was involved. At the Chichén Itzá ball court, the captain of one of the teams (whether winner or loser is not known) is depicted being decapitated. No evidence shows that human sacrifice was involved in the Classic Maya game. Marvin Cohodas thinks that the game was played during calendrical celebrations of solstices and equinoxes. By the sixteenth century, the game was utilized as a ceremonial war, a sort of Mesoamerican trial by battle, where issues were resolved by a contest between champions.

The Postclassic game used stone-ring goals set in the sides of the court; no goals have been found in the Classic Maya area. Ball-court markers have been found at Copán, and the so-called column altars at Tikal may have been ball-court markers.

Commerce and Trade

The Classic Maya cities were not parochial or provincial sites merely subsisting on local agriculture, but mercantile centers whose prosperity rose and fell with the success of the trade and commerce.

Christopher Jones feels that the rise and demise of the Classic Maya was inextricably interwoven with trade and commerce. He begins with the elementary concept that as wealth develops, so does the demand for goods that are not produced locally, especially exotic goods that derive their value in part from scarcity. So it was when the great civilization of Teotihuacán developed in central Mexico during the Maya Preclassic. This civilization created a demand for goods that could be supplied from the Maya area: jade, obsidian, quetzal feathers, cacao beans, cotton, and sea shells.

Jones suggests that the Maya cities developed along trade routes: Tikal, because it was in the portage area between the east-west rivers from the Caribbean coast and the Pasión and Usumacinta River area; Copán, because of its location on the Copán River; and Quiriguá on the Motagua. These cities flourished because of the trade with each other and with central Mexico.

Jones also argues that the Classic Maya cities declined and were abandoned in large measure because trade routes and, we may suppose, the demand for trade goods changed, leaving them isolated. As canoes became adapted to seacoast travel, coastal cities in Yucatán became more important than the old river towns. About A.D. 800, trade to and from the Maya lowlands was disturbed by pressures from outside the area. That disruption was one of the central factors in the decline and demise of Classic Maya civilization in the ninth century.

In both the Preclassic and the Classic periods, three southern Mesoamerican trade routes existed. The Pacific coast route went south across the Isthmus of Tehuantepec, then southeast along the Pacific coast, west of the mountains to Kaminaljuyú and El Salvador. This route began in Olmec times and continued through the Maya Classic.

The middle route from Palenque to Copán utilized the Usumacinta River through the Pasión River to the Motagua River, then downriver to the Bay of Honduras, or to the Copán River and into Copán. As part of the middle route, trade crossed by portage through Tikal east to what is now Belize (Altun Há and Xunántunich) and the sea.

The Caribbean-gulf route was the sea route from Honduras to Yucatán and the Veracruz area, with cross routes up the Motagua and inland from Chetumal Bay.

These routes continued north to Monte Albán in Oaxaca, the Mexican highlands, and Teotihuacán. The items traded were obsidian, jade, ceramics, shells, feathers, jaguar skins, cotton, bark paper, cacao, and salt. In the Classic period, food may have been a principal item of trade.

In the Late Classic period, Tikal and other Maya sites might have become so populous that it was necessary to import substantial quantities of food.

The Maya lowlands contain evidence of very early trade in obsidian and quartzite, perhaps as early as Tikal's beginnings between 700 and 600 B.C. From the beginning of the Classic period (A.D. 250), Tikal tombs reveal trade in sea shells, stingray spines, jade, greenstone, and pottery.

The Tikal area was possibly settled by people moving down the Motagua River from the Guatemala highland area and into the Petén lowlands, where they retained trade relations with the highland people. From as early as 50 B.C., tombs in the North Acropolis contain items similar to those of the same period found at Kaminaljuyú and demonstrate continuing ties with the Guatemala highlands. In addition to trade items, another tie may be the custom of ancestor veneration present at both sites. There is no way to determine whether there was a highland-lowland migration or merely close contacts.

The change in Tikal rulers, which occurred when Jaguar Paw's family rule terminated (about A.D. 379) with the accession of Curl Nose, may have been influenced by merchants from Teotihuacán to the Guatemala highlands and Kaminaljuyú. Even then, business affected politics.

Three basic resources were essential to the survival of a Maya center: mineral salt, obsidian for sharp cutting tools, and volcanic stone for grinding implements. None of these items are available in the Maya lowlands, while all three are available in the Guatemala highlands, so trade was imperative.

During Classic Maya times, trade moved from the Guatemala highlands and the Pacific coastal area through Copán down the Motagua River to the Maya lowlands and to the Maya centers located in what is now Belize. Quiriguá, located on the Motagua, was a stopping point along the route up and down the river. In A.D. 737, Quiriguá became free from the domination of Copán, which may have jeopardized Copán as a trade center. Quiriguá was still flourishing in the early ninth century after Copán had begun to decline.

The bulk of the commerce by land went along

trails through the brush and jungle, and, in the northern lowlands at least, along an extensive system of paved roadways called *sacbes* (*sacbeob* in Maya, "white roads"). The network of rivers carried commerce throughout the central Maya area, and a large volume of commerce went by sea around the Yucatán peninsula south along the coast of Belize to the Motagua River. Throughout Precolumbian times, trade and commerce appeared to have been carried on among the various Mesoamerican peoples.

On his fourth voyage to the New World, Columbus described a Maya vessel carrying passengers and a cargo that included

> cotton mantles, *huipils* (blouses) and loincloths, all with multicolor designs, *macanas* (wooden swords with pieces of flint or obsidian glued into slots down each side), little copper axes and bells, plates and forges to melt copper, razors and knives of copper, and hatchets of a sharp, bright-yellow stone with wooden hafts and large quantities of cacao (Thompson 1966: 221).

These were goods from the Postclassic period, for the Classic Maya did not utilize copper.

Yucatán was a significant source of salt for Mesoamerica and also exported honey, cotton, mantles, and slaves. Quetzal feathers, jade, flint, shells, and obsidian were traded. Obsidian cores the size of a fist were bartered; from them a sharp cutting edge could be separated by one well-placed blow, producing a razor or knife.

Maya currency used in trade included spondylus shell beads, jade, and—most important—cacao beans, the universal currency of the region. A load of beans contained about 24,000 individual beans, which, in the early sixteenth century, was "worth about $9.50 on the isthmus, but nearly double that in Mexico City" (Thompson 1966: 220).

Government and Society

Throughout the ancient Maya realm, civil (and perhaps religious) power was in the hands of hereditary nobles. The Maya were governed by an elite class who were born to power. Palenque, we know, was governed by a series of rulers from one family, who exercised a combination of civil and ecclesiastical authority. At Tikal, Copán, and Quiriguá, the kings were rulers by divine right who, together with the nobles, were the administrators of nearly all facets of government. These rulers portrayed themselves as descended from or closely associated with the deity we call God K.

In the Postclassic era of Chichén Itzá, the Mexican warrior class wielded a proportionately greater share of power than the priests. In Yucatán, at the time of the Conquest, each area was governed by a *halach uinic* ("real man"), who inherited his post through the male line.

Society was complex. At the top was the aristocracy of civil, military, and religious leaders. Next in the social order were the artisans and merchants. At the bottom were the peasants, who lived in the nearby countryside raising crops.

Archaeological evidence from the Classic period, especially in the Maya lowlands, suggests high social status for the nobles. The burials, particularly, indicate the wealth of the kings and nobles. The magnificent architecture and sculpture demonstrate that the priests and nobles had a large force of laborers who could be called upon for the heavy work and a corps of expert artisans for the design and art.

Feudalism

The organization of Maya society may have resembled European medieval feudalism to the extent that the nobles owned or controlled the land and produced the food. These elite families owed allegiance to the king, and in turn were owed allegiance by the people who worked the land. The right of ownership of the land and control of the people probably passed by inheritance. If the system produced a surplus, it was owned by the lords. As Gordon Willey suggests, "A wide variety of evidence suggests a good 'fit' of this feudal model to the Classic Maya" (Willey 1981: 409).

Using architectural size and complexity as a means of comparison, Classic Maya sites may be hierarchically ordered, with the major centers at the administrative apex and a descending order of smaller and architecturally less complex sites. This system is analogous to the royal, ducal, and baronial structural levels of feudal Europe. In addition, glyphic evidence shows that Maya kings and their families traced their genealogies to the gods, which gave them a religiously sanctioned status for retention of power (Adams and Smith 1981: 335).

Tikal, Copán, and Quiriguá were political centers that functioned as the main residence of the king, where he was surrounded by lesser chiefs and nobles. From these centers, they administered outlying agricultural lands, either directly or through lesser nobles living in scattered minor centers.

Commerce and the production of goods were probably also controlled by noble families. Although craft production was probably at the household level, the production and distribution was part of an integrated system. The centers, both major and minor, combined religious ceremony with markets, both of which were administered by the nobles (Freidel 1981: 371). If we add to the local ceremonies and markets more elaborate religious holidays and markets at the larger centers, and extend the process on an interregional basis—say Tikal with Quiriguá or Quiriguá with Copán, or even the Petén with the Guatemala or Mexican highlands—a model for the production and distribution of food and goods becomes clear and reasonable.

Warfare

Sylvanus G. Morley, who wrote his classic, *The Ancient Maya*, in 1946, believed the Maya to be a peaceful people. He suggested "a near absence of war" and "comparative tranquility in the central Maya area during Classic times" (Morley 1956: 58). Modern research has changed this view, as Michael Coe's 1966 description attests:

> The Maya were obsessed with war. The Annals of the Cakchiquels and the Popol Vuh speak of little but intertribal conflict among the highlanders, while the 16 states of Yucatán were

Illustration 28. Raid on an enemy village to obtain captives for sacrifice, from the Bonampak murals. From Thompson, *Rise and Fall of Maya Civilization*, p. 95.

constantly battling with each other over boundaries and lineage honour. To this sanguinary record we must add the testimony of the Classic monuments and their inscriptions. From these and from the eyewitness descriptions of the *conquistadores* we can see how Maya warfare was waged. The *holcan* or "braves" were the footsoldiers; they wore cuirasses of quilted cotton or of tapir hide and carried thrusting spears with flint points, darts-with-*atlatl*, and in late Post-Classic times, the bow-and-arrow. Hostilities typically began with an unannounced guerrilla raid into the enemy camp to take captives, but more formal battle opened with the dreadful din of drums, whistles, shell trumpets, and war cries. On either side of the war leaders and the idols carried into the combat under the care of the priests were the two flanks of infantry, from which rained darts, arrows, and stones flung from slings. Once the enemy had penetrated into home territory however, irregular warfare was substituted, with

ambuscades and all kinds of traps.
Lesser captives ended up as slaves,
but the nobles and war leaders had
their hearts torn out on the sacrificial
stone (Coe 1966: 147).

This picture of Postclassic warfare has been
extended back into the Classic period, when in-
cessant and apparently nonterritorial war was
waged.

Deities and Myths

The Maya considered Itzamná to be their principal deity. He was the creator of the universe
and was worshiped as the god of harvest, sun,
earth, and rain. Also of substantial importance
in the Maya pantheon were the deities of the
sun and moon: Kinich Ahau, lord of the sun,
and Ix Chel, goddess of the moon.

The Chacs, gods of rain, are popular deities
among present-day Maya, and the Chacs appear, with their characteristic long noses, on the
facades of many Classic Maya structures in Yucatán.

At Tikal, Copán, and Quiriguá, four deities
appear most frequently in the iconography of
the stelae, lintels, and buildings: the three gods
of the Palenque Triad of deities (GI, the Fish
God; GII, God K, or the Flare God; and GIII,
Jaguar God of the underworld), and the Sun
God, or Kinich Ahau.

In addition to these deities, the bloodletting
symbol of the Quadripartite Badge is an important manifestation of the Maya relationship to
the gods; it was the obligation of the Maya lord
to nourish the gods by giving his blood.

Each of these deities has certain recognizable
characteristics:

GI. The GI glyph exhibits several of the identifying characteristics of the god: a big god eye,
Roman nose, a tau tooth, a fish barbel extending
from a cheek, and a shell ear. He is associated
with Hunahpú of the Hero Twins.

GII. The GII glyph shows the primary mark
that identifies GII or God K—the flare in the
form of a pine torch, a cigar, or an axe in his
forehead. He is also shown with an obsidian
mirror in his forehead, and often with a serpent
foot.

Illustration 29. God GI, the Fish God. From
Michael D. Coe, *Maya Scribe*, p. 108.

Illustration 30. GII (God K) and Jester God. From
Robertson, *Primera Mesa Redonda de Palenque, I.*

God K and the Jester God have been identified
as closely connected with rulership, and God K
has been identified with the "Smoking (or Obsidian) Mirror," the prototype of the Aztec god,
Tezcatlipoca.

35

GI   GII

GII   a   GIII

b

Illustration 31. (a) Glyphs representing GI, GII, and GIII, the Palenque Triad. From *Segunda Mesa Redonda de Palenque*, vol. 3, p. 10. Drawings by Linda Schele. (b) Cruller, one of GIII's attributes.

GIII. The Jaguar God of the underworld can be identified by his jaguar ear, a tau tooth, a cruller in his forehead, and gathered hair. He is associated with the Hero Twin, Xbalanqué.

Sun God. The Sun God, who appears frequently at Quiriguá, is often referred to as Kinich Ahau. Thompson saw Kinich Ahau as an aspect of Itzamná, the greatest of all the gods. This representation of the Sun God is seen often on the regalia of rulers, especially on the loincloth.

Cauac Monster. The rulers of the Classic period in the lowlands employed representations of the Cauac Monster on their stelae to "symbolize their own role as the rightfully dynastic inheritors of the office of sacrificial intercession with the divine ancestors and Underworld rulers" (Tate 1980: 2).

The Cauac Monster is the god of storm and lightning and the manifestation of the earth as the core. The characteristics of the Cauac Monster include a stepcurl forehead with a niche in the center; eyes that may relate to the jaguar, or vegetation or water symbols; a nose represented by a curling line; generally no lower jaw; a broad central tooth and curling fangs; and an open mouth. The most pronounced characteristic is the "bunch of grapes" symbol, which is also a part of the Cauac day-sign glyph T528, from which the Cauac Monster gets its name.

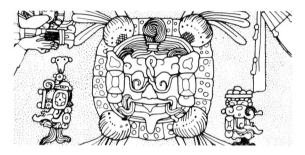

Illustration 32. Jaguar God of the underworld (center). From Ferguson and Royce, *Maya Ruins of Mexico in Color*, p. 56. Drawing by Linda Schele.

Illustration 33. Sun God (three faces) Stela F, Quiriguá.

36

Illustration 34.   Glyph T528 (Cauac).

Carolyn Tate concludes that the Cauac monster represents or symbolizes the transformation that the Maya believed affected all forms of life within the earth. The Cauac Monster also referred to the earth as the home of deceased deified ancestors and deities, who required nourishment by bloodletting. We may therefore associate the Cauac Monster with sacrifice and bloodletting, cycles of time, and the regeneration of life.

The Maya universe was filled with a great number of deities, perhaps even thousands, considering the various aspects of each deity. "Each was not only one but four individuals, separately assigned to the color-directions" (Coe 1966: 151). Many had counterparts in the opposite sex, and each astronomical god had an underworld counterpart. As each god died, he passed beneath the earth to reappear in the heavens in the same way as the sun sets and rises. Illustration 36 depicts the major gods of the Maya pantheon.

Maya religion was not based on the contrast between good and evil, and apparently most of the Maya deities were considered to embody a duality of good and evil. The god of rain, for example, was probably considered benevolent as long as the rains came in the normal amounts at normal times, but the same god became malevolent when the area was struck by a hurricane. In the same way, the Sun God was probably considered perverse during periods of drought.

The *Popol Vuh* of the Maya commanded man to nourish the gods with blood. The Maya honored this injunction with their bloodletting ceremonies.

The priests bore the responsibility for the relationship of the Maya to their gods. In addition, according to Landa, they directed the "compu-

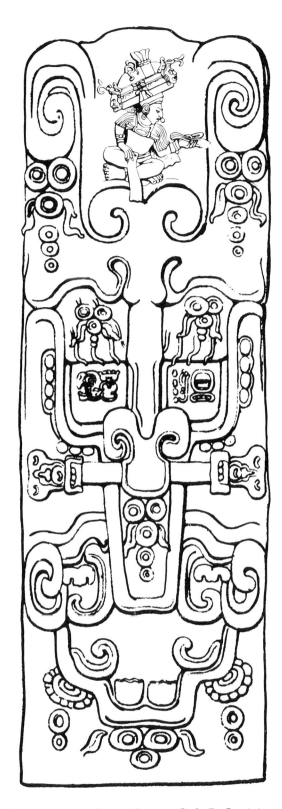

Illustration 35.   Cauac Monster (Stela B, Copán). From Francis Robicsek, *Copán, Home of the Mayan Gods*, p. 75.

37

Illustration 36. Gods of the Maya pantheon with their name glyphs, from the Dresden Codex; (a) Death God, (b) Chaac, the Rain God, (c) North Star God, (d) Itzamná, (e) Maize God, (f) Sun God, (g) Young Moon Goddess, (h) Bolon Dzacab, (i) Ek Chuab, the Merchant God, (j) Ixchel, Goddess of Medicine and Childbirth. From Ferguson and Royce, *Maya Ruins of Mexico in Color*, p. 10.

tation of the years, months, and days, the festivals and the ceremonies, the administration of the sacraments, the fateful days and seasons, their methods of divination and their prophecies, events, and the cures of diseases and their antiquities and how to read and write the letters and characters" (Coe 1966: 153).

Both ritual acts and the details were governed by the calendar. Rituals involved bathing, abstinence from food and sexual contact, and sacrifice. As we have seen, self-mutilation was carried out by piercing the ears, cheeks, lips, tongue, and penis, and spattering the blood on the face or body of the representation of a god. Animal and human sacrifices were performed, the human sacrificial victims generally being prisoners of war, slaves, or children. Special rites were performed in connection with military campaigns, as well as on behalf of hunters, farmers, fishermen, and artisans.

Origins of Maya Symbolism

David Freidel's excavation of Temple 5C at Cerros in northern Belize revealed at Structure 5C-2nd four great masks from Late Preclassic times. With the iconography of these masks as a starting point, David Freidel and Linda Schele have developed a hypothesis that these masks incorporate much of the symbolism utilized by the lowland Maya kings during the Classic period to demonstrate publicly the legitimacy of their rule.

On each side of the pyramid stairway at Cerros are two masks, one above the other. The lower two masks are composites embodying two faces. One of the lower masks has jaguar characteristics and sun symbolism, which the later Maya associated with the underworld at sunrise and sunset.

The temple itself is aligned north and south and sits on a promontory extending northward

38

Illustration 37. Cerros, Belize.

into Chetumal Bay. From the plaza in front of the temple, the people could see the sun's daily cycle. The iconography on the masks framing the east and west sides of the temple stairway symbolized the physical passage of the sun from east to west. It also symbolized Venus as the morning star preceding the sun at sunrise and as the evening star following the sun after sunset. To the Maya, it was a schematic representation of the sun's passage.

If we visualize the king standing on the stairway between the east and west masks, we can see that he becomes central to both the physical and symbolic representation of solar movement.

Schele feels that this concept of the role of the king as an integral part of the sun's passage was much more than a religious concept: rather, it was a Maya rationale of the way his cosmos worked—a set of principles in which he believed, much the same as twentieth-century man conceives the universe to operate according to the laws of nuclear physics. This symbolism became a major element of the Maya culture in Classic times.

From the iconography that appears on these stucco masks came the earplug assemblage (a square plug with a central hole and four corner holes), a serpent muzzle with knots above and below, and the antecedents of symbols representing the Palenque Triad of gods (GI, God K, and GIII) and the Jester God, the god so closely connected with the legitimacy of Maya kings. From the long-nosed god represented on the upper mask (GI or Venus) developed the sky band and the double-headed ceremonial serpent bar. Much of the iconography of the headdress and the chin strap can be traced to these masks. The *Kin* glyph, which represents the sun, appears on the lower right mask, and the Venus sign appears on the upper right mask. The elements of the Quadripartite Badge are also found on these masks. All are symbols of kingship, and all are found in Classic times throughout the lowland Maya area. It is remarkable that here at Cerros on this Preclassic temple, 5C-2nd, built between 50 B.C. and A.D. 25 are found almost all of the iconographic elements later used in Classic times by Maya kings to demonstrate their right to rule.

During the Middle Preclassic period from 1000 to 300 B.C., the regional interaction in the lowlands—both trade and war—produced a change from an essentially egalitarian society to what Freidel terms a low-profile, self-effacing elite. Between 300 B.C. and A.D. 1, agricultural ridged or raised fields (hydraulic system) were developed, which led to the production of a surplus of food. At the same time, a class society emerged that incorporated the concept that the rulers were the descendants of the gods. Freidel and Schele have further concluded that the Preclassic cultures of the Maya lowlands probably spoke the root languages of the modern Chol and Yucatec, or at least the lowland Preclassic Maya probably used mutually understandable languages. These three elements: food, a class society, and communication through language and trade made possible a flowering of culture that took place in the lowlands in Late Preclassic times.

At Cerros, Freidel says, "This period, which lasted for a relatively short time from 50 B.C. to about A.D. 25, involved such an explosive transformation that it is fitting to speak of massive urban renewal" (Freidel, Robertson, and Cliff 1982: 12). Evidence of this cultural explosion, which embraced and included the symbolism found at Cerros, can be found at Tikal, Cuello, Uaxactún, Lamanaí, Mirador, and other sites during this period of the Late Preclassic.

At Cerros, the Freidel-Schele hypothesis suggests that the Preclassic Maya set in place on the facade of Temple 5C-2nd a public charter of kingship and a public definition of reality. These symbols were adopted by the Maya in cities all over the lowlands area, where they continued to be utilized by the Maya for nearly a thousand years.

Cosmology

The Book of Chilam Balam of Chumayel, also known as the *Book of the Prophet Balam,* was written in the Maya language using European script early in the sixteenth century in Yucatán. It articulates the Maya concept of cosmology, which envisioned that the universe consisted of thirteen layers above the earth and nine layers of inferno below. Each layer above and below had its own deities.

The earth itself was thought by the Maya to have been destroyed several times. After the last destruction, the gods set up four great ceiba trees of abundance (each surmounted by a bird) at the four cardinal quarters of the world. From these quarters came the winds; in them were located the four great jars of water that supplied the rains. The Maya connected the four cardinal points with a system of color symbolism: red for the east; white, the north; black, the west; and yellow, the south. In the exact center of the earth,

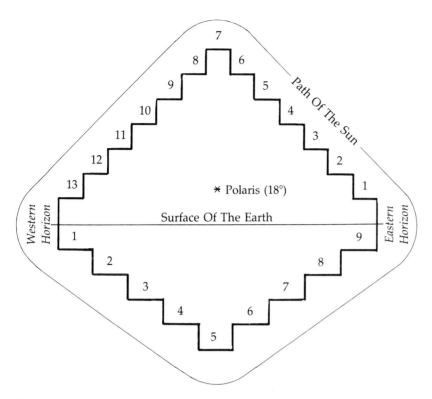

Illustration 38.   Maya upperworld and underworld.

the ceiba, the sacred tree of the Maya, stood with its roots in the underworld and its trunk and branches piercing the layers of the sky.

In order to support the sky, the gods placed four *bacabs,* representatives of the gods, at each cardinal point, and they, too, were distinguished by the red, white, black, and yellow colors assigned to each direction. In Yucatán, the *bacabs* may have been considered to be *chacs* or rain gods during the Classic period. But more likely the *bacabs* are manifestations of the Old Shell-back God, known as God N.

Generally speaking, the sky with its thirteen gods stood for goodness and light, while the underworld with its association with disease and death represented the powers of evil and darkness. In addition, as Thompson says:

> At the same time, there exists in Maya thought a sexual drama: the sky is male, the earth female, and their intercourse mystically brings life to the world. Similarly, light is male and darkness, female. The day 4 Ahau,

day of the Sun god, is creation (in Maya thought, darkness preceded creation); the day 1 Ahau, Venus at heliacal rising, emerging from the underworld, represents darkness. In the creation story of the Quiché in the Popol Vuh, the people anxiously wait in darkness for the rising of the morning star, harbinger of the light to come to the world (Thompson 1970: 196).

Thompson also tells us:

> There were thirteen "layers" of heaven and nine of the underworld . . . the thirteen celestial layers were arranged as six steps ascending from the eastern horizon to the seventh, the zenith, whence six more steps led down to the western horizon. Similarly, four more steps led down from the western horizon to the nadir of the underworld, whence four more steps ascended to the eastern horizon. (Thompson 1976: 195)

In effect, there were only seven upperworld layers and five underworld layers. The sun was considered by the Maya to follow these stepped layers from sunrise to sunset and sunset to sunrise. Polaris, the north star, is shown at 18 degrees above the horizon, which is its approximate position in the Maya area and indicates north in the diagram of the Maya cosmos shown in Illustration 38.

The sun was considered to be a god. At sunrise, he was fleshed and remained so during his journey across the daytime sky; as he made the passage, he went from young to old. At sunset, the Sun God descended into the underworld, land of the dead, where he became skeletal as he passed through the layers of the underworld. In the morning he became fleshed again as he arose from the land of the dead to cross the daytime sky.

The Hero Twins, Myth of the Underworld

In three scholarly and well illustrated books—*The Maya Scribe and His World* (1977), *Lords of the Underworld* (1978), and *Old Gods and Young Heroes* (1982)—Michael Coe discusses the Classic Maya concept of death and the underworld as evidenced by scenes painted or carved on Classic Maya funerary ceramics.

The myth of the Hero Twins, Hunahpú (pronounced hoón-a-poó) and Xbalanqué (pronounced sh-baá-lan-kay), and their conquest of the lords of Xibalba, the Maya underworld, is related in the Quiché Maya epic, the *Popol Vuh*. Although the *Popol Vuh* was written after the Spanish Conquest, eight hundred years after the close of the Classic Maya era, the discovery and analysis of the scenes on Classic Maya painted ceramics now tie the myth of the Hero Twins to Classic Maya times. Michael Coe suggests that the "Harrowing of Hell" by the Hero Twins related in the *Popol Vuh* (M. Coe 1977: 12) preserves one of many myths of the Classic Maya.

The word *Xibalba* (pronounced shee-baal-baa) is derived from the root *xib* ("fear, terror, trembling with fright") and represented an underworld, the entrance to which emitted a stench of rotting corpses and clotting blood (M. Coe 1977: 12).

The tale begins when the father and uncle of the Hero Twins, Hun Hunahpú and Vucub Hunahpú, annoy the lords of the underworld by playing the ball game. They are summoned to the underworld, where they are humiliated and sacrificed. The head of Hun Hunahpú is placed in a calabash tree. Later, the disembodied head spits into the hand of a daughter of one of the lords of Xibalba, causing her to become pregnant with the Hero Twins. She escapes from the underworld and takes refuge with the twins' prospective grandmother.

The Hero Twins, Hunahpú and Xbalanqué, grow up to be handsome young men, who are experts at the ball game and with the blow gun. Their playing of the ball game annoys the lords of Xibalba, who summon the twins to the underworld. After many adventures, the Hero Twins overcome the lords of the underworld and rise into the sky to become the sun and moon.

Michael Coe points out that the *Popol Vuh* myth can be seen in many details of Maya vase painting, but the references are often highly metaphorical. One episode of the adventures of the Hero Twins seems to be represented on Museum of Primitive Arts Vase No. 4 (Coe 1978). The episode is described in the Recinos translation of the *Popol Vuh*:

> And the lord said to them: "Cut my dog into pieces and let him be brought back to life by you," he said to them.
>
> "Very well," they answered, and cut the dog into bits. Instantly they brought him back to life. The dog was truly full of joy when he was brought back to life, and wagged his tail when they revived him.
>
> The lord said to them then: "Burn my house now!" Thus he said to them. Instantly they put fire to the lord's house, and although all the lords were assembled together within the house, they were not burned. Quickly it was whole again, and not for one instant was the house of Hun-Camé destroyed.
>
> All of the lords were amazed, and in the same way the [boys'] dances gave them much pleasure.

42

Illustration 39. Vase in codex style. Hunapú (left) as GI and Xbalanqué as GIII in the form of a jaguar before Hun-Camé (One Death) King of the underworld. Rollout photograph © Justin Kerr 1976.

Then they were told by the lord: "Now kill a man, sacrifice him, but do not let him die," he told them. "Very well," they answered. And seizing a man, they quickly sacrificed him, and raising his heart on high, they held it so that all the lords could see it.

Again Hun-Camé and Vucub Came were amazed. A moment afterward the man was brought back to life by them [the boys], and his heart was filled with joy when he was revived.

The lords were astounded. "Sacrifice yourselves now, let us see it! We really like your dances!" said the lords. And they proceeded to sacrifice each other. Hunahpú was sacrificed by Xbalanqué; one by one his arms and his legs were sliced off; his head was cut from his body and carried away; his heart was torn from his breast and thrown onto the grass. All the Lords of Xibalba were fascinated. They looked on in wonder, but really it was only the dance of one man; it was Xbalanqué.

"Get up!" he said, and instantly [Hunahpú] returned to life. They [the boys] were very happy and the lords were also happy. In truth, what they did gladdened the hearts of Hun-Camé and Vucub-Camé, and the latter felt as though they themselves were dancing.

Then their hearts were filled with desire and longing by the dances of Hunahpú and Xbalanqué; and Hun-Camé and Vucub-Camé gave their commands.

"Do the same with us! Sacrifice us!" they said. "Cut us into pieces, one by one!" Hun-Camé and Vucub-Camé said to Hunahpú and Xbalanqué.

"Very well; afterward you will come back to life again. Perchance, did you not bring us here in order that we should entertain you, the lords, and your sons, and vassals?" they said to the lords.

And so it happened that they first sacrificed the one, who was the chief [and Lord of Xibalba], the one called Hun-Camé, king of Xibalba.

And when Hun-Camé was dead, they overpowered Vucub-Camé, and they did not bring either of them back to life (Recinos 1950: 158).

The central element of the myth of the Hero Twins appears to have been similar to that of most other cultures—if the right prescription is

43

followed, death can be overcome. The Maya lords likewise probably believed that by conquering the underworld, as the Hero Twins did, they would become gods.

Numeration and Computation of Time

The ancient Maya were excellent mathematicians, having developed a system of numeration that included the concept of zero. They used a vertical vigesimal positional system of numeration, as distinguished from the horizontal decimal positional system we use. In our system, the positions to the left of the decimal point increase by tens. In the Maya system, the values of the positions increase by twenties from bottom to top.

In writing their numbers, the Maya used the dot with a numerical value of 1, and the bar with a numerical value of 5. Varying combinations of these two symbols created the written numbers from 1 to 19. These combinations of bars and dots make up the so-called normal forms of Maya numbers. In addition to the normal bar and dot forms of the numbers, a second method for writing numbers was used in the inscriptions employing different types of human heads in profile to represent the numbers. These are referred to as head variant numbers. The symbols for the numbers 1 to 19 are shown in Illustration 42.

Any positional numerical system must have a character or symbol to maintain the positions of the various orders and to indicate that no units of that order are involved. In the codices, the extant written records of the ancient Maya, the figure used was a stylized shell. Signs for zero found in the codices appear in Illustration 40.

In the mathematical computations shown in the codices, a purely vigesimal system was used, progressing from the bottom up as 1s, 20s, 400s, 8,000s, 160,000s and so on, as shown in Illustration 41, in which column four—the sum of the three preceding columns was obtained by combining the bars and dots of columns one, two, and three.

In counting time—the count of the days, so important to the Maya—a somewhat different

Illustration 40. Maya zero signs. From S. G. Morley, *An Introduction to the Study of Maya Hieroglyphs*, Fig. 46.

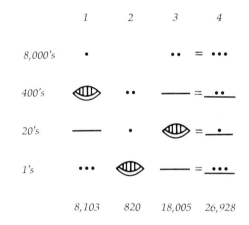

Illustration 41. Vigesimal computation. From Ferguson and Royce, *Maya Ruins of Mexico in Color*, p. 11.

system was used. The Maya Long Count was a consecutive count of elapsed days from a fixed date in the past, in the same way that our culture uses the birth of Christ as a starting point. As a starting point, the Maya used a date calculated to be August 11, 3114 B.C., according to our calendar, using the Goodman-Martinez-Thompson correlation.

In the time count, only eighteen units of the second order make one unit of the third order. Thus, the third order is 360s, approximating the number of days in the solar year, instead of 400s, as in a purely vigesimal system. Above the third order, the system again proceeds vigesimally with 7,200s, 144,000s, and so on.

It should be noted that if the tun is considered to be the basic unit, the system may be conceived as purely vigesimal. Thus, 20 tuns equal 1 katun; 400 tuns equal 1 baktun; 8,000 tuns equal 1 piktun, and so on. Evidence reveals that the Maya thought of the Long Count in exactly this manner.

In the codices, the time counts, like the mathematical notations, are wholly positional. This is not true, however, of the time counts in the carved inscriptions. In the inscriptions, the normal bar and dot numbers were affixed either above or to the left of glyphs representing various Maya time periods. These time periods are:

large element above it containing a curling infix, as shown in Illustration 45.

Both the normal form numbers (bar and dot) and the the head variant numbers are affixed either above or on the left of glyphs for day and month names, giving the day name and the number of the day in the month, as well as being affixed to period glyphs.

When we write a Maya Long Count number using arabic numerals, we write in descending orders of time periods from left to right. Thus, 9.18.10.0.0 10 Ahau 8 Zac, is calculated as 9 baktuns (9 × 144,000 = 1,296,000), plus 18 katuns (18 × 7,200 = 129,600), plus 10 tuns (10 × 360

		1 Kin		=	1 day
20 Kins	=	1 Uinal		=	20 days
18 Uinals	=	1 Tun		=	360 days
20 Tuns	=	1 Katun (20 Tuns)		=	7200 days
20 Katuns	=	1 Baktun (400 Tuns)		=	144,000 days
20 Baktuns	=	1 Piktun (8000 Tuns)		=	2,880,000 days
20 Piktuns	=	1 Calabtun (16,000 Tuns)		=	57,600,000 days
20 Calabtun	=	1 Kinchiltun (320,000 Tuns)		=	1,152,000,000 days
20 Kinchiltun	=	1 Alautun (6,400,000 Tuns)		=	23,040,000,000 days

In the inscriptions, a single column of glyphs is read from top to bottom. With two or more columns, the glyphs are read from left to right and top to bottom by columns of twos. The ordinary Long Count dates are inscribed in order from the largest unit to the smallest; however, in some supplementary series, the order may be reversed. Nevertheless, if, for example, the number 9 is affixed as a coefficient of the glyph for baktun, it signifies 3,600 tuns or 1,296,000 days (9 × 144,000 = 1,296,000), regardless of its position in the inscriptions.

The signs for zero in the inscriptions are also different from those found in the codices. In the inscriptions , the signs shown in Illustration 44 were affixed to a time period glyph to indicate that no units of that order are included.

Another sign for zero, used in the inscriptions expressing the idea of "ending" or "end of" in period-ending dates, is the clasped hand with a

= 3,600), plus 0 uinals, plus 0 kin equals 1,429,200 days that have elapsed since the starting point of the current Maya era.

This calculation can also be made by tuns as follows: 9 baktuns (9 × 400 = 3,600 tuns), plus 18 katuns (18 × 20 = 360 tuns), plus 10 tuns, equals 3,970 tuns, equals 3,970 × 360 = 1,429,200 days, plus 0 uinals, plus 0 kins makes a total of 1,429,200 days. The day reached at the end of these 1,429,200 days is 10 Ahau 8 Zac, which, according to the Goodman-Martinez-Thompson correlation, would be August 19, A.D. 800 in the Gregorian calendar.

The starting point or base date of the current Maya era is almost universally accepted as 13.0.0.0.0. 4 Ahau 8 Cumku. However, the problem of correlating Maya dates with the Gregorian calendar has proved extremely difficult. The two most widely used correlations are the Spinden correlation and the Goodman-Martinez-

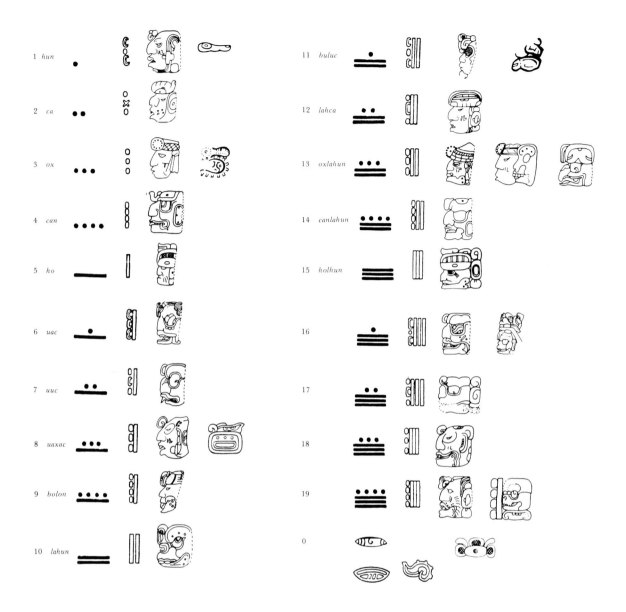

1 *hun*	•			
2 *ca*	••			
3 *ox*	•••			
4 *can*	••••			
5 *ho*	—			
6 *uac*	— •			
7 *uuc*	— ••			
8 *uaxac*	— •••			
9 *bolon*	— ••••			
10 *lahun*	═			
11 *buluc*	═ •			
12 *lahca*	═ ••			
13 *oxlahun*	═ •••			
14 *canlahun*	═ ••••			
15 *holhun*	≡			
16	≡ •			
17	≡ ••			
18	≡ •••			
19	≡ ••••			
0				

Illustration 42. Maya numerals (1-19). From D. H. Kelley, *Deciphering the Maya Script*, p. 22.

Thompson correlation, usually referred to as the Thompson correlation, or the GMT correlation. The Spinden correlation would place the Maya Long Count dates 260 years earlier than the GMT correlation. While both of these correlations have had, and continue to have, support among Mayanists, the majority favor the GMT correlation, which is used throughout this book. By the GMT correlation, the base date, 13.0.0.0.0. 4 Ahau 8 Cumku is August 11, 3114 B.C., in the Gregorian calendar.

As recently as 1980, David H. Kelley said, "I think it extremely unlikely that the widely accepted Thompson correlation is correct, but do not yet have any counter-proposal, as my own attempts to reach a solution also show inexplicable flaws" (Kelley 1980: S5).

The Maya used a Calendar Round of 52 years. It consisted of two permutating cycles, one of 260 days, the other a vague year of 365 days. The 260-day count meshed with a 365-day solar year composed of 18 months of 20 days each,

46

Day Signs   Month Signs

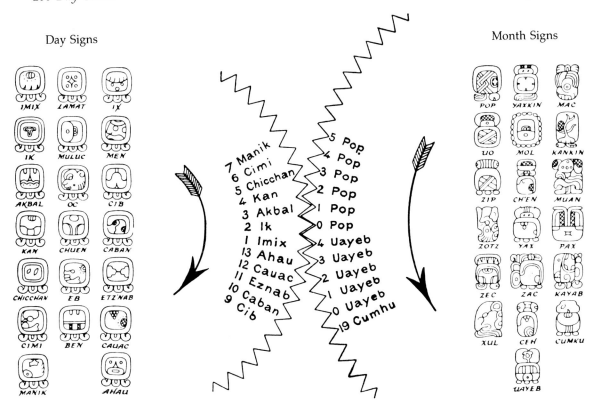

Illustration 43.   The 260 day–365 day time wheels.

with 5 unlucky days added at the end. Each day was considered to be a god with its own omens and associations. The 20-day periods were a "kind of perpetual fortune-telling machine guiding the destinies of the Maya" (M. Coe 1966: 55).

The Maya living in the Guatemala highlands, who were under Olmec influence, began using their calendar in its final form by the first century B.C., and usage gradually spread to the Petén area. The Long Count system was based on elapsed days so that it would be accurate over great periods of time. In addition, the Maya faced the problem of coordinating their lunar calendar with the solar calendar. About A.D. 682, the Maya at Copán began calculating with the formula 149 moons = 4,400 days, a time-computing system that was eventually adopted by most of the other Maya centers.

The texts in the Group of the Cross in Palenque suggest that the Palencanos were inter-

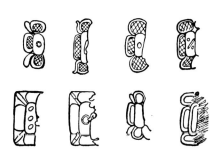

Illustration 44.   Zero affixes. From Morley, *An Introduction to the Study of Maya Hieroglyphs*, Fig. 47.

Illustration 45.   Period-ending zero signs. From Morley, *An Introduction to the Study of Maya Hieroglyphs*, Fig. 54.

ested in calculating the accumulated error in the 365-day calendar, which produced a one-day drift every four solar years. Some of the dates in the Group of the Cross are very near to the amount of time (1,508 years of 365 days and 1,507 years of 365.2422 days) that it takes for a day to drift entirely around the 365-day calendar to return to its original position in the solar year.

The birth of the Palenque Triad of Gods occurred one-half of one of these adjustment cycles after 4 Ahau 8 Cumku; thus, if the era began on a summer solstice, the god would have been born near the winter solstice. In addition, other historical dates celebrated the tropical year (including leap-day calculations) and anniversaries of major dynastic events.

Astronomy

Astronomy was of great interest to Maya scholars, who recognized that the planet Venus was both a morning and an evening star. Many generations of observing and record keeping were required for the Maya to arrive at the figure of 584 days for the Venus year—an error of only one day in 6,000 years.

The Maya envisioned Venus as the evening star pushing the sun into the underworld and as the morning star pulling it up. In observing the association of the sun and Venus either as the evening or morning star, the logic of this concept becomes immediately apparent.

These astronomers also evolved tables for predicting when (but not where) solar eclipses might be visible, and they calculated the lunar revolution to average 29.53020 days, compared with the actual average of 29.53059. Their calculations often went millions of years into the past or the future. Very often they deliberately calculated the intervals between contemporary and ancient dates so that both occupied the same station in several cycles: cycles of the moon, Venus, the sun, eclipses, and nonastronomical cycles not yet fully understood. Recent evidence suggests that the Maya used the Venus cycle as a stimulus for war, and that other astronomical observations, especially those of Jupiter, played a part in ritual events.

Hieroglyphic Writing

During the Late Preclassic period (200 B.C.–A.D. 150), most of the peoples of southern Mesoamerica used basically the same calendric system. The names of the days and months varied from area to area, but the base date (13.0.0.0.0 4 Ahau 8 Cumku in Yucatec Maya) seems to have been generally utilized for Long Count notations.

Although the calendrics showed similarity, Schele and other epigraphers believe that the peoples of Abaj Takalik, Kaminaljuyú, Izapa, and other sites used script that varied from site to site and from language to language. The earliest examples of the Maya writing system to include both calendric notation and recognizable signs appear to have developed in the lowlands during the first three hundred years of the Christian era.

The earliest evidence of clearly identifiable Maya glyphs appears on the stucco facade of Structure 5C-2nd at Cerros in northern Belize. David Freidel estimates the erection date of the temple to have been about 50 B.C. Friedel says: "I now have a solid C14 date on a termination ritual carried out on one of the pyramids at Cerros that places abandonment of the site before the time of Christ. I estimate that 5C-2nd is at least 50 years older" (Freidel 1981). William Coe indicates the presence of a painted Akbal glyph on Building 5A-Sub. 10-1st at Tikal is contemporaneous with the Cerros glyphs. The next known use of Maya glyphs appears on Tikal Stela 29—Tikal's earliest dated monument—which bears the Maya Long Count date 8.12.14.8.15 (A.D. 292). By that time, the glyphic writing system had been fully matured. This date opens the Classic Maya period. The stela itself is now housed in the Tikal Museum.

The famous Leiden Plaque (Ill. 118), now generally accepted as being from Tikal, is a third piece of evidence of early Maya hieroglyphic writing. It records the accession date of a ruler of Tikal, possibly Jaguar Paw, in 8.14.3.1.12 (A.D. 320).

Existing Maya hieroglyphic writing is found on stelae and altars, on the walls and lintels of public buildings, and in the illuminated manuscripts called codices. Four codices are extant—the Dresden, Paris, Madrid, and the recently authenticated Grolier. This body of glyphs (except for the Grolier Codex) constitutes the source of Thompson's *Catalogue of Maya Hieroglyphs.*

The glyphs on ceramics recovered primarily from graves are, in many cases, different from those of other sources. Thompson dismissed them as purely decorative, but they are now considered to be additions to the body of known glyphs, although most of them are not yet understood.

Additional hieroglyphic texts or portions of texts continue to be gleaned from various sources, many of which contain new and heretofore unknown glyphs. In the early 1980s, Emilio Bernabe Pop discovered a mile-deep cave in southeast Guatemala near the Belize border at Naj Tunich. The cave contains a number of painted glyphs, some hitherto unknown or used in new configurations.

In his sixteenth-century *Relación de las Cosas de Yucatán*, Bishop Landa explained the Maya calendric system. When these writings were rediscovered in the latter part of the nineteenth century, Mayanists were able to read the dates, and were struck by the plethora of dates contained in the inscriptions on buildings and stelae. They concluded that the Maya were particularly concerned with the passage of time itself, a sort of time-for-time's-sake record. What they did not know then was the tendency of the Maya to tie events in time to the several cycles of solar and lunar time contained in Maya calendrics, and a tendency toward redundancy encouraged by use of couplets in describing events.

The tendancy for rulers, such as Rameses II, Caesar Augustus, Napoleon, and Lincoln, and their peoples to make public declarations in stone of lineages and exploits is well known. This custom of people to so honor their rulers prompted Tatianna Proskouriakoff to speculate that stelae containing three successive dates all within the span of a normal lifetime could refer to the birth, accession, and death of a king. In 1960, she published "Historical Implications of a Pattern of Dates at Piedras Negras, Guatemala," a brilliant piece of scholarship in which she demonstrated that the glyphs on stelae were historical records involving real people, not simply calendric notations, as previous Mayanists thought. In the years following the Proskouriakoff breakthrough, the Maya glyphs have been translated bit by bit. It is now known that the bulk of the glyphic writing on the stelae and public buildings are public and semipublic declarations designed to demonstrate the legitimacy of the ruler's authority and to proclaim his successes in office. Generally, the legitimacy of rulership is demonstrated by showing the king's descent from historical, legendary, or mythical ancestry. As a result of this propensity on the part of Maya kings, particularly at Palenque, we now have a wealth of Maya history, legend, mythology, and poetry.

The redundancy and couplet structure used in describing the events of the rulers' lives confused early Mayanists because the inscriptions are not only history, they are also literature, reflecting formal literary convention and oral tradition. As Schele says, the Maya were not time freaks, as early scholars thought, they used time as a framework within which to demonstrate the king's relationship to his ancestors and gods.

Illustration 47 shows the accession record of Chan-Bahlum from the Tablet of the Foliated Cross at Palenque. The text records the birth and accession of Chan-Bahlum and links his accession to an event celebrated six years later by the gods of the Palenque Triad: GI, GII, and GIII.

Recent Discoveries at the Cave of Naj Tunich (Stone House)

Naj Tunich, a cave recently discovered in the Petén area of eastern Guatemala, contains magnificent Classic Maya paintings and glyphic texts done near the middle of the eighth century A.D. George E. Stuart wrote an excellent article in the August 1981 *National Geographic*, entitled "Maya Art Treasures in Cave."

Shown here from the Passage of Rites room in the cave are two figures: at the top a Maya wearing a headdress and loincloth sits tailor fashion with a conch shell in front of him. The lower figure is a standing ballplayer wearing a chest protector and kneepad faces a ball topped by the number 9.

As George Stuart suggests, these figures embody Maya underworld (Xibalba) symbolism. The conch shells' association with the sea relates the figures to the underworld. The ball game is an integral part of the myth of the Hero Twins' struggle with the lords of the underworld, and the number 9 may relate to the number of levels of the underworld. The Maya may have considered the cave itself as an entrance to Xibalba.

The glyphic texts here depicted do not equate well with other known Classic Maya texts. David Stuart, an epigrapher who was a part of the expedition to Naj Tunich reported in the August 1981 *National Geographic,* suggested in a personal communication that the texts that appear in the cave are not standard and are difficult to make out. He has been able to identify glyphs that make reference to persons, events, and dates but little more than that. In addition, several "impossible dates" are noted—that is, dates such as February 30 would be in our calendar. Such impossible dates are not unusual in Maya texts, and no one knows whether they were mistakes or were done deliberately.

Illustration 46.   Naj Tunich, glyphs, ballplayer and seated figure. Photograph by Wilbur E. Garrett, © 1981 National Geographic Society.

Illustration 47.   Panel from the Temple of the
Foliated Cross, Palenque, recording the accession of
Chan-Bahlum. From Ferguson and Royce, *Maya
Ruins of Mexico in Color*, p. 54. Drawing by Linda
Schele.

Tikal Area

The ruins of Tikal are located in the rain forest of northern Guatemala about 60 miles east of the Belize border, 40 miles by road northeast of Flores, and about 190 air miles north of Guatemala City. Santa Elena has a new jet airport on the mainland just off the island town of Flores.

Flores was Tayasal, one of the last areas conquered by the Spaniards. Tayasal, an island on Lake Petén Itzá, was occupied in the Postclassic period by the Itza from Yucatán. When Hernan Cortez encountered it in 1524, he was received by King Canek. Although the Spaniards made various attempts to take Tayasal, it was not finally conquered until 1697—173 years after the Cortez visit.

Today the village of Tikal surrounds an airport (built in 1951) near the archaeological site. In Tikal, an excellent small museum named for S. G. Morley contains many well-displayed artifacts from the ruins. Several small hostelries and the Aviateca office are grouped around the west threshold of the airstrip. The entrance to the ruins is about 300 yards to the west of the village.

Archaeological work has been going on at Tikal since the middle of the nineteenth century. In 1853, the Berlin Academy of Science published an account of the explorations of Modesto Mendez and Ambrosio Tut, officials of the government of Guatemala. In the 1870s, a Swiss, Gustav Bernoulli, explored the site. He arranged for the removal of the lintels from Temples I and IV, now in the Museum fur Volkerkunde in Basel, Switzerland. It is sad they are not *in situ,* but at least they have been preserved. A. P. Maudslay, an Englishman who also worked extensively at Copán and Quiriguá, arrived in 1881. Teobert Maler visited Tikal twice, in 1895 and 1904. He was followed by A. M. Tozzer; together they published a Peabody Museum report on Tikal in 1911. S. G. Morley made several visits to Tikal from 1914 to 1928. These pioneers have been remembered by having Tikal monuments named in their honor.

In 1956, the University Museum of the University of Pennsylvania began an eleven-year program of restoration and study, under the di-

Illustration 48. Airstrip at Tikal, Guatemala, showing the Bonanza used by the authors.

Illustration 49. Aviateca Office, Tikal.

rection of William R. Coe and Edwin M. Shook. This project continued for thirteen seasons until 1969, with restoration funds from many sources. The Guatemalan government provided large sums for restoration and continues to do so.

Tikal, one of the major archaeological sites of the world, is located in a magnificent setting and is exciting to behold. This magnificent flower of the jungle is an indigenous New World blossom and should be visited, at some time, by every *aficionado* of Precolumbian culture.

Illustration 50.   Aerial View of the Island of Flores,
Guatemala, the Maya city of Tayasal.

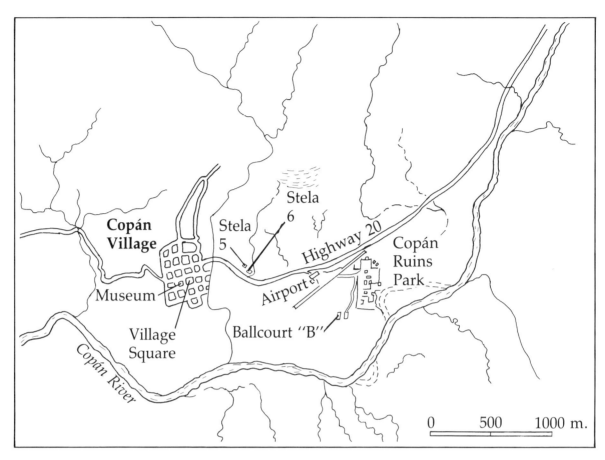

Illustration 51.   Copán River Valley, Honduras, C.A.

Copán Area

Copán, the southernmost of the principal Maya Classic period sites, is situated in a mountain valley on the western edge of Honduras, not more than four or five miles from the Guatemalan border and near the picturesque Spanish colonial town now called "Ruinas de Copán." The ruins are a mile east of the town of Copán on Highway 10—the only road in or out of Copán except for the road leading into Guatemala. In town, with its entrance facing the church across the main plaza, is the Regional Museum of Mayan Archaeology, which houses a number of artifacts from the Copán ruins.

Don Diego García de Palacio wrote to Philip II of Spain in 1576, saying:

> Near here and in Copán, the first town within the province of Honduras, on the road to the city of

San Pedro, we came across certain ruins and remains of what seems to have been a great civilization. There are structures built with such skill and splendor that it seems that they could have never been built by the natives of that province. They are located on the banks of a beautiful river in an extensive and well-chosen plain, which enjoys a temperate climate, is fertile and abounding in fish and game. Amongst the ruins there are mounds which appear to have been made by man, as well as many other remarkable things (Nuñez C. 1975: 9).

Alfred P. Maudslay studied the ruins between 1891 and 1894 and made the drawings of the stelae that are included in this book. He was followed by Herbert J. Spinden in 1913. Sylvanus G. Morley and the Carnegie Institution

54

Illustration 52.   Village square, Copán Ruinas,
Honduras.

of Washington, together with the Honduran government, began the excavation and restoration of Copán in 1935. Gustav Strömsvik restored the stelae. Most of the restoration work around the central plaza of the ruins was done prior to 1942. Recent restoration has been done by the Honduran government under the direction first of Claude Baudez, then of William Sanders. The ruins are now a part of an archaeological zone operated by the National Institute of Anthropology and History (INAH) of Honduras.

The ruins are located in a valley about eight miles long and a mile and a half wide; it is cut by the Copán River flowing northwest into the Motagua River in Guatemala. The valley is about two thousand feet above sea level and surrounded on all sides by tree-covered mountains, which rise a thousand feet from the valley floor. The climate is warm and dry in the winter and warm and rainy in the summer. This is mountain country, neither jungle nor rain forest.

Along the road from the town to the ruins are two stelae: Stela 6, dated A.D. 692, and Stela 5, dated A.D. 706. On the north side of the ruins running parallel to the road is the Copán airstrip (a short grass strip designed for light aircraft), which one must cross to enter the ruins. The reception committee is composed of the ticket taker and several beautiful and vocal macaws.

Outside the park, about one-fourth mile south of the park entrance, is the recently restored Ball Court B, accessible by a trail leading to the southwest (Ill. 54). This I-shaped court with two walled end zones was discovered in 1978 and excavated by Bill Fash. It has no markers nor any stone or stucco floor. Its three phases of construction all took place in the Late Classic. Inside the park is the core of the magnificent ruins of the Classic Maya civilization of Copán.

Illustration 53. Stela 5 near Copán ruins.

Illustration 54. Aerial view of Copán's Ball Court B.

Illustration 55.   Stela 6 on the road to Copán ruins.

Illustration 56.   Macaws at the entrance to Copán ruins.

Illustration 57.   Cessna 185 used by the authors on the Copán airstrip at the entrance to the ruins.

Quiriguá Area

In a small island of primeval forest of giant ceibas, mahoganies, and cohune palms within a sea of banana plants are the ruins of Quiriguá, Guatemala (Ill. 58). Quiriguá is about 135 miles northeast of Guatemala City, where the Motagua River valley between the Sierra del Espíritu Santo Mountains on the southeast and the Montaña del Mico range on the northwest make a flood plain five or six miles wide. The continuous overflow of the valley by the Motagua River creating rich alluvial soil, coupled with the hot, moist climate, make this an area ideal for growing bananas.

In 1910, the United Fruit Company set aside the area that is now the Quiriguá Park, about three miles east of Los Amates, a small Guatemalan village. In the 1930s, the only way a visitor could reach the ruins was by rail. The service by rail still exists and is used by workers in the banana plantations. Illustration 60 shows workers loading the train at the entrance to the ruins.

The restoration has been done recently by the University of Pennsylvania, as the sign in Illustration 59 indicates. Original work was done in the nineteenth century by A. P. Maudslay. In 1883, Maudslay spent three months in the ruins making plaster reproductions of the monuments and drawings of the sculptures and the hieroglyphic inscriptions. In the decade before 1920, the Archaeological Institute of America sent several expeditions to Quiriguá, with S. G. Morley on the staff. Morley also did research at Quiriguá sponsored by the Carnegie Institution of Washington between 1915 and 1934. Gustav Strömsvik repaired and re-erected several of the giant stelae.

The towering forest enshrouds the ruins and blocks out the evidence of modern man, so that the atmosphere of a visit to Quiriguá approximates that of a thousand years ago, when ancient Quiriguá was a powerful Maya trading center on the Motagua River.

Illustration 58. "Ruins of Quiriguá" with a background of banana plants.

Illustration 59. Sign at the entrance to the Quiriguá, Guatemala, ruins.

Illustration 60. Railroad built by the United Fruit Company at the Quiriguá ruins.

Architecture

The spectacular architectural achievements of the Maya have long been the subject of attention and admiration. Classic Maya architecture had certain diagnostic features that spanned the region throughout the Classic period.

1. A rubble- or earth-filled substructure subdivided into terraced levels
2. One or more stairways leading from plaza spaces to the temple above
3. Corbeled vaults
4. Stucco veneer over the stone masonry
5. Roof combs
6. Exterior and interior relief sculpture
7. Frontality in temple architecture
8. Restricted interior space
9. Outward-looking architecture that functioned as a stage for ritual activity.

Modifications of both style and construction techniques appeared from area to area and from one period to another. Some of these differences and common features are discussed below in relation to the sites pictured in this volume. Additional details are given in the descriptions of the various sites and individual buildings.

Tikal Architecture: The massive pyramids whose crowning temples and roof combs thrust above the rain forest are the hallmark of Tikal architecture. Six of these great monuments can be seen rising above the Guatemalan jungle—Temples I through V and the Temple of the Inscriptions (Temple VI).

The Tikal pyramids were constructed like wedding cakes, with a series of terraces one above the other. These terraces were interlocked with interior retaining walls to contain the rubble fill as each terrace was constructed. The exterior of the pyramid was faced with masonry blocks held together with mortar. The top of each terrace was leveled and a plaster floor laid; stairways on the outside of the pyramid connected the terraces.

Nicholas Hellmuth suggests that a hundred men could build a terrace (such as those utilized in the pyramid structures supporting King Ah Cacaw's Temples I and II in the Great Plaza) in two months, and that a pyramid, temple, and

Illustration 61.   Tropical entrance to Quiriguá ruins.

Illustration 62.   In the village of Quiriguá, just west of the ruins.

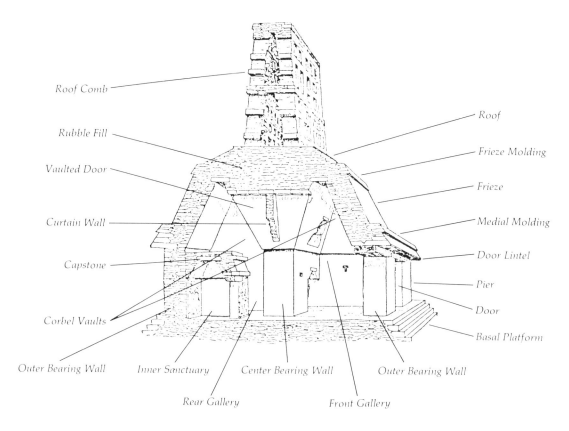

Roof Comb

Rubble Fill

Vaulted Door

Curtain Wall

Capstone

Corbel Vaults

Roof

Frieze Molding

Frieze

Medial Molding

Door Lintel

Pier

Door

Basal Platform

Outer Bearing Wall   Inner Sanctuary   Center Bearing Wall   Outer Bearing Wall

Rear Gallery   Front Gallery

Illustration 63.   Temple of the Cross, Palenque.
From Ferguson and Royce, *Maya Ruins of Mexico in Color*, p. 237.

roof comb could be completed within two years (Hellmuth 1976: 27).

These huge terraced pyramids were the platforms for the construction of temples. The temples were built with one or three doors on one side only. The interiors were composed of one or more narrow, high-vaulted rooms. To the twentieth-century observer, the temple rooms seem inordinately small and dark, particularly in view of the overall size of the structure. It must be remembered, however, that Maya pyramid-temples were not constructed for interior use, but rather for exterior visual effect. A most important space was that of the doors, over which carved wooden lintels were mounted.

The Maya used the corbeled vault. The vault was formed by insetting each row of stone masonry on the vault walls so that the walls slanted inward until they came together at the top, upon which a horizontal row of capstones was laid.

Illustration 64.   Corbeled vault.

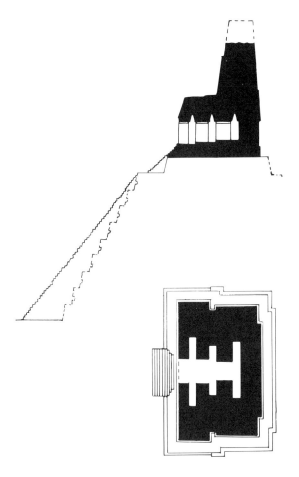

Illustration 65. Temple I, Tikal. From *Primera Mesa Redonda de Palenque*, vol. 2, p. 84. Drawing by Paul Gendrop.

Illustration 66. Temple II, Tikal. From T. Proskouriakoff, *An Album of Maya Architecture*, p. 9.

It was not a true arch, because it employed no keystone. The rubble in the surrounding walls provided the lateral support. The doors were capped with a wooden or stone lintel.

The massive stone roof combs were constructed to tower high above the rear of the temple. The temple and roof comb together made up approximately one-third the total height of a structure. The Temple of the Giant Jaguar (Temple I) on the east side of the Great Plaza is an example of this one-third–two-thirds proportion. The pyramid is approximately a hundred feet high and the temple and roof comb total fifty feet in height.

The sculptured stone roof combs were a principal element of the Tikal temple-pyramid. They were brightly painted (generally red, but often

with a combination of colors), and are believed to have depicted the lord to whom the temple was dedicated. The lord was portrayed in painted stone on the roof comb, towering above the city like a multistoried poster of Lenin. The temple-pyramid was plastered with white stucco and rose from a white-paved plaza below to support the temple with its garish red roof comb thrusting 150 feet in the air. These lithic edifices towered above the jungle to pay proper tribute to the deceased kings, whose funerary monuments they were.

A second principal type of Tikal architecture is the truncated pyramid, a pyramid lacking the temple crown. The earliest known is the Preclassic Lost World Pyramid (5C-54). When this pyramid was recently stripped during archaeological investigation, the construction revealed it to be a radial pyramid with four stairways. To the west of the Lost World Pyramid is an altar with four stairways. Another pyramid without a temple built in Early Classic times is located on the south side of the Great Plaza.

Smaller pyramids without temples with four stairways leading to a platform are part of the twin-pyramid complexes constructed in the Late Classic Period, as shown in Illustration 69.

Palace or range-type structures are a third category of construction at Tikal. They are long rectangular structures of one, two, and even five stories constructed with corbeled vaults to create long, narrow rooms. The construction method used to build the palace buildings is the same as for the temple buildings; each building is essentially a rectangular pile of rubble faced on the outside with stone, and containing on the inside a series of narrow, high-vaulted chambers with the doors as the only openings.

These range-type structures were the residences and administrative centers used by the ruler, the nobles, and their retinue. The Central Acropolis is the most obvious residential and administrative area. The Palace of the Windows, Group G Structures, and Structure 5D-91 in the Plaza of the Seven Temples are other residential buildings.

If we assume that all phases of the government were under the direct control of the ruler, a divine-right monarch, who with his staff managed obeisance to the gods, public building, food production, trade and commerce, and the military, we can envision the necessity for public buildings to house and office the bureaucrats needed to administer a city-state composed of perhaps more than 100,000 subjects.

Copán Architecture: Late Classic architecture at Copán employed terraced pyramids topped by range-type buildings without roof combs. The pyramids were constructed of rubble and faced with stone, as were the pyramids of Tikal.

Copán has a man-made acropolis, which supported the Eastern and Western Courts, Pyramid Structure 16, the beautifully adorned Structure 11 (Temple of the Inscriptions), Structure 22 (Temple of Meditation), and the recently

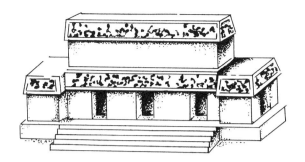

Illustration 67. Palace or range-type structure, Tikal (5D-65). Drawing by M. Remmert.

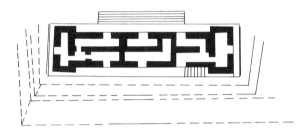

Illustration 68. Plan of Maler's Palace. Drawing by M. Remmert (after W.R. Coe).

restored Structure 18. The most unique and exciting aspect of the Copán ruins is the sculpture. In the words of Tatiana Proskouriakoff, "In most Petén cities architectural decoration was executed in stucco, and sculpture is largely confined to stelae and altars, whereas at Copán stone carvings, often in full round, adorned every important building" (Proskouriakoff 1963: 31).

The Temple of the Inscriptions was designed and constructed so as to effectively block off the acropolis from the plaza level below. It is a range-type building which faces the Court of the Hieroglyphic Stairway to the north, with no passageway through to the south side. The south face of the Temple of the Inscriptions surmounts the Reviewing Stand, which faces south overlooking the Western Court.

The Eastern Court (bounded by the Jaguar Stairway, Temple of Meditation, and a stairway on the east side) creates a rectangular amphitheatre surrounded by steps, from which spectators could view ceremonies.

The acropolis area is effectively isolated from the plaza floor to the north indicating that this

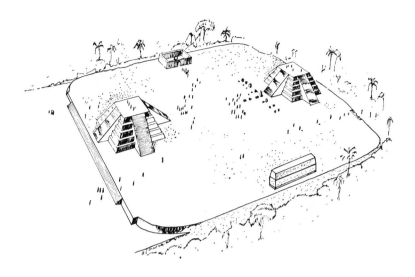

Illustration 69.   Twin-Pyramid Complex. From
George Kubler, *The Art and Architecture of Ancient
America,* p. 132.

Illustration 70.   Acropolis, Copán. From
Proskouriakoff, *Album of Maya Architecture,* p. 33.

area may have been reserved for the ruler and nobility. None of the buildings on the acropolis, however, seem suitable for either residential or administrative functions, so it appears that the rulers and city-state administrators lived and had their offices in another area. There are some unexcavated range-type or "palace structures" in the Cemetery Group located south of the acropolis, and evidence of elite residences have been found to the northeast of the site.

The Hieroglyphic Stairway, the steps of which are formed by thousands of separate glyph blocks, is Copán's most celebrated construction. The stairway faces the Court of the Hieroglyphic Stairway, which is partially enclosed by the ball court on the north and the grand stairway of the Temple of the Inscriptions on the south.

The Court of the Hieroglyphic Stairway, the Central Court, and the Great Plaza constitute the plaza area. Steps which appear to have been designed as grandstands for spectators surrounded the three plazas. The plaza area contains structures that, by their nature, were essentially public structures: the ball court, the radial pyramid (Structure 4 with its four stairways), and the autonomous stelae and altars that are scattered through the plaza area.

The ball court is particularly elaborate. The playing area is flanked on the east and west by range-type buildings, which were probably used by the players and participants in the ball game ceremonies.

These structures were all constructed late in the history of Copán. All of the stelae in the Great Plaza, except Stela I, were constructed after A.D. 730. The temples on the acropolis—Temple of the Inscriptions, Temple of Meditation, and Temple 18—were all constructed in the eighth century A.D.

At Tikal, the architecture reveals the development from Early to Late Classic times, but at Copán the ruins exhibit only the last great burst of architectural achievement at the end of the Golden Age of the Maya.

Quiriguá Architecture: The energy of the Quiriguá rulers went into the construction of stelae rather than into great temple pyramids. As Michael Coe says, "Quiriguá contains a few archi-

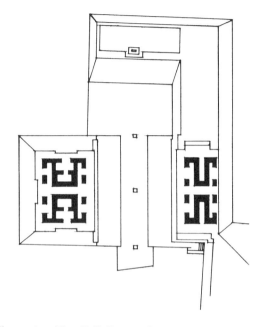

Illustration 71.   Ball Court, Copán. From Andrews, *Maya Cities,* p. 48.

tectural groups of no great distinction. Its enormous sandstone stelae, however, are quite another matter; indeed, Stela E, erected late in the eighth century, might claim to be the greatest stone monument of the New World, its shaft measuring 35 feet in height" (M. Coe 1980: 88).

The acropolis at Quiriguá is composed of range-type single-story buildings facing a court surrounded by a stairway. This technique is similar to that used to construct the Eastern Court and the Great Plaza at Copán. At both sites the steps were utilized on occasion as grandstand seats to view the spectacle in the center of the plaza. While the Quiriguá acropolis represents a sequence of construction from A.D. 550 to 850, the basic design of the structures facing the court remained unchanged.

Quiriguá's acropolis, like Tikal's central acropolis, was designed in the Late Classic period

Illustration 72. Range-type building, reviewing stand, and south elevation of Temple of the Inscriptions, Copán. From Proskouriakoff, *Album of Maya Architecture,* p. 49.

for elite residential use. According to Robert J. Sharer, "The large masonry structures of the Acropolis are considered to be primarily residential because they have multiple rooms and usually possess benches, windows, and curtain holders' (notches in doorways, presumably to hold textile curtains)" (Sharer 1978: 60). Nothing in the acropolis at Copán compares with the residential aspect of this architecture.

The basic organization of the site, however, is similar to Copán's. There is a man-made acropolis at the south end of a north-south-oriented assemblage of structures. The design is linear with a raised elite area on the south (the acropolis) and a public area to the north with stelae, a ball court, and a radial temple.

Building methods were essentially equivalent in all the sites discussed in this book. The buildings are rubble-filled mounds faced with stone

and incorporate small rooms constructed with corbeled vaults.

A unique feature of construction at Quiriguá, was the use of marble during the final building stage (A.D. 810–850). Structure 1B-5 (Temple 5), the largest building at Quiriguá, was built of marble and rhyolite. As far as we know, this is the only example of the use of marble by the Classic Maya.

Ceramics, Stratigraphy, and Carbon-14 Testing as Archaeological Tools

One key to determining the development of any ancient civilization is the record left by bits and pieces of pottery vessels. Since pottery sherds do not disintegrate, ceramic types and styles found in various strata can be employed to correlate the time period in which the people lived

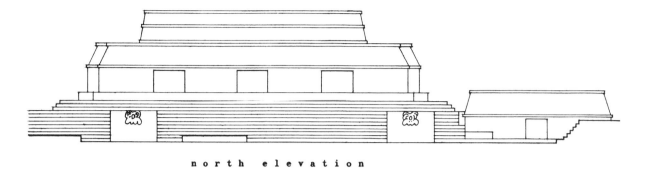

north elevation

Illustration 73. Palaces of Jade Sky (Str. 1B-1) and Cauac Sky (Str. 1B-2), Quiriguá. From Andrews, *Maya Cities*, Fig. 145.

with their level of cultural development. Mayanists utilize ceramic complexes, beginning with the Swasey complex at Cuello, in Belize, around 2500 B.C., as time frames for subdividing larger periods. The appendix includes a chronology for Tikal of ceramic complexes and horizons.

An example of the employment of pottery to give a historical perspective is one taken from "The Rise of Maya Civilization: A Summary View," wherein Willey concludes that the earliest real evidence of Maya Petén area occupation comes from Xe and Eb pottery. Xe pottery is described as being unslipped monochrome ware that was occasionally incised and punctated and that featured flaring sided, flange-rim plates and *tecomate* (neckless) jars. From an analysis of these sherds he concludes:

> Xe and Eb sites are small and few.
> They are in effect, small refuse areas
> and house locations found beneath
> later cultural deposits at Altar, Seibal,
> and Tikal. The inferences drawn from
> this are that the first Petén settlers
> were few in number and widely
> scattered. It is highly probable that
> these people were farmers. They built
> perishable houses either on the
> ground level or on very low artificial
> platforms (Willey 1977: 386).

Another way ceramic analysis helps reconstruct the history of a people is by indicating the presence or absence of nonlocal pottery. This characteristic is valuable in determining the ex-

ternal influence on the development of a particular culture.

Ceramics are analyzed by studying the paste (clay type), surface treatment, shape, size, and assumed use of vessels. Were they cooking pots, eating plates, storage vessels, or sumptuary wares for burial or trade? The color (monochrome or polychrome), decorative patterns, the fineness of the ware, and the method of firing are important keys to identifying the complex or horizon to which the ceramic can be assigned. Over a period of time, the shape may remain the same, but the surface treatment changes; or the size or shape may slowly evolve. Archaeologists develop ceramic sequences by plotting the ways in which pottery production and decoration change over time in a particular site or region.

Once a ceramic sequence has been established, it can be used as a technique to verify the chronological placement of parts of a site. For example, by carefully comparing and cataloging pieces of pottery found directly beneath the foundation of a plaza, the archaeologist can determine when the construction was begun.

One method archaeologists use to prepare a site history is to cut trenches at appropriate points to determine the stratigraphic record. Digging a trench to bedrock indicates that nothing older lies beneath that point. From a comparison of ceramics found from bedrock upwards, layer by layer, one group of pottery sherds above another, the history of the people who lived at that site over the centuries can, at least in general

66

terms, be laid out. A delightful description of stratigraphic methodology is found in *The Source*, a novel by James Michener. The first chapter chronicles the trenching process for fifteen layers, strata by strata, from modern times down to 10,000 B.C.

Radiocarbon (C^{14}) dating involves the determination of the approximate age of organic materials by measuring the deterioration of the radioactive isotope of carbon (C^{14}) as it compares with ordinary carbon (C^{12}). Living organisms absorb both C^{12} and C^{14}. At death, C^{14} is no longer absorbed into the body, and, being unstable, it begins to decay at a predictable rate. By comparing the relative amounts of stable C^{12} and unstable C^{14}, then applying the known rate of decay, scientists can compute the relative age of an organic sample. Such dates will be expressed as a date along with a range of possible error—plus or minus ($\pm$) a number of years depending upon the actual age of the sample.

In the Maya area particularly, C^{14} has proven to be a valuable tool as an adjunct to the ceramic and stratigraphic method of dating. In 1959, the University of Pennsylvania laboratory ran thirty-three counts of samples from ten beams in a Tikal temple. The series averaged A.D. 746, with a leeway of thirty-four years on either side. The Maya date, based on hieroglyphic inscriptions, indicated A.D. 741.

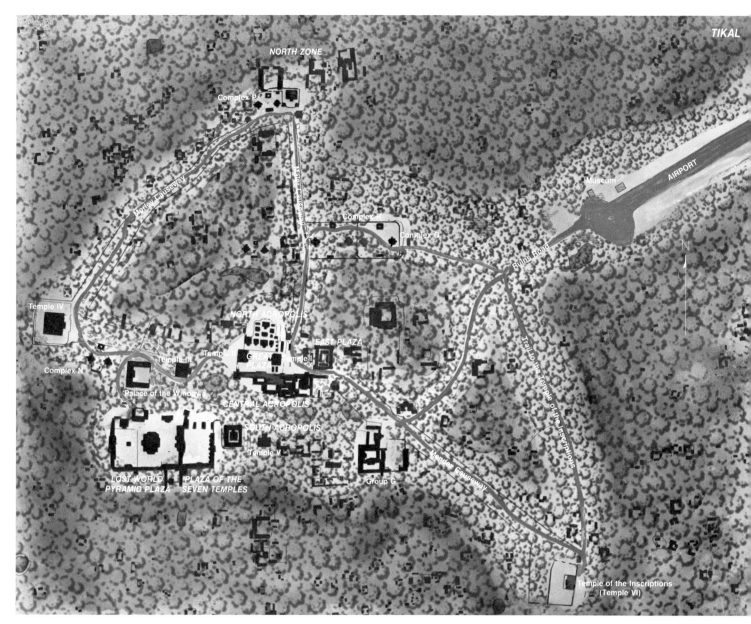

Illustration 74. Plat of Tikal ruins.

Tikal

Introduction

When approaching Tikal from the air, the first glimpse of the ruins are the temple pyramids thrusting through the solid tropical ocean green of the rain forest. In the center is the cluster of the Great Plaza temple-pyramids, which are the most striking remains of this ninth-century Maya city.

These ruins are ancient and alien—the civilization was dead by the time of Charlemagne. Their appearance is so striking to the twentieth-century eye that the science-fiction movie *Star Wars* made in the 1970s used Tikal to represent the hidden Rebel base on the fourth moon of the planet Yavin.

Imagine the city in its heyday. It was stuccoed and plastered white. It was a gleaming, spar-kling island of white in a sea of green forest and cultivated land. Jutting from the white plazas were temples painted red, crowned with red roof combs, here and there trimmed with blue. Paved streets crisscrossed the city, and huge reservoirs of water were scattered throughout the area. In the center of the city was a huge market. From the temples, smoke from burning copal joined the smoke from hundreds of cooking fires wafting upward to disappear in the blue sky.

The Great Plaza, enclosed on the east by the Temple of the Giant Jaguar (Temple I) and on the west by the Temple of the Masks (Temple II), both constructed by the ruler Ah Cacaw in the Late Maya Classic period (ca. A.D. 700), is now the focal point of restored Tikal. To the west is the Temple of the Jaguar Priest (Temple III),

Illustration 75.   Aerial view of Tikal from the west.
Temple IV is in the foreground and the Tikal
airstrip in the background.

the last of the pyramid-temples constructed by
the Maya of Tikal, built during the reign of Chitam (ca. A.D. 810). To the far west is the gigantic
Temple IV built by Ruler B (ca. A.D. 750). Just
south of the Great Plaza is the unexcavated Temple V, and farther to the southeast is the Temple
of the Inscriptions (Temple VI), constructed by
Ruler B and reworked by Chitam.

The Tikal park area, which lies to the west of
the airport, is only a small portion of ancient
Tikal. Hidden under the canopy of the rain forest
are more than 3,000 structures and 200 stone
monuments. In its golden age in the Late Classic, Tikal may have had a population of more
than 50,000 people. William R. Coe says, "Perhaps as many as 10,000 earlier platforms and
buildings lie sealed beneath the surface features
mapped during 1957 to 1960" (Coe 1967: 21).

During the eighth century A.D., Tikal supported
a population estimated at 1,550 to 1,800 people
per square mile in the central area and 260 per
square mile in the peripheral area (Rice and Puleston 1981: 144); today there are less than two.

Tikal's beginnings can be traced back to 750
B.C. during the middle Preclassic phase (ca. 1000–
300 B.C.). The period up to A.D. 250 is called the
Preclassic period; the years from A.D. 250 to 475
encompass the Early Classic, A.D. 475 to 681 the
Middle Classic, and A.D. 681 to 810 the Late Classic. Most of the stuctures that have been restored
are of the Late Classic, period from around A.D.
700 to 800. Tikal's classic civilization, along with
all of the Maya Classic civilization, died about
A.D. 900.

The University Museum of the University of
Pennsylvania conducted a fifteen-year excava-

70

Illustration 76.   Tikal Great Plaza from the southwest.

tion and consolidation project beginning in 1956, under the direction of Edwin M. Shook and William R. Coe. Since then, excavation and restoration have been conducted by the Instituto de Antropología e Historia de Guatemala.

Recent research by Christopher Jones, Clemency Coggins, Flora Clancy, Linda Schele, and others has identified and placed in chronological context a number of Tikal rulers. The dates of some are fixed with certainty—Curl Nose, Stormy Sky, Ah Cacaw (Ruler A), Ruler B, and Chitam (Ruler C). Others are more speculative. Jaguar Paw, the first identified ruler, is known to have existed, but it is only a hypothesis that he is the ruler depicted on the Leiden Plaque (see Ill. 118). Surely others ruled between Jaguar Paw and Chitam, and we know of rulers before Jaguar Paw (ca. A.D. 320 and after Chitam (A.D. 768).

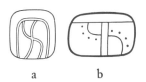

a   b

Illustration 77.   Glyph T 573 (Hel).

In 1979, Berthold Riese suggested that the *hel* glyph (T 573a), which regularly appears with the names of Tikal rulers coupled with a number, indicates the sequence of rulers. Jones concurs in this concept. Stela 22 at Tikal is an example. The *hel* glyph, which David Kelley translates "successor in office," appears with the numbers 9 and 20. Jones concludes that Chitam, who appears on Stela 22, was, therefore, the twenty-

Illustration 78.   Curl Nose name glyph, left. Glyph T 561 (Sky), right.

ninth ruler of Tikal. But twenty-nine Tikal rulers have not as yet been identified, and whether this line represents actual or mythological rulers is not known. The Temple of the Inscriptions records a dynastic succession, which began in Olmec times, and must include a series of legendary, if not mythological, rulers.

The identity and order of succession of the Tikal rulers is an evolving discipline requiring the deciphering of the monument inscriptions. Some of the stelae have been badly damaged, and many of the glyphs are eroded. Some of the dates are incomplete and some of the name glyphs are missing so that any conclusion requires substantial interpretation. Suffice it to say, because the record left on the monuments of Tikal is sketchy and often equivocal, there is no unanimity among Mayanists with respect to the rulers of Tikal.

The list of Tikal rulers (p. 74) is based upon personal communications with Linda Schele and Cristopher Jones and upon Jones's *The Monuments and Inscriptions of Tikal: The Carved Monuments.*

The names given these rulers are not their actual names, but are identifiers given by Mayanists for convenience, based upon the reading of the name glyphs. The name Curl Nose (or Curl Snout) is descriptive of his name glyph. Stormy Sky's name glyph is described by Clemency Coggins: "The name consists of a cleft sky glyph surmounted by a long-nosed deity figure with arms out to either side, bent at the elbows with hands raised to the sky. Its forehead is emblazoned with a large cartouche in which a smoking axe is hafted" (Coggins 1976: 265). Coggins argues that the same deity appears on the top of Stela 4; she identifies this deity as Tlaloc,

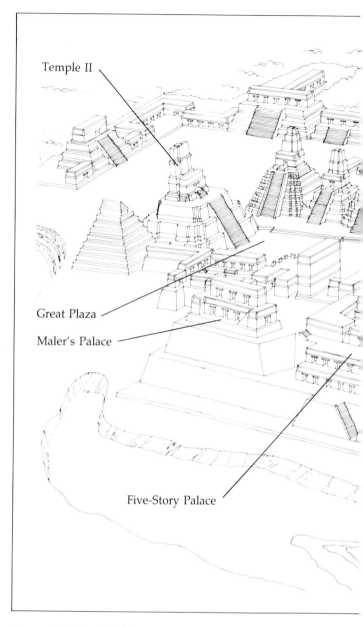

Illustration 79.   Tikal Central Area. From Doris Heyden and Paul Gendrop, *Pre-Columbian Architecture of Mesoamerica*, p. 107.

the Storm God—hence the name "Stormy Sky." Other Mayanists consider the god on the glyph and on Stela 4 to be God K and would name the ruler "God K, Cleft Sky." But the name Stormy Sky is generally accepted.

Ruler B could be named "Half-darkened Kin" or "Half-darkened Sun" because his name glyph

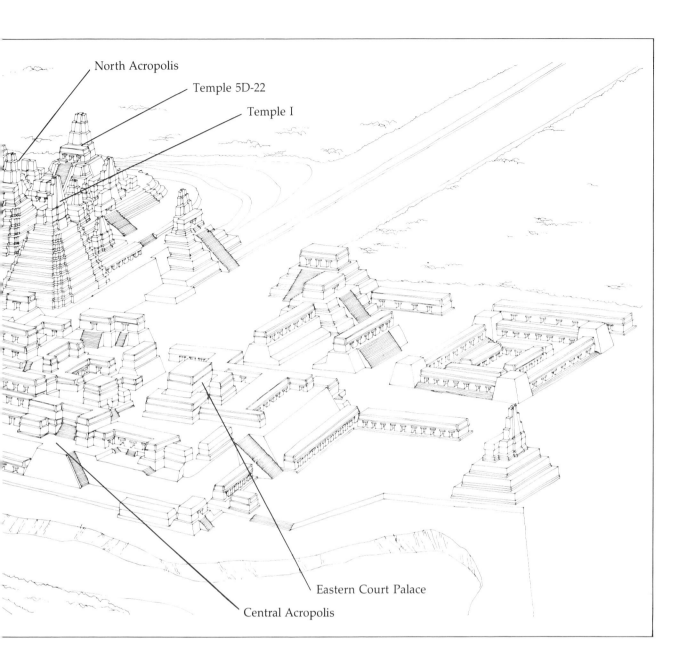

North Acropolis

Temple 5D-22

Temple I

Eastern Court Palace

Central Acropolis

includes a sun half darkened by cross hatch. Ruler C is called "Chitam" by Schele because that is the Mayan word for "peccary," the animal that appears in Ruler C's name glyph.

Tikal was an urban center and the seat of authority for the area. The government was headed by a ruler considered by himself and his subjects to be a direct descendant of the gods. His deceased parents were gods. Jones envisions the government to have been conducted in all phases by the ruler—a kind of divine dictatorship. R. E. W. Adams and Woodruff D. Smith suggest that Classic Maya society was essentially feudalistic, similar to medieval Europe and Japan

73

Tikal Rulers

Ruler	Where Portrayed	Ruled
Jaguar Paw	Leiden Plaque? Stelae 29?, 31	ca. A.D. 320
Curl Nose	Stelae 4, 18	ca. A.D. 379–426
Stormy Sky	Stela 31, possibly stelae 1, 2, 28	ca. A.D. 426–457
Kan Chitam (Kan Boar)	Stelae 9, 13	ca A.D. 457–488
Jaguar Paw Skull	Stelae 3, 7, 15, 27	ca A.D. 488
Bird Claw	Stela 8	ca. A.D. 497
Curl Head	Stelae 10, 12	ca. A.D. 528
Double Bird	Stela 17	ca. A.D. 538
Shield Skull (Father of Ah Cacaw)	Temple I, Lintel 3	Before A.D. 682
Ah Cacaw (Ruler A)	Stelae 16, 30, Lintel 3, Temple I	From A.D. 682
Ruler B (Half-darkened Sun)	Stelae 5, 20, 21, Lintels 2 & 3, Temple IV	From A.D. 734
Chitam (Ruler C)	Stelae 19, 22	From A.D. 768 to 790
Stela 24 Ruler	Stela 24	ca. A.D. 810
Stela 11 Ruler	Stela 11	ca. A.D. 869

(Adams and Smith 1981: 336). The king, the nobles, and their retinue of administrators lived and ran the government from the Central Acropolis, Group G, and the Palace of the Windows.

Evidence seems to indicate that the ruling elite of Tikal came from the area of Kaminaljuyú about the time of Christ, but glyphic inscriptions and the burial paraphernalia found in tombs do not provide historical information about Tikal previous to the end of the third century A.D. Jaguar Paw is believed to be the ruler referred to on the Leiden Plaque (see Ill. 118), who became king of Tikal in 8.14.3.1.12 (A.D. 320) and died before A.D. 378. He probably was the last of the local Tikal rulers, whose family had ruled Tikal for several hundred years.

Jaguar Paw was followed by Curl Nose, who seems to represent the Teotihuacán connection. Teotihuacán, in the Mexican highlands, as-sumed some political and economic control over Kaminaljuyú during the middle of the fourth century A.D., and Curl Snout may have been a trade emissary from the highlands. He was very likely also of noble birth, and possibly of combined Mexican and Kaminaljuyú parentage; the latter would have related him to the ruling families of Tikal. Although the threat of military force may have been real, Curl Snout might have attained dynastic as well as economic power at Tikal by marrying the daughter of Jaguar Paw (Coggins 1976: 259).

Curl Nose was followed by Stormy Sky in A.D. 426. These three early rulers—Jaguar Paw, Curl Nose, and Stormy Sky—are named in the inscriptions on the magnificent Stela 31, which is now located in the Tikal Museum. Stormy Sky, a member of the old Tikal nobility, is credited with synthesizing the Teotihuacán and Maya cultures and returning Tikal to local rule.

Little is actually known about the history of Tikal from the death of Stormy Sky in about A.D. 457 to the accession of Ah Cacaw (Ruler A) in A.D. 682. With Ah Cacaw began the golden age of Tikal, which continued during the reigns of his son, Ruler B (Half-darkened sun) and grandson, Chitam. During this hundred years, the great temple-pyramids, which dominate the Tikal ruins, were constructed. After Chitam, who became king in A.D. 768, the curtain comes down. We know Tikal continued to function until well into the ninth century A.D., but beyond that, little is known.

The Great Plaza, which has been excavated, was not the hub of Tikal. The center of the basically radial design of the city was just to the east in the unexcavated East Plaza, where the Mendez and Maler causeways intersect. The Great Plaza, with Temples I and II and the North Acropolis, were the west boundary of the East Plaza.

The East plaza contained a ball court and was the central marketplace area—a public area of Tikal, as opposed to the Great Plaza, which appears to have been an elite ceremonial area constructed for the rulers. The huge palace complex (Central Acropolis), which flanked the Great Plaza on the south, combined elite housing and administrative buildings.

Leaving the museum-airport area on the way toward the Great Plaza, visitors find themselves in a tunnel of green. The jungle closes overhead, and the sides of the trail are thick with a foliage of ferns and tropical plants.

In this setting, it is easy to imagine life a thousand years ago. Although the Classic Maya civilization is long dead, the surroundings of Tikal have changed little. The Maya ruins were abandoned in all their glory and have not been covered by the accumulated remains left by subsequent inhabitants, as is the case in Europe and the Middle East. The jungle has covered the buildings, but when the vegetation is removed, much of the architecture remains almost as it was when Maya lords lived in this beautiful city.

The jungle teems with life. Huge butterflies, twice the size of those in the temperate zones, flash blue and gold around the flowering shrubs. Overhead, flowering flamingo trees create a halo of color around the temple-pyramids. Wild orchids cling to the high branches. In the winter, Tikal is home to migratory birds from North America, including hummingbirds, finches, and warblers. Big green Amazon parrots fly in formation, one behind the other, complaining to each other in raucous tones. "Banana-bill," the keel-billed toucan, with his yellow cheeks and long canoe-shaped green bill, appears occasionally. His scratchy froglike voice joins with the more melodious sounds of the other birds in the jungle.

Occasionally, a troupe of spider monkeys bursts through the trees, raising a big commotion, and then is gone. Sometimes the roar of the howler monkey, like the sound of an enraged bull, reverberates through the forest.

Often in the mornings, low clouds from the Caribbean Sea roll across Belize, a few miles to the east, and settle over Tikal at treetop height. Then the jungle drips, and the fog makes it look like an Oriental painting. Generally by ten o'clock, the fog is gone and the tropical sun is turned off and on by broken cloud layers that drift by. When not obscured, the sun is like a floodlight, filling the monuments with highlights and shadows.

In the afternoon, it may rain with tropical warmth and gentleness; afterwards the water drops from leaf to leaf, and the forest gives off a damp odor, which is faintly musty and faintly tart, like the taste of a ripe papaya.

Illustrations 80 and 81.   Tikal Great Plaza from the
southwest.

76

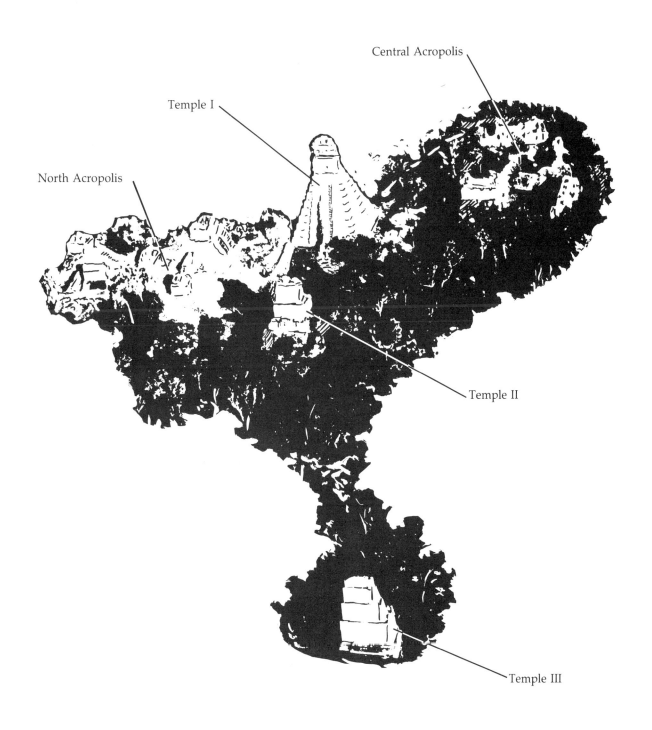

North Acropolis

Temple I

Central Acropolis

Temple II

Temple III

Illustration 82.   Great Plaza of Tikal. Temple I on
the right and Temple II on the left, the North
Acropolis in the center background.

Great Plaza

Illustration 82 shows an aerial view of the Great
Plaza of Tikal from the south, with a portion of
the palace in the foreground, Temple I on the
right, Temple II on the left, and the North Acropolis in the background. The floor of the plaza
is roughly the size of two parallel football fields,
about 400 feet by 250 feet. Seventy stelae and
altars are located in the plaza and on the terrace to the north. A great stairway leading to the
acropolis terrace flanks the north side of the plaza.
The stairway and terrace constitute the entrance
to the North Acropolis.

The plaza was in use from about 150 B.C. until
Tikal was abandoned. Over a period of a thousand years, four plaster floors were laid one above
the other. The latest floor, constructed about A.D.
700, is surrounded by the restored ruins of the
Late Classic monuments that are visible today.

Given sufficient energy and no problems with
acrophobia, one can climb the steep stairway of
Temple I for an orientation view of the Great
Plaza. From the steps of the temple at the pyramid's top the North Acropolis is visible on the
right, the Great Plaza stelae below, Temple II
across the plaza to the west, and the Central
Acropolis on the left.

A climb to the top of the stairway flanking the
south side of the plaza provides a view of the
stelae and North acropolis in front, Temple I to
the east, and Temple II to the west.

Great Plaza Structures

In Early Classic times (A.D. 250 to 475), the Great
Plaza was a paved area between the North Acropolis and the Palace Group (Central Acropolis). The North Acropolis had its beginnings
in the second century B.C. and is basically a group

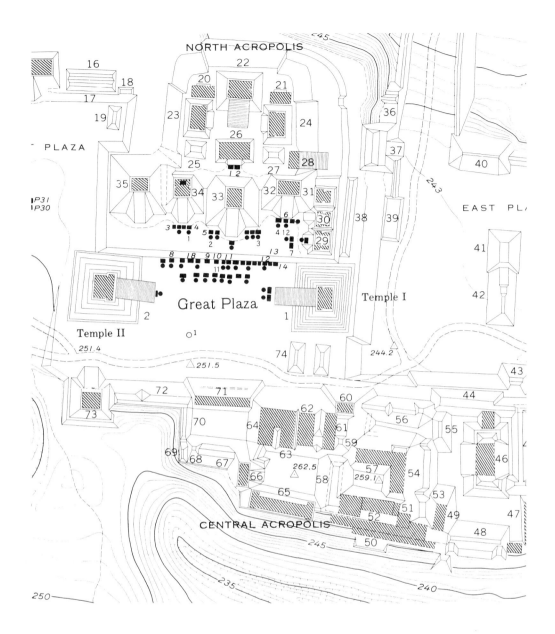

NORTH ACROPOLIS

PLAZA

Great Plaza

Temple I

Temple II

EAST PL

CENTRAL ACROPOLIS

Illustration 83.   Plat of Great Plaza, Tikal. From
Carr and Hazard, *Tikal Reports Number 11.*

of funerary monuments erected by a succession
of rulers to venerate their ancestors. It has been
rebuilt over and over again by succeeding rulers.
The monuments now standing represent the last
of the construction, except for the front and center temple-pyramid called Structure 5D-33, which
was rebuilt for the third time, probably by Ah
Cacaw. This temple-pyramid was disassembled
by the University Museum of the University of

Pennsylvania project, leaving only portions of
it and its two prior constructions visible. When
standing, 5D-33, towered some one hundred feet
above the plaza floor and was part of a three-
pyramid-temple complex surrounding the Great
Plaza—Temple I, Temple II, and 5D-33. In effect,
this huge pyramid screened off from the plaza
the North Acropolis structures which had been
built in earlier times.

Illustration 84.   Central Acropolis and Temple I, a view from the northwest. From the left to right are Temple I, the Ball Court, and the Central Acropolis.

The Temple of the Giant Jaguar (Temple I) rises on the east side of the plaza facing the Temple of the Masks (Temple II) on the west. Ah Cacaw is credited with building both of these colossal edifices, which seal the Great Plaza on the east and west sides.

On the south, the Palace Group (Central Acropolis) represents the culmination of centuries of building. William Coe says, "It has been estimated that the visible final stage of the Central Acropolis, an incomparable architectural achievement in ancient America, incorporated 42 individual structures, with some five hundred years of building activity in this final stage alone, while centuries of construction underlie this prodigious achievement" (W. Coe 1967: 71) This area housed the rulers and functioned as an administrative center for the government.

On the floor of the plaza and on the terrace to the north are stelae, some originally placed by the Classic Maya and some reset in Postclassic times. The stelae provide a record in stone of some of the great Indians who ruled this city. Normally, an altar was erected with each stela; if the stela was carved, the altar was also carved.

If a stela was to be removed, the custom at Tikal was to "kill" it ritually by breaking it, smashing the face, and then caching it. Stelae

80

Illustration 85.   Central Acropolis (foreground),
Great Plaza, and North Acropolis.

inscriptions constituted only a partial record of
events in Maya history. Full records were probably kept in folded books or codices, which have
long since been destroyed. Many of the stelae
seen in the Great Plaza were retrieved and re-
erected by Postclassic people after having been
broken during Classic times.

Illustrations 86 and 87.   Stelae Row, Great Plaza.

Stela 3

Stela 4

Stela 5

Stela 8

Stela 18

Stela 9

Stela 10

Stela 11

Stela 12

Stela 13

Illustration 88.   Temple of the Giant Jaguar (Temple I).

Temple I

In the late afternoon when the sun is just right, the massive outline of Ah Cacaw, sitting tailor fashion on his throne, stands out on the roof comb of Temple I. The date of his accession—9.12.9.17.16 (A.D. 682)—as ruler of Tikal appears on Lintel 3 of Temple I. In Tikal's halcyon days of the eighth century A.D., Ah Cacaw's figure was painted in bright contrasting colors of red

and cream and overlooked the Great Plaza and the western portion of his great city. The surrounding figures may have been finished in green or blue.

His temple-pyramid consists of nine terraces topped by a single-doored temple, which supports the roof comb. Its popular name is "Temple of the Giant Jaguar" because of the figures on one of the lintels found in the temple. Archaeologists have designated it as 5D-1 or Temple I. The silhouette of this pyramid is one of the best known of any Precolumbian monument, and is the hallmark of Guatemala.

Temple I was built about A.D. 700. Prior to the construction of the pyramid, a twenty-foot-deep excavation was made in the Great Plaza, and a vaulted grave chamber, fourteen and a half feet by eight feet by thirteen feet high, was constructed to be the tomb of Ah Cacaw. Over the grave (designated Burial 116), Temple I was built. Included in the grave were the remains of Ah Cacaw and numerous pieces of jade jewelry, bracelets, necklaces, ear ornaments, and head-dress decorations. Also included in the burial were ceramics and bone artifacts. The tomb has been reassembled at the Tikal Museum.

The pyramid has nine terraces with horizontal grooves on the lower portion of each terrace and inset or recessed corners. These architectural techniques were employed by the Maya to create a chiaroscuro or shadow effect both vertically and horizontally to enhance the overall impact of the building, which thrusts upward 145 feet above the floor of the plaza.

Only the first few steps of the formal stairway have been restored. The Maya built the now visible stairway as a workmen's stairway, used in the construction of the pyramid and the upper temple.

At the time of Ah Cacaw's death, Temple II had probably been completed and Temple I was under construction.

Illustration 89.   Temple II from the Central
Acropolis.

Temple II

Temple II, which seals the west entrance to the
Great Plaza, was erected by Ah Cacaw about
A.D. 700. It originally stood nearly 140 feet above
the plaza. Also known as the Temple of the Masks,
Temple II has two hugh masks located on each
side of the stairway at the top of the third terrace
just below the temple portal. The masks are still
in place, but only a few details can now be distinguished. Between the masks in front of the
temple door, the Maya constructed a platform.

William Coe considers the platform to be a reviewing stand, which allowed the priests or rulers to see and be seen by the people in the plaza
below. On the sides are stairways leading from
terrace to terrace indicating that the temple was
utilized as a grandstand.

Behind the reviewing platform is the entrance
to the three-room temple. The roof comb was
adorned with a massive face with earplugs on
each side, the details of which can still be dis-
cerned.

At the foot of the stairway stands the large,

Illustration 90.   Temple II, aerial view from the northeast.

uncarved Stela P83 and its altar, the largest stone monument found at Tikal, originally more than eleven feet high. The portrait of a woman, possibly the wife or mother of Ah Cacaw, appears on the lintel of Temple II. Although no tomb was found by trenching, Coggins feels that Temple II was constructed as a memorial to Ah Cacaw's wife, and that she may be buried somewhere in it or under it.

Illustration 91.   Temple II on the west side of the Great Plaza.

Great Plaza, Stela 3

In this book, we have elected to consider the stelae located in the Great Plaza in numerical order. This decision has advantages and disadvantages. The advantage is that the location of the stelae follow a more or less logical placement order around the plaza. The disadvantage is that moving from one to another means jumping back and forth in time. Stela 3 is dated A.D. 488; Stela 4, a century older, is dated A.D. 379. Stela 5 then jumps ahead 350 years to A.D. 744. An analogy would be first studying William Penn (A.D. 1700), then Captain John Smith (A.D. 1607), followed by Gerald Ford (A.D. 1975). The temporal sequence is given with the list of rulers in the introduction to this section.

Jaguar Paw Skull appears on Stelae 3 and 7. He was the successor to and son of Kan Chitam (Kan Boar), who was memorialized on Stelae 9 and 13, and was possibly the father of Curl Head, his successor, who appears on Stelae 10 and 12.

Stelae 3 was erected in the northwest corner of the Great Plaza on the terrace in front of Structure 5D-34 (the structure on the west side in the front row of the North Acropolis) next to its steps. The Maya Long Count date is 9.2.13.0.0 (A.D. 488).

The figure, carved with simplicity and clarity, does not have all the allegorical iconography incorporated on Stormy Sky's Stela 31 (now in the Tikal Museum), carved only forty-three years earlier in A.D. 445. Jaguar Paw Skull is shown in profile wearing a feathered headdress and holding a staff. He wears sandals, a heavy jade necklace, a back rack, and an elaborate loincloth. The stela displays no sky figure—that is, no ancestor or deity figure appears on top of the stela above the figure. The ruler stands upon a mat-type basal band, which is either the emblem glyph of Tikal or, perhaps, a pine torch. A trace of red paint is still visible. Originally, all of Tikal's carved monuments were painted red.

Coggins suggests that the method of presentation of Jaguar Paw Skull on this stela is similar to the flanking figures on Stela 31 in the Tikal Museum, from which she concludes, following Tatiana Proskouriakoff, that Jaguar Paw Skull was a foreigner, a ruler from a line of rulers who

Illustration 92.   Stela 3.

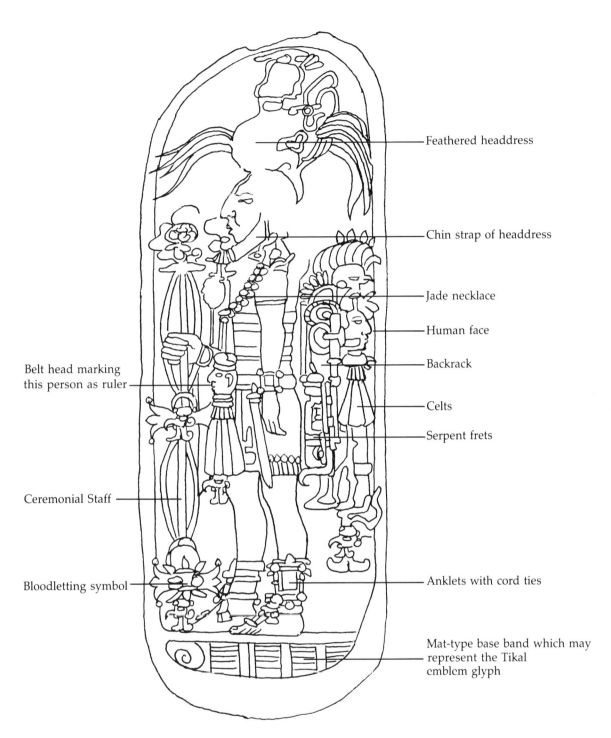

Feathered headdress

Chin strap of headdress

Jade necklace

Human face

Backrack

Belt head marking
this person as ruler

Celts

Serpent frets

Ceremonial Staff

Bloodletting symbol

Anklets with cord ties

Mat-type base band which may
represent the Tikal
emblem glyph

Illustration 93.   Stela 3, Tikal. Drawing by Lisa
Ferguson; iconography interpreted by Schele.

were not of old Tikal lineage. These rulers, with Mexican attributes, may have come to Tikal through Kaminaljuyú. The line began with Curl Nose (Stelae 4 and 18), who may have represented an incursion into Tikal by a dynasty oriented to trade and commerce. Jaguar Paw, for whom no stela has been found, may have been the last of the local chieftains.

The glyphs pictured on the east side of Stela 3 display the long count date 9.2.13.0.0 (A.D. 488). The date begins with the topmost glyph on the right: 9 (●●●●), followed in the frame below on the left with 2 (●●), and next to it on the right, 13 (●●●). These glyphs are followed by zero indicators and the name of the day, the age of the moon and other data, and a verb. The other side of the stela names the protagonist, with Jaguar Paw Skull's name glyph occurring as the first glyph in the right column. The last five glyphs in the west side text named Jaguar Paw Skull as the son of Kan Chitam.

Stela 4

Ruler Curl Nose appears on Stelae 4 and 18. He was the father of Stormy Sky, Tikal's brilliant ruler of the Early Classic period. Curl Nose followed Jaguar Paw and, as mentioned in the discussion of Stela 3, may have been the first king in a line of rulers who replaced the local Jaguar Paw dynasty. Stormy Sky, successor to Curl Nose, does not appear on any stelae still found in the Great Plaza. He appears or is referred to on Stelae 1, 2, 28, and 31, all of which are now in the Tikal Museum.

Curl Nose's Stela 4 stands on the North Acropolis terrace in front of Temple 5D-34, the partially restored temple in the front row on the west side. The stela depicts the accession of the ruler Curl Nose on a calculated date of 8.17.2.16.17 (A.D. 379). Curl Nose is named for the long-snouted animal in his name glyph appearing on the back of Stela 4 as the right-most glyph in the third row. He appears seated with his legs hanging down and with a frontal view of his upper body and face. He holds a jaguar deity in his right hand and wears a jaguar headdress with a panache of feathers and a necklace of pecten shells. Over his head is a God K deity figure with an axe in its forehead, which symbolizes an ancestor figure.

Curl Nose was possibly non-Mayan—a foreigner—thought to have come from Kaminaljuyú, a site near present-day Guatemala City, which at the time was under the influence of Teotihuacán in the Mexican highlands. With the accession of Curl Nose, many non-Maya traits appear in the sculpture of Tikal, which point to some sort of association with Teotihuacán, probably via Kaminaljuyú. Some Mayanists believe that he married the daughter of Jaguar Paw. Although no evidence indicates that his power was achieved through military force, his accession broke the established Tikal tradition, and it may have been implemented by the threat of force.

Illustration 94.　Stela 4, Tikal.

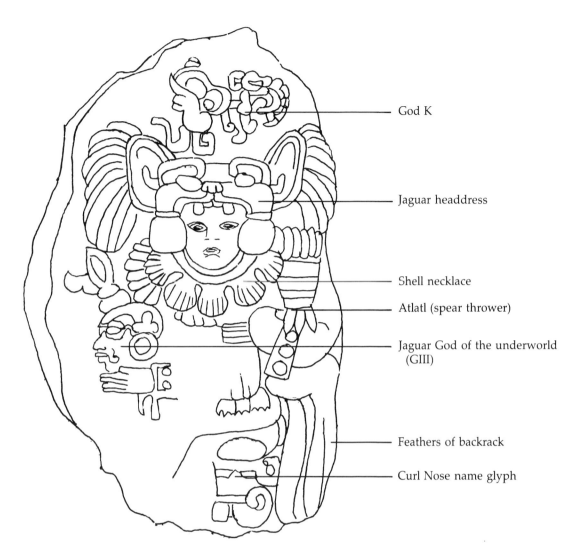

God K

Jaguar headdress

Shell necklace

Atlatl (spear thrower)

Jaguar God of the underworld
(GIII)

Feathers of backrack

Curl Nose name glyph

Illustration 95.   Stela 4, Tikal. Drawing by Lisa
Ferguson; iconography interpreted by Schele.

Stela 5

Stela 5 shows Ruler B (Half-darkened sun) standing over a belly-down captive. The captive's legs and a rope are visible at the base of the stela. Ruler B acceded to the throne of Tikal on 9.15.3.6.8. (A.D. 734). The *hel* glyph is associated with the 27 glyph on the west side of the stela, eight blocks from the bottom, which would indicate Ruler B to be the twenty-seventh ruler of Tikal. His father was Ah Cacaw, who appears on Stela 16 in Complex N in front of Temple IV. Ruler B was followed by his son, Chitam (the twenty-ninth ruler), who appears on Stela 22 in Complex Q. Ruler 28 is unknown, although Jones considers him to have been a brother or uncle of Chitam. Schele tentatively suggests he may be named on the Hummingbird Vase (Ill. 12) from Burial 196 as Mah K'ina Ah Chac K'in.

Stela 5 is located on the terrace in front of Structure 5D-33 of the North Acropolis. The stela, dated 9.15.13.0.0 (A.D. 744), records Ruler B's accession in A.D. 734. His name is recorded on the west side of the stela in the fourth, fifth, and sixth rows from the top. His genealogy is also included on the east side, with his mother shown in rows 7 to 9, and his father, Ah Cacaw, in rows 10 to 12. The last glyph on the east side is the Tikal emblem glyph.

Ruler B wears an ornate back rack with a display of feathers from his headdress down his back. Over his shoulders he wears a short jade cape trimmed with feathers. On his left wrist is a bracelet with crossed bands and jade disks. Below his belt are Oliva shells; below the face on the front of his belt are two celts and a piece of mat marking him as Ahau Pop, "Lord of the Mat Throne." He wears a jaguar skin shirt complete with tail.

Illustration 96. Glyphs designating Ruler B as the twenty-seventh ruler of Tikal. After W. R. Coe, *American Antiquity* 42 (1), Fig. 14.

Illustration 97.   Stela 5 and glyphs, Tikal.

Illustration 98.   Stela 5, Tikal.

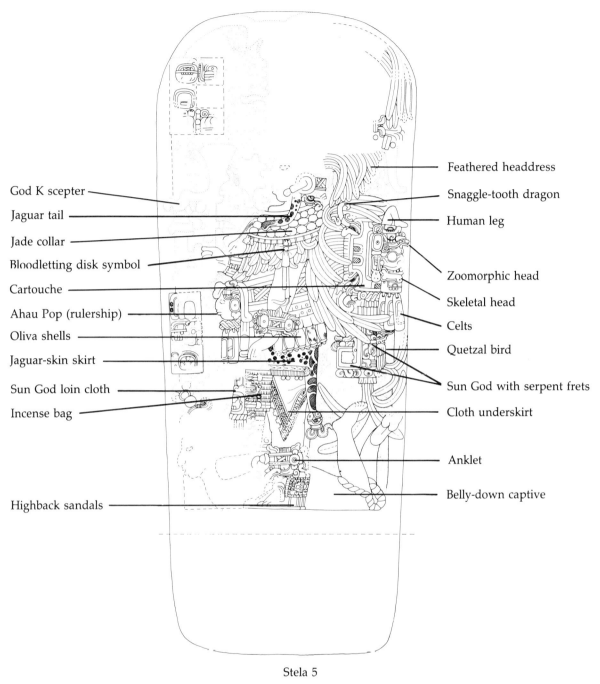

God K scepter

Jaguar tail

Jade collar

Bloodletting disk symbol

Cartouche

Ahau Pop (rulership)

Oliva shells

Jaguar-skin skirt

Sun God loin cloth

Incense bag

Highback sandals

Feathered headdress

Snaggle-tooth dragon

Human leg

Zoomorphic head

Skeletal head

Celts

Quetzal bird

Sun God with serpent frets

Cloth underskirt

Anklet

Belly-down captive

Stela 5

Illustration 99.   Stela 5, Tikal. From W. R. Coe,
American Antiquity, 42: 1, Fig. 13. Iconography
interpreted by Schele.

Stela 7

Jaguar Paw Skull appears on Stela 7, as well as on Stela 3. He was the son of Kan Chitam (Kan Boar) (Stelae 9 and 13), and was possibly followed by Bird Claw (Stela 8).

Stela 7 is badly damaged. W. R. Coe reports that it was found as a mass of fragments. It was restored and reset near where it was found on the terrace in the northeast corner of the Great Plaza, in front of the west-facing unexcavated mound (Structure 5D-29) located just to the north of Temple I. This stela was erected to celebrate the katun ending 9.3.0.0.0 2 Ahau 18 Muan (A.D. 495). Both Kan Chitam's and Jaguar Paw Skull's glyphs appear on it.

Coggins suggests that Jaguar Paw Skull was related to the old Tikal Jaguar Paw family that ruled Tikal before Curl Nose became ruler in A.D. 379—a little more than a hundred years earlier. Tikal's history is clouded during the period following the death of the great ruler, Stormy Sky, in about A.D. 457. No important burials occurred for some seventy years. Tikal seems to have been isolated during that time.

On Stela 7, Jaguar Paw Skull holds a staff in his right hand and an incense bag (probably copal) in his left hand. His headdress is a turban. The three-knot bloodletting symbol appears on his staff.

Stela 7 is a limestone shaft carved in low relief with the ruler on the front and glyphs on each side. Jaguar Paw Skull's name glyph appears fourth from the bottom following the Tikal emblem glyph on the east side, where it appears in a phrase naming him as the father of Jaguar Paw Skull.

Illustration 100.   Stela 7, Tikal.

Stela 8

Stela 8, located at plaza level in the northwest corner of the Great Plaza, has been dated 9.3.2.0.0 (A.D. 497). Linda Schele has tentatively identified the figure as Bird Claw, who succeeded Jaguar Paw Skull. Bird Claw's name glyph appears on the east side, the third group from the bottom. Jones does not believe the bird claw glyph designates a ruler.

The badly eroded stela shows the ruler facing west. In his right hand he holds a staff with three-bloodletting knot symbols (see Ill. 101). The stela is a limestone shaft with the profile figure in low relief and with glyphs on the east and west sides.

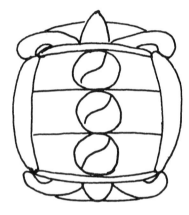

Illustration 101.   Bloodletting knots (Stela 8).

Illustration 102.   Stela 8, Tikal.

100

Stela 9

Illustration 103 shows Stela 9, with Ruler Kan Chitam, who also appears on Stela 13. He followed, but was not the son of, the great Stormy Sky (Stelae 1, 2, 28 and 31 in the Tikal Museum), and was followed by Jaguar Paw Skull (Stelae 3 and 7).

Located on the north side at plaza level in the center of the Great Plaza, Stela 9 is easily identified by the uncarved circular flint stone at the top. No one knows why this piece of stone was not removed when the stela was carved.

Stela 9 is a limestone shaft, which depicts Kan Chitam within a frame. The monument is dated 9.2.0.0.0 (A.D. 475). The figure wears a radial headdress with feathers and carries a simple paper- or cloth-wrapped staff. His cape is made of layers of cropped feathers falling from his shoulders with a jaguar tail at the bottom. Down the back are three jaguar heads, each with feathers on its nose and possibly smoke emanating from each head. A face on his loincloth appears above a cluster of celts and below the mat symbol of royalty. Traces of red paint are still visible.

On the east side of the monument are seven well-preserved glyphs. On the bottom is the Tikal emblem glyph; next above is the name glyph of the ruler, Kan Chitam. Above Kan Chitam's name glyph is a ruler's title glyph, and above this is a glyph indicating the deity GIII. GIII, the Jaguar God of the underworld, is identified by a cruller in his forehead and a jaguar ear. On the west side, beginning at the top, the glyphs indicate the end of the second katun, 4 Ahau 13 Uo, giving the date 9.2.0.0.0.

Illustration 103.   Stela 9, Tikal.

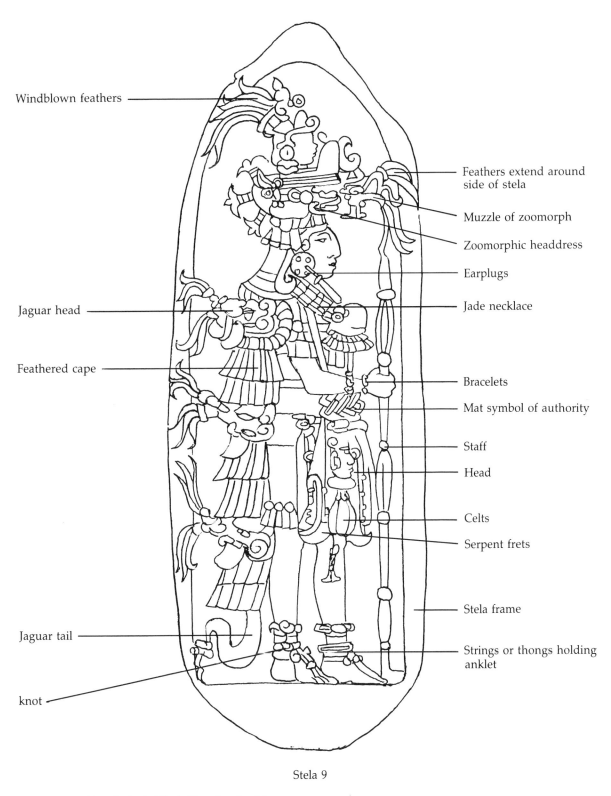

Windblown feathers

Feathers extend around side of stela

Muzzle of zoomorph

Zoomorphic headdress

Earplugs

Jaguar head

Jade necklace

Feathered cape

Bracelets

Mat symbol of authority

Staff

Head

Celts

Serpent frets

Stela frame

Jaguar tail

Strings or thongs holding anklet

knot

Stela 9

Illustration 104.   Stela 9, Tikal. Drawing by Lisa Ferguson; iconography interpreted by Schele.

Illustration 105.   Stela 9 glyphs, Tikal.

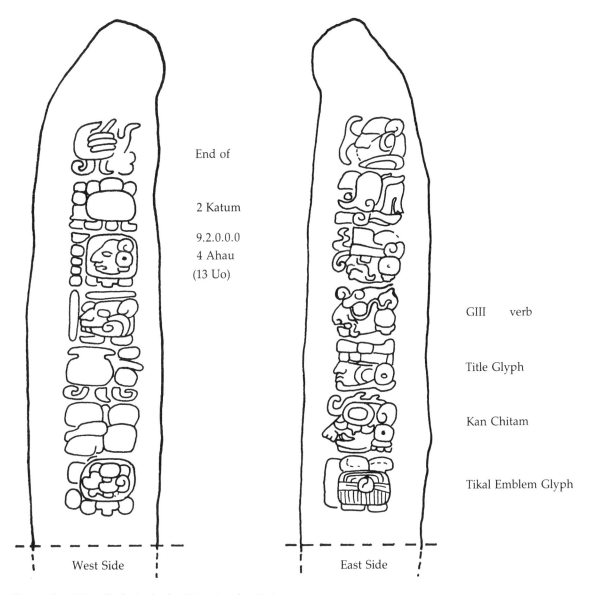

End of

2 Katum

9.2.0.0.0
4 Ahau
(13 Uo)

GIII   verb

Title Glyph

Kan Chitam

Tikal Emblem Glyph

West Side

East Side

Illustration 106.   Stela 9 glyphs. Drawing by D. J.
Reents; iconography interpreted by Schele.

Stela 10

Linda Schele feels that Stela 10 portrays Ruler Curl Head. In the surviving monuments, he is the next ruler following Bird Claw, who appears on Stela 8 in the Great Plaza. Curl Head had acceded by about A.D. 528, which is the date of Stela 12, a companion stela to Stela 10. Jones, however, has concluded that both Stela 10 and Stela 12 are possibly Jaguar Paw Skull's.

Stela 10 is located at plaza level in the center of the north side of the Great Plaza. Stela 10 represents a substantial change in style from earlier stelae. It marks a partial return to the old Maya tradition except for the deep carving. It is the first representation of the belly-down captive since the Leiden Plaque (A.D. 320), which is shown in Illustration 118.

The carving is in deep relief, similar to the Copán style of monument carving. The figure, carved in a full frontal view, stands over a bound belly-down captive and wears a large feathered headdress, a jade cape, and pectoral. Around his waist is a kind of short skirt, fringed around the bottom, with hanging celts (which are possibly jade). He wears a loincloth with elaborate dangles on each side. In his right hand he holds a bannerlike object, and he probably held a copal bag in his left hand.

Illustration 107. Stela 10, Tikal.

106

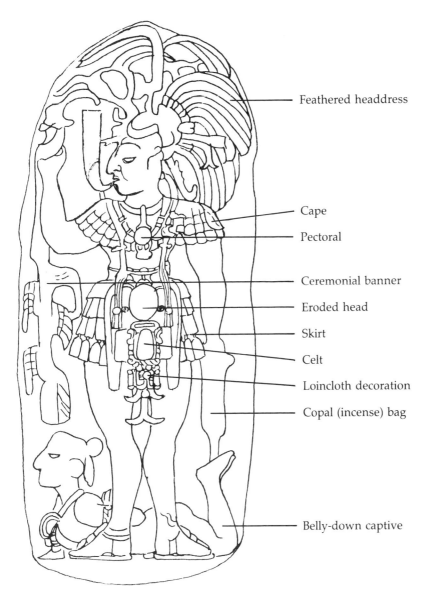

Feathered headdress

Cape

Pectoral

Ceremonial banner

Eroded head

Skirt

Celt

Loincloth decoration

Copal (incense) bag

Belly-down captive

Illustration 108.   Stela 10, Tikal. Drawing by Lisa
Ferguson; iconography interpreted by Schele.

107

Stela 11

Stela 11 now stands in the center of Stela Row in the Great Plaza. It bears the date 10.2.0.0.0. (A.D. 869). The figure represented is unknown because the glyphs are eroded and unreadable. Chitam, Tikal's last identified ruler, acceded to power in A.D. 768, a hundred years before this stela was carved; it therefore belonged to an as-yet-unknown subsequent ruler, who has been named Stela 11 Ruler.

The survival of a Tikal emblem glyph on Stela 11 indicates a continuation of Tikal traditions. A belly-down captive figure appears at the base of the shaft, and the ruler is performing the traditional scattering gesture. The stela was cut from bedded limestone and carved with a geometrically designed border.

This stela depicts the Stela 11 Ruler's inauguration, as there is some rulership iconography present. The figure holds a ceremonial bar with a series of three bloodletting knots. He wears a jade collar with cylinder and bead bangles. His belt bears crossed bands. On his loincloth are representations of the Sun God and square-nosed serpents (Ill. 109). This loincloth is similar to those found at Quiriguá. On the back rack appear hanging celts, below which is a quetzal bird.

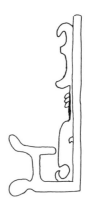

Illustration 109. Square-nosed serpent.

Illustration 110. Stela 11, Tikal, and altar with
Stela 10 in the background.

Stela 12

Stelae 10 and 12 depict Curl Head, according to Schele. He followed Bird Claw. Jones, however, suggests both Stelae 10 and 12 may be attributable to Jaguar Paw Skull, as he may have ruled to A.D. 537. Stela 12 is located in the northeast corner of the Great Plaza. It is dated 9.4.13.0.0 (A.D. 527). The figure on Stela 12 faces east (to the left), while the figure on its companion, Stela 10, faces west (to the right). Only a portion of Stela 12 is in place; the figure is cut off at the knees.

On the back of the stela, the glyphs 13 Ahau 13 Yaxkin can be deciphered, as can the 9.4.13.0.0 date. The glyphs that appear in the photograph are, as yet, undeciphered.

Illustration 112.   Stela 12, Tikal.

Illustration 111.   Stela 12, Tikal.

110

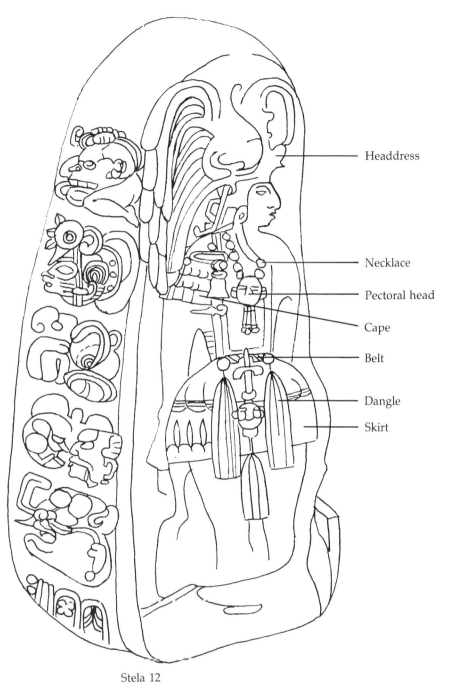

Headdress

Necklace

Pectoral head

Cape

Belt

Dangle

Skirt

Stela 12

Illustration 113.   Stela 12, Tikal. Drawing by Lisa
Ferguson; iconography interpreted by Schele.

Stela 13

Kan Chitam (Kan Boar) appears on Stela 13 and Stela 9. He followed Stormy Sky, and in turn was succeeded by Jaguar Paw Skull. Stela 9 is dated A.D. 475, but no date appears on Stela 13. Jones suggests the date should be around 9.2.0.0.0 (A.D. 475).

The third glyph from the bottom on the west (left) side is Kan Chitam's name glyph. The east side of the stela records Kan Chitam's parents. Stormy Sky's glyph, however, is not certain. It may appear in outline at the top of the east side.

The figure is carved in high relief wearing a clearly outlined cape and holding a simple staff. He holds an incense bag in his right hand. A jade necklace hangs around his neck, below which is a woven mat—a Maya symbol of authority and power. Traces of red paint, which once covered all of Tikal's stelae, are visible.

This is a small stela, smaller than Stormy Sky's stelae displayed in the museum. The figure is rendered simply, and the ruler is emphasized rather than his regalia. The Tikal stelae erected around A.D. 500 were different in style than stelae being erected at other Maya sites during the period. At that time, Tikal was outside the mainstream of Maya stelae fashion; not until the time of Ah Cacaw did Tikal begin to catch up.

Illustration 114.   Stela 13, Tikal.

112

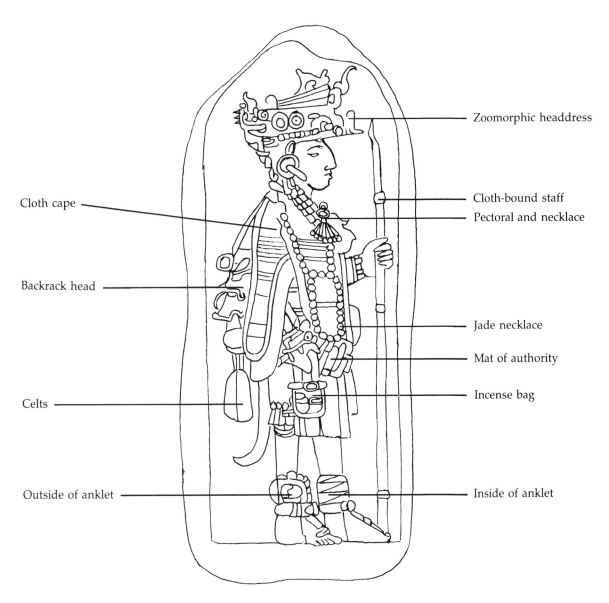

Cloth cape

Backrack head

Celts

Outside of anklet

Zoomorphic headdress

Cloth-bound staff
Pectoral and necklace

Jade necklace

Mat of authority

Incense bag

Inside of anklet

Illustration 115.   Stela 13, Tikal. Drawing by Lisa
Ferguson; iconography interpreted by Schele.

Stela 18

Stelae 18 and 4 depict Curl Nose, who became king in A.D. 379. The stela possibly commemorated the 8.18.0.0.0 (A.D. 396) katun ending. Curl Nose is the Early Classic period ruler who followed Jaguar Paw, preceded the great Stormy Sky, and who may have been the progenitor of a new dynasty at Tikal.

Stela 18, now located on plaza level just west of center on the north side of the Great Plaza, was not originally erected here, but was brought in and set up in Postclassic times. The stela has been broken in half, and only the lower portion remains. Despite this, we can reconstruct the figure and the iconography. The ruler was seated on his name glyph, Curl Nose, with his hip and legs in profile and his torso in front view. The name glyph depicts a zoomorphic mask with a snarling creature with a curled-up snout. The human face at the rear of his body, marking him as an Ahau Pop, is attached to his loincloth just above three pendants. Above this head is his crooked arm in which rested a full-figure effigy of which only the legs survive.

Also visible is a major costume motif of the Maya, a belt chain with the head of a deity at the end of the chain, appearing in the same way as on the Leiden Plaque.

Stelae 18 and Stela 4 were carved in the Early Classic tradition with a figure on the front, nothing on the sides, and glyphs on the back. Stela 18 is made of true limestone cut into a form that approximates a shaft. Imperfections in the stone were not removed.

Illustration 116.   Stela 18, Tikal.

114

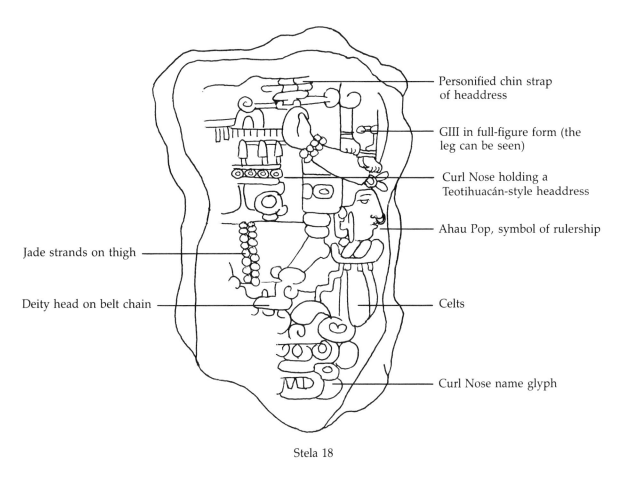

Personified chin strap
of headdress

GIII in full-figure form (the
leg can be seen)

Curl Nose holding a
Teotihuacán-style headdress

Ahau Pop, symbol of rulership

Jade strands on thigh

Celts

Deity head on belt chain

Curl Nose name glyph

Stela 18

Illustration 117.   Stela 18, Tikal. Drawing by Lisa
Ferguson; iconography interpreted by Schele.

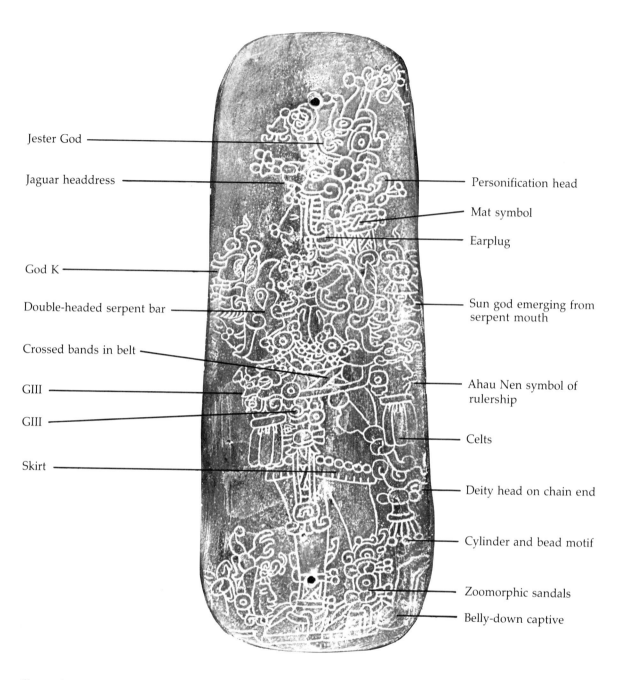

Jester God

Jaguar headdress

Personification head

Mat symbol

Earplug

God K

Double-headed serpent bar

Sun god emerging from serpent mouth

Crossed bands in belt

GIII

Ahau Nen symbol of rulership

GIII

Celts

Skirt

Deity head on chain end

Cylinder and bead motif

Zoomorphic sandals

Belly-down captive

Illustration 118. Leiden Plaque (8.14.3.1.12 [A.D. 320]). Courtesy Rijksmuseum, Leiden; iconography and hieroglyphs interpreted by Schele.

116

Initial Series Introductory Glyph

8 Baktun

14 Katuns

3 Tuns

1 Uinal

12 Kins

1 Eb

G5/ seating of

Yaxkin/ he was seated

Office/ name

Sky/Tikal EG (early Classic version)

117

Illustration 119.   Great Plaza Ball Court.

Ball Court, Great Plaza (5D-74)

The Great Plaza ball court is nestled between Temple I and the Central Acropolis Palace. It was built in Late Classic times. The playing area, only about ten and a half feet by forty-four and a half feet, is located between two parallel ranges with horizontal benches and sloping playing walls. On the south terraces of Temple I, which rises to the north of this ball court, stairways lead from terrace to terrace, creating a grandstand effect ideal for viewing the game.

The ball court has been only partially excavated and stabilized. The tree growing out of the east wall is a reminder that the rain forest can quickly cover any structure. The basic design of the court is similar to other ball courts in the Petén area. On each end of the court sides are small stairways.

Other ball courts have been discovered at Tikal. At the north end of the Plaza of the Seven Temples is a triple ball court, and a larger, more elaborate court is located in the East Plaza. Jones indicates that the court in the East Plaza had a gallery with round columns constructed on the court sides overlooking the playing alley.

The ball game was played throughout Mesoamerica, but the rules of the game varied from site to site and from period to period. The game was ceremonial, as well as for sport. There is evidence that human sacrifice was connected with the Classic Maya game at Tikal as it was with the Mexicanized-Maya (Toltec) game at Chichén Itzá.

The funerary vases discovered in Classic Maya tombs of the Petén area indicate that the game there was played with a large solid rubber ball, probably bigger than a basketball, and was

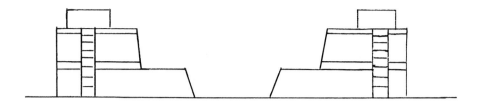

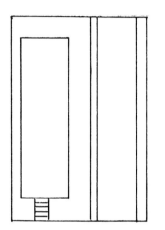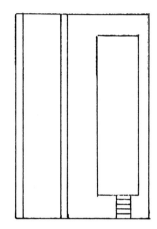

Illustration 120.   Great Plaza Ball Court.

played without the use of hands. The vases also show that the players wore protective pads of leather, wood, or basketry on their hips and knees. Considering that the ball was of solid rubber (not filled with air), it would have been a heavy and dangerous flying missile. Body protection would have been a necessity. Illustration 234 is a drawing of a Classic Maya ballplayer.

Illustration 121. North Acropolis, center background, with Temple I on the right.

North Acropolis

The North Acropolis consisted of temple-crowned pyramids built either to house royal tombs or as temples dedicated to royal ancestors. They were built either by the lord himself during his lifetime or by his progeny or successors in veneration of deceased lords, who were assumed to have conquered death to become deities to be worshipped by the living lords.

In the Petén, pyramids generally were freestanding, rubble filled, faced with limestone, and usually terraced. They had a single stairway reaching the flat top of the pyramid, which served as a platform for a temple. On these pyramids, the Maya constructed a small corbel-vaulted temple containing one, two, or three small rooms. Architecture was designed for exterior use, and little importance was placed upon interior space in relationship to the mass of the construction.

The visible structures in the North Acropolis

of Tikal were built during Early and Middle Classic times—long before Ah Cacaw's Temple I and Temple II.

An aerial view shows the Central Acropolis Palace in the foreground and Temple I to the right. Temple 22, the largest temple still standing in the North Acropolis, is in the center background. A long east-west stairway constitutes the entrance to the North Terrace. Stelae and altars line the terrace and the plaza below.

The earliest construction dates to around 200 B.C. and, in all, the North Acropolis contains portions of as many as a hundred structures. The Acropolis from south to north, beginning with 5D-26 and Temples 25 and 27 which flank it, consists of a great masonry and rubble-filled platform, which serves as a base for Temple 22 and the four partially restored temples that surround it. The unrestored temple to the west of the North Terrace and just north of Temple II is Temple 35. Together with the front row of Tem-

120

Illustration 122.   Great Plaza. From *Tikal Reports, No. 11.*

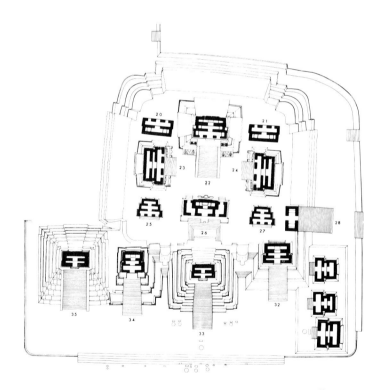

Illustration 123.   North Acropolis in A.D. 800. From William
R. Coe, *A Handbook of the Ancient Maya Ruins*, p. 42.

Illustrations 124 and 125.   North Acropolis, aerial
view from the west.

ples 32, 33, and 34, it is based at the North Terrace level and abuts the Great Platform.

The Early Classic Maya ruler, Jaguar Paw, who
became king in about A.D. 320, was buried under
Temple 26. Stormy Sky, who died in 9.1.1.10.10
(A.D. 457), was buried under Temple 33. Cut into
the bedrock under Temple 34 is Burial 10, the
tomb of Curl Nose. This ruler was buried with
nine retainers, who were sacrificed to accom-
pany the deceased through the dreaded underworld.

In Curl Nose's tomb, beautifully painted Teotihuacán-style pottery was found. Some evidence suggests a connection between Curl Nose
and Kaminaljuyú, a Maya site located where
Guatemala City now stands. In the Early Classic
Period, Kaminaljuyú was heavily influenced by
the central Mexican center, Teotihuacán.

In addition to the royal tombs, other tombs
have been discovered in the North Acropolis.

About 70 percent of the pyramid-temples cover
tombs; the remainder were ceremonial structures, perhaps dedicated to ancestors or to Maya
deities.

The North Acropolis, although in ruins, appears today as it did during the Late Classic
Period, except that the central front pyramid-
temple (Structure 5D-33-1st) which was nearly
110 feet high, has been disassembled because
archaeologists found that this temple had de-
teriorated to the point that stabilization was im-
practical. Temple 33 was composed of three
temples built one above the other. All three are
partially visible today. On the platform of the
earliest temple, designated 5D-33-3rd, one of the
terraces is faced on the east and west by masks
of long-nosed gods. These masks may be seen
by descending the stairway to the left of the
main stairway leading up to Temple 33.

Burial 48 was one of three tombs found during

122

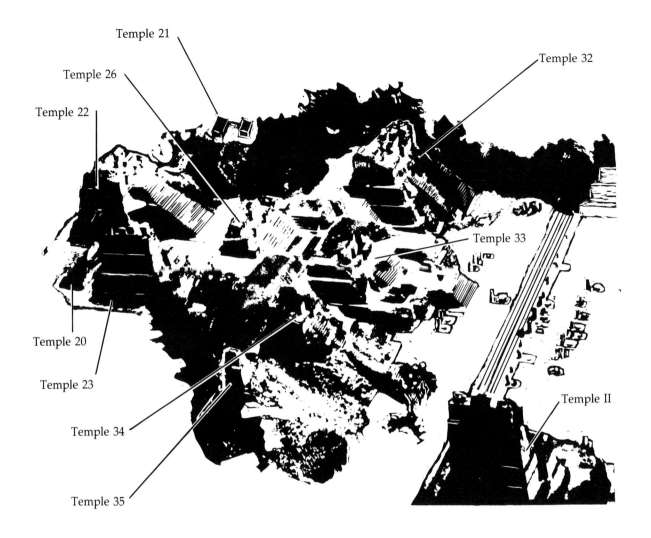

Temple 21
Temple 26
Temple 22
Temple 32
Temple 33
Temple 20
Temple 23
Temple II
Temple 34
Temple 35

archaeological tunneling under 5D-33. It was a chamber cut into bedrock prior to the construction of the stairway from the North Terrace to the Acropolis. This was the tomb of Stormy Sky, probably Curl Nose's son and successor. The glyphic text painted on the walls of the tomb indicated a Long Count date equivalent to March 18, A.D. 457. The extraordinarily well-preserved Stela 31 depicting Stormy Sky, now located in the Tikal Museum, was found in the excavation of Structure 33.

In *Tikal, A Handbook of the Ancient Maya Ruins* (1967), W. R. Coe describes the construction of the Late Classic Temple 5D-33-1st (the last constructed of the three temples known as 33). He says the Maya first constructed a forty-foot flat-topped pyramid over Temple 33-2nd, which completely buried it. A construction stairway, like the stairway on Temple I, was built up its south side from the North Terrace. The construction stairway enabled workmen to carry up the mortar, mud, and rubble to make the fill, and the stone blocks to retain it. This fill, held together by cut-stone blocks, constituted the core of the pyramid. When the first core had been completed for Structure 33, it too was gradually interred beneath a second core with its own construction stairway; the pyramid was then built in ever higher and narrower stages, eventually reaching a height of sixty-two feet. Evidence suggests that as they built the substructures of this pyramid, the Maya completed each of the

123

masonry faces of the inner pyramids. Each terrace level consisted of dozens of walled-up blocks of fill. Most of the blocks of fill were rectangular, but in the lower stages of the pyramid they were curved. Some can be seen today radiating from the core-pyramid of 33-2nd (Coe 1967: 48).

Most of the construction of the North Acropolis was done in Preclassic times, prior to the Early Classic period. Fifteen of the twenty floors and six of the eight reconstructions were completed before A.D. 250. An estimated date of about 700 B.C. is assigned to the founding of Tikal, but the earliest radiocarbon date, 588 B.C. ± fifty-three years, came from the North Acropolis.

The earliest cut-stone masonry and lime plaster yet discovered is in the North Acropolis in 5D-Sub 14, very close to bedrock, dating to around 200 B.C. By the time of Christ, three substantial temples and two smaller ones stood on the North Acropolis, constituting a standard ceremonial assemblage organized on a north-south axis. This construction is now buried deep within the acropolis. By A.D.1, the monumental architecture, developed to mark the graves of the elite dead, employed apron panels, and offset back panels with great stucco masks on the buildings. One of these masks is preserved just west of the stairway of Temple 22, in addition to the two masks preserved in Temple 33.

According to W. R. Coe (1967: 43), "By about A.D. 250 the North Acropolis started to take on its now visible form. All buildings then extant were razed and a completely new Acropolis platform was built. Four vaulted buildings were then constructed on this platform." These four Early Classic buildings, which formed a quadrangle, were later covered by the major structures, Temple 22 to the north, Temple 23 to the west, Temple 24 on the east, and Temple 26 as the entrance to the ceremonial assemblage on the south.

Structure 5D-22 itself was built over three times, the final construction being completed in the fifth century A.D. Visible are portions of the second reconstruction of about A.D. 350. The A.D. 250 construction is completely covered.

Taken as a whole, the North Acropolis at Tikal must be considered as one of the great feats of human construction. It represents a thousand

Illustration 126.   North Acropolis Pyramid 5D-33 before disassembly. From *Expedition*, 8 (1), Fall 1965, p. 43.

years of continuous construction. In the Late Classic period, when it stood partially painted a garish red rising above the green of the jungle, it was as imposing as anything constructed prior to the eighth century A.D. anywhere in the world.

Ah Cacaw's (Ruler A) construction began a new era at Tikal. To visualize central Tikal before Ah Cacaw, one should view the North Acropolis from the top of the steps of the Central Acropolis on the south side of the Great Plaza. Visualize the Plaza and the North Acropolis as if Temple I, Temple II, and the remains of the front and center Temple 5D-33 on the North Acropolis are all absent. This is the way central Tikal appeared before Ah Cacaw. At that time Structure 5D-22 to the far north dominated the North Acropolis, and the North Acropolis dominated the Great Plaza.

Then visualize the front and center temple-pyramid (5D-33) in its original form, more than a hundred feet high, here shown in Illustration

Illustration 127.   Long-nosed God, Temple 5D-33-
3rd.

Illustration 128.   Deity mask, Structure 5D-22.

126, before it was taken down by the archaeologists. This temple-pyramid effectively sealed off the North Acropolis. Its construction began the new era at Tikal.

Structure 5D-33, Temple I, and Temple II were built by Ah Cacaw in the eighth century A.D. With their construction, the Great Plaza, with Structure 5D-33 on the north and Temple I and Temple II to the east and west, became a new ceremonial assemblage, which changed the focus of Tikal from the North Acropolis to the Great Plaza and triggered the expansion of all Tikal, including the paved causeways, the great market to the east, and the twin-pyramid complexes. The Late Classic rulers, beginning with Ah Cacaw, transformed Tikal.

Illustration 129.   Teotihuacán Building, Structure 5D-43.

Teotihuacán Building (5D-43)

The three-stairwayed Structure 5D-43 was part of the East Plaza. It was built against the east portion of the Central Acropolis located just behind Temple I. Its style is Late Classic, with a platform supporting a two-room building.

It is called the Teotihuacán Building because of its similarity to the architectural style called "talud-tablero" of Teotihuacán in the Valley of Mexico.

The double circles are generally considered to be manifestations of the Mexican rain god, Tlaloc, but the double circles are also associated with the serpent in Maya iconography, as on the lintel on Tikal Temple IV. Tlaloc is also associated with Maya bloodletting. Although the Teotihuacán Building has been so called because of the Mexican talud-tablero-like iconography, it may be that the iconography is actually Mayan.

Illustration 130.   Talud-tablero-type architecture.

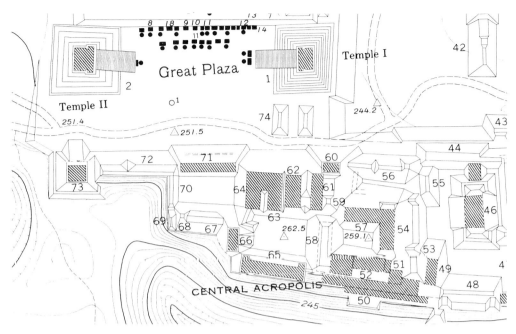

Illustration 131. Central Acropolis and Great Plaza. From *Tikal Reports No. 11.*

Central Acropolis (Aerial View)

The Central Acropolis or palace area is some seven hundred feet long east to west and covers about four acres. In the Late Classic period, it was composed of range-type buildings, some multistoried, surrounding six courts on various levels. Of these six courts, only three have been excavated—from west to east, Courts 2, 4, and 6, going in sequence from higher to lower elevations. Court 5D-2, at the center of Illustration 132, is directly to the south of Temple I and may be reached by climbing the stairway that rises from the south side of the Great Plaza.

Court 2, dominated by Maler's Palace on the south, is further surrounded on the west by Structure 5D-66, on the north by Structures 5D-63 and 62, and on the east by the unexcavated mound of 5D-58. A pathway goes downhill through unexcavated Court 3 with the five-story highrise buildings, 5D-50 and 52 on the right (to the south). The path comes to the top of a flight of stairs leading to the smaller Court 4, which is surrounded by Structures 5D-51, 122, and 49.

A final stairway on the north side of Court 4 leads down to the large Court 6, the Great East-ern Court. On the west side of this court is a complex of two one-story structures, 5D-128 and 53, and the two-story 5D-54. The effect of this combination is a four-story building. Across the court to the east is 5D-46, which has an interior winding stairway leading to the second floor. A pathway from the north end of Court 6 leads down to what was originally the base level of the East Plaza of Tikal. The back of Temple I is to the west.

The Central Acropolis buildings were used by the upper echelon of Maya society as residences and for running the government. The structures that face the Great Plaza and the East Plaza seem to lend themselves to administrative functions, whether religious or secular, but the rest of the complex, which is made up of many-roomed buildings opening onto courts of various levels, certainly seems to justify the buildings being called palaces.

When we consider that the rulers and their retinue probably had numerous servants to prepare food, tend to dress and toilet, and to minister to every physical need, plus a tropical climate suitable for year-round outdoor living, the concept of these small-roomed buildings as palaces

129

Illustration 132.   Central Acropolis (west to east).

becomes meaningful. Visualize the rooms of these buildings stuccoed, painted, and furnished with mats and draperies and other accoutrements available to the nobles, and the nobles with a vast multitude of servants to minister to them. These Indians lived in a style unsurpassed by any ninth-century kings of Europe.

Peter Harrison, who wrote his doctoral dissertation for the University of Pennsylvania on the Central Acropolis during the period of excavation at Tikal, believes that the buildings served several diverse functions. His research led him to conclude that the Central Acropolis buildings could have been utilized for the following functions: houses of lords, boys' pre-marriage houses, priests' residences or training schools, men's ritual houses, special oratories, and storerooms. He suggests that the storerooms might have been used for the storage of merchant's goods, weapons, and codices.

To the south and just below the Central Ac-ropolis is a ravine where the Palace Reservoir may have been, with stairways leading down to the water. While it appears that at no time was the entire ravine dammed and filled with water, William Coe indicates that the small reservoir probably contained a supply sufficient to have met the needs of those residents of the Central Acropolis. Along the terrace near the reservoir have been found the remains of what may have been the communal kitchen, which served the priests, young men, and trainees.

All that can be seen in the aerial photo is Late Classic period construction with the exception of the Great Eastern Court Palace 5D-46 located at the lower portion of the picture. The palace was built over earlier construction.

Illustration 133.   Central Acropolis (north to south).

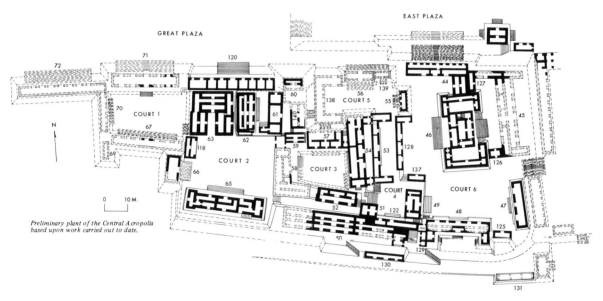

Illustration 134.   Plat of Palace area (Central Acropolis). From W. R. Coe, *Tikal*, p. 54.

131

Court 2 and Structures 5D-62 and 5D-63 (Central Acropolis)

Court 2 is the highest court of the Central Acropolis. Over the centuries the Maya built, filled, and rebuilt, until the present commanding level was reached in the Classic period. The floor of the court is thirty to fifty feet above bedrock.

Palace 5D-62 (to the right) has three long, narrow vaulted chambers with three doors on the east side, which open onto a stairway leading to a small court. Another stairway on the southeast corner reaches the second floor. Palace 5D-63, built after 5D-62, is a U-shaped structure with nine ground-floor rooms. After it was completed in its present location, it was altered by changing the location of doorways and by the addition of benches and windows.

Both Palaces 62 and Palace 63 rest upon platforms, which have as their footing the surface level of Court 1 to the west, some sixteen feet below the level of Court 2. By its location and design, the U-shaped building on the northwest corner of Court 2 suggests that it may have been used by the priests as living quarters and robing rooms for ceremonies to be performed in the Great Plaza and in the North Acropolis. The two-story building just to the east is similar in form to the lower portion of the five-story palace; it was probably used to house elite single males before marriage.

Illustration 135.   Court 2, Structure 5D-62.

Illustration 136.   Court 2, Structure 5D-63.

132

Illustration 137.   Court 2.

Maler's Palace (Central Acropolis, 5D-65)

Malers Palace has three doors facing Court 2. It was so well constructed that it never collapsed nor had to be restored. Teobert Maler, an early explorer of Tikal, used the building as a residence in 1895 and again in 1904. It was originally a two-story building; the second story can be reached by a stone stairway at the southeast corner of the building. From that vantage point, the vegetation-covered roof comb of Temple V is visible above the treetops.

Above the three doorways are traces of a carved frieze, which originally ran around the entire palace. Holes above the doorways probably supported curtains or a canopy to cover the forecourt.

The interior platforms could have been used for sleeping or as thrones for the rulers. The polychrome vases found in tombs of the period show rulers sitting tailor fashion on raised daises similar to those in the Maler Palace. The wall plaster, floors, benches, and some of the lintels over the doorways are original. This building, according to Peter Harrison, was probably used by the high priests as a residence.

Illustration 138.   Maler's Palace.

Illustration 139.   Maler's Palace interior.

Illustration 140.   Court 2, Temple 5D-66.

Structure 5D-66 (Court 2, Central Acropolis)

Structure 5D-66 is something of an enigma. It is considered to have been the last building constructed around Court 2. Unlike the palace, it is a single-room, single-door building set upon a pyramid at the top of a long, narrow stairway, all of which suggest that it was a temple or a shrine, not living quarters. Coe says, however, that during restoration no caches or burials were found, which distinguishes this little building from the funerary temples of the North Acropolis. Another unique characteristic is that only the rear portion was vaulted, while the front was either left open or supported a thatched structure. Structure 5D-66 was probably an oratory, serving the residents of the palace area.

Illustration 141. Five-story Palace.

Five-Story Palace, Central Acropolis (5D-50 and 5D-52)

The Five-Story Palace combines Structures 5D-50, which constitutes the lower two stories, and 5D-52, the upper three storeis. The upper story of Palace 52 may be reached by a stairway on the northwest corner. The rooms on the south side of the top story contain the original stone thrones and wooden beams carved of chicoza-pote.

Directly below this point, to the south of the Central Acropolis, was the Palace Reservoir. Stairways led down from the palace to a ravine below. The intial construction of this complex is thought to have begun about A.D. 650. The first story of the upper building was the first con-structed and contains vestiges of a medial frieze. The portion shown in Illustration 143 is probably a representation of the Sun God.

Harrison suggests that the lower portion of the Five-Story Palace may have been utilized to house the young sons of the elite before their marriages—a sort of bachelor's quarters—and that the upper story (the interior of which is pictured in Ill. 142) was designed as a residence for the high priests.

Illustration 142.   Five-story Palace Interior.

Illustration 143.   Five-story Palace Sun God.

138

Illustration 144.   Central Acropolis, Court 6, and structures 128, 53 and 54 in foreground. Five-Story Palace to the left. Court 2 and Temple II in background.

Court 6, West Side, Buildings 5D-128, 5D-53, and 5D-54 (Central Acropolis)

The lower building (5D-128) on the Court 6 level was constructed in a U-shaped pattern. The next story up is 5D-53, on the level of Court 4. Court 4 joins Court 6 by a stairway at the southwest corner (to the left of the picture) of Court 6. Above is 5D-54. These buildings were not connected by stairways of access, but were reached only from the separate courts. This construction leads us to believe that each elevation had a separate function. Harrison assigns the upper story to the high priests.

The lower building (5D-128), located directly across the court from the palace, was part of the Great Eastern Court Palace complex, as were the other buildings that open onto Court 6—the royal court. Harrison concludes that Structures 5D-47 and 5D-125, in the southeast corner of Court 6, were utilized for storage. 5D-53, just above 5D-128, is of similar construction and may also have been a part of the palace complex.

Illustration 145. Great Eastern Court Palace
(Structure 5D-46).

Great Eastern Court Palace, (Central Acropolis, Court 6, 5D-46)

The Great Eastern Court Palace was built in Early Classic times—before A.D. 600—and was continually occupied as a residence until Tikal was abandoned, before A.D. 900. It is a two-story building located on the east side of Court 6 with an interior stairway, which reaches the upper story. In Late Classic times, patios, with rooms on three sides, were added on the north and south. The palace was reached by broad stairways on the east and west.

William Coe reports that excavation beneath the west stairs yielded flint and shell objects, medallions of jade, as well as mosaics of shell, pyrite, and obsidian. Four Late Classic burials were found beneath the stairway on the east side of the palace.

Of all the buildings that make up the Central Acropolis, the Great Eastern Court Palace is most characteristically a ruler's palace. We may well imagine that rulers Jaguar Paw, Curl Nose, Stormy Sky, Ah Cacaw, Ruler B, Chitam, and other kings of Tikal may have lived there either temporarily or permanently during, perhaps, six hundred years of its use. Adams and Smith suggest that "the living accommodations at the Maya centers were not intended for continuous occupation by members of the Maya elite but rather were temporary quarters to be occupied whenever business, war, or religious ceremonies required attendance in the urban center" (Adams and Smith 1981: 343); otherwise they lived in the suburbs.

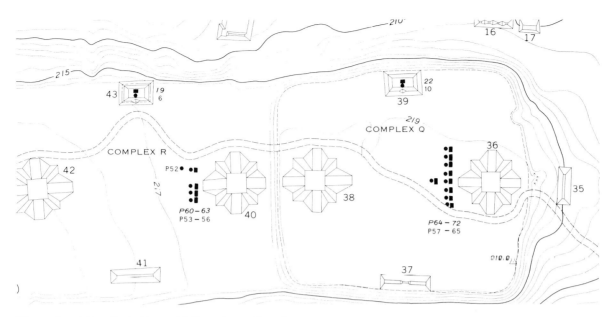

Illustration 146. Twin-Pyramid Complexes Q and R. From *Tikal Reports, No. 11.*

Twin-Pyramid Complex Q

Just west of the airport and the Tikal Park Head-quarters, the road through the jungle branches to the right (north) and passes through Twin-pyramid Complexes Q and R before it turns south to the Great Plaza. The eastern radial (four-stair-wayed) temple at Complex Q has been partially restored with a row of uncarved stelae and altars. On the north side of this complex are Stela 22 and Altar 10. The western temple is unexcavated. Complex Q was constructed in 9.17.0.0.0 (A.D. 771) by Chitam.

Twin-pyramid complexes were constructed for public celebration of katun endings. The Maya katun ritual began in the Middle Classic period around A.D. 600. A twin-pyramid complex would be utilized for a twenty-year period, then another complex would be constructed.

The twin-pyramid complex, as shown in Illustration 146, was composed of two radial pyramids lacking temples or other structures on top, one on the east and one on the west. On the north side of the area was an open-walled enclosure with a stela and altar, which commemorated the katun ending. On the south was a low stone range-type structure with nine door-

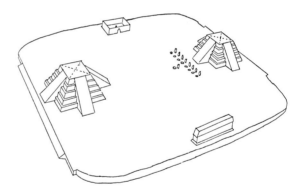

Illustration 147. Twin-Pyramid Complex. Drawing by Marvin Cohodas, *Segunda Mesa Redonda,* vol. 4, p. 218.

ways. The entire complex was constructed on a low platform of fill.

These twin-pyramid complexes were, according to Jones, probably employed in connection with large public functions involving cosmic order and the passage of historical time. Tikal had nine such complexes.

Illustration 148.   Complex Q Pyramid.

Illustration 149.   Complex Q Pyramid and stelae.

Illustration 150.   Stela 22 and Altar 10, Tikal.

Illustration 151.   Stela 22, Tikal.

Stela 22 and Altar 10

Stela 22 and Altar 10 are located in the reconstructed unroofed enclosure on the north side of Twin-pyramid Complex Q (originally designated "Group E" by Morley). The stela, dated 9.17.0.0.0 (A.D. 771) was constructed by Chitam (Ruler C), who "was seated as *batab*" (became ruler) of Tikal on 9.16.17.16.4 (A.D. 768), as indicated on Stela 22, and ruled until A.D. 790 or later.

Chitam is shown in profile wearing a feathered headdress and an elaborate backrack, holding a ceremonial bar in his left arm, and scattering seeds, corn, copal, or perhaps blood with his right hand. The Perforator God is depicted on the anklets and wristlets. This stela follows the style of Ruler B's Stela 21 located at the Temple of Inscriptions. The belly-down prisoner on the much-eroded Altar 10 is similar to the one on Ruler B's Altar 9.

Coe reads the hieroglyphic text from the upper left of Stela 22 as follows:

> The first glyph records the day 13 Ahau ( ), followed by the month 18 Cumku ( ); the left hand glyph in the second row is the katun

glyphs surmounted by the number 17 ( ) or 17th Katun, while the second glyph, to the right in this row, records that the Haab, or Tun, is completed. These four glyphs state that a day in a 52-year cycle, 13 Ahau 18 Cumku, completes Katun 17 of an implied Baktun 9; in other words, 9.17.0.0.0 (W. Coe 1967: 86).

Schele has interpreted the glyphs that appear on Stela 22. The stela celebrates the end of the seventeenth katun (A.D. 771) and relates this katun-ending date to the accession of Chitam, son of Ruler B.

144

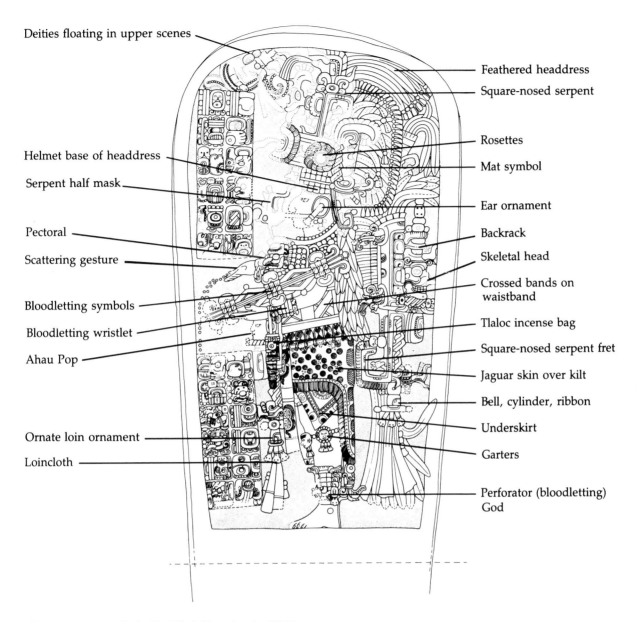

Deities floating in upper scenes

Feathered headdress

Square-nosed serpent

Rosettes

Mat symbol

Helmet base of headdress

Serpent half mask

Ear ornament

Pectoral

Backrack

Scattering gesture

Skeletal head

Crossed bands on waistband

Bloodletting symbols

Tlaloc incense bag

Bloodletting wristlet

Square-nosed serpent fret

Ahau Pop

Jaguar skin over kilt

Bell, cylinder, ribbon

Underskirt

Ornate loin ornament

Garters

Loincloth

Perforator (bloodletting) God

Illustration 152. Stela 22, Tikal. Drawing by W. R. Coe, *American Antiquity* Jan. 1977, p. 31; iconography interpreted by Schele.

145

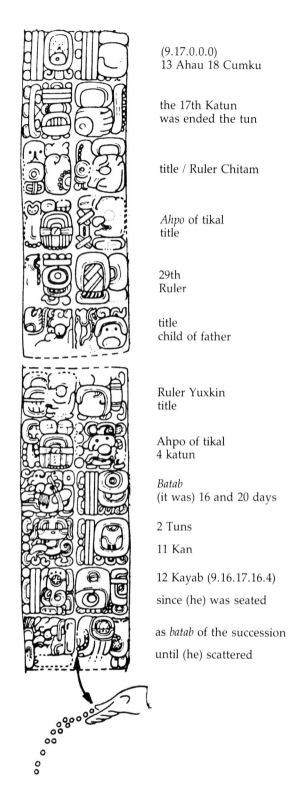

(9.17.0.0.0)
13 Ahau 18 Cumku

the 17th Katun
was ended the tun

title / Ruler Chitam

Ahpo of tikal
title

29th
Ruler

title
child of father

Ruler Yuxkin
title

Ahpo of tikal
4 katun

Batab
(it was) 16 and 20 days

2 Tuns

11 Kan

12 Kayab (9.16.17.16.4)

since (he) was seated

as *batab* of the succession

until (he) scattered

Illustration 153. Interpretation of Stela 22 glyphs.
Drawing by W. R. Coe, Linda Schele, from *Maya
Hieroglyphic Writing Workshop,* p. 51.

Structure 5D-73

The trail from the Great Plaza west to Temple III leads around the south side of Temple II, between it and the unexcavated Pyramid 73. Structure 5D-73 supported no temple, but enclosed Burial 196. The tomb contained an enormous quantity of jade jewelry, stingray spines, shell objects, and other jewelry. Clemency Coggins suggests that the tomb was a burial of a member of Ah Cacaw's family. She says, "The richness of this tomb, its close relationship in both construction methods and in tomb furnishings to Burial 116 [Temple I] and its location, all strongly suggest this was the tomb of a younger son of Ruler A [Ah Cacaw]—a younger brother of Ruler B" (Coggins 1975: 554).

William Coe suggests that an even more important person was buried here—Ruler B himself. The burial is comparable in many ways to Ah Cacaw's tomb under Temple I which contained a stingray spine bearing an inscription dated ca. A.D. 755. Ruler B was the twenty-seventh ruler of Tikal and Chitam (Ruler C) was the twenty-ninth, so it is possible that A.D. 755 could be the date of his death.

Complex R, Stela 19

Stela 19 and Altar 6 are found along the north loop road, west of Complex Q, next to the Maler Causeway. Stela 19 is part of Twin-pyramid Complex R built by Chitam (Ruler C) in celebration of the date 9.18.0.0.0 (A.D. 790). It is the latest twin-pyramid complex found at Tikal.

The figure has been badly defaced but appears to be in the same style as Chitam's Stela 22, located to the east in Complex Q. The stela is carved in low relief from bedded limestone quarried and cut to the size required for the finished monument.

Illustration 154.   Stela 19, Tikal.

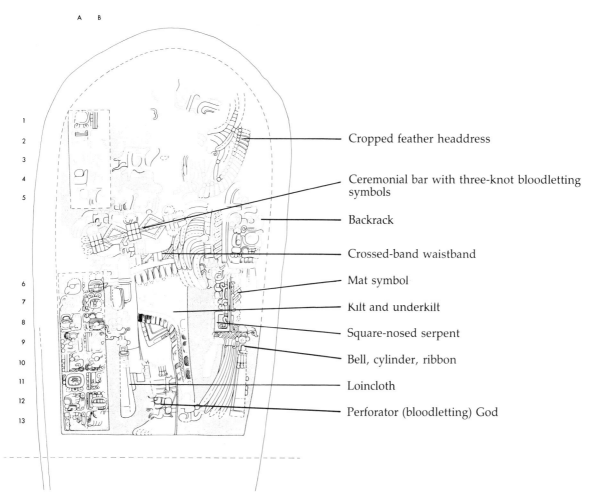

A B

Cropped feather headdress

Ceremonial bar with three-knot bloodletting symbols

Backrack

Crossed-band waistband

Mat symbol

Kilt and underkilt

Square-nosed serpent

Bell, cylinder, ribbon

Loincloth

Perforator (bloodletting) God

Illustration 155. Stela 19, Tikal. Drawing by W. R. Coe, *American Antiquity,* Jan. 1977, p. 57; iconography interpreted by Schele.

Illustration 156.   Temple II with Temple III in background.

Temple III

The trail west leads to the unrestored Temple III about two hundred yards away. It is possible to climb the pyramid for a view of Lintel 2, which is still in place.

Known as the Temple of the Jaguar Priest because of the principal figure on the lintel in the temple, Temple III is probably the last pyramid and temple constructed by the Maya of Tikal. Stela 24 at the base of the pyramid provides the accepted date of construction—9.19.0.0.0 (A.D. 810)—but it is not known if Chitam was still in office. The Stela 24 ruler may be Chitam or, possibly, his brother.

Illustration 157.   Altar 7, Tikal.

Stela 24 and Altar 7

Stela 24 and Altar 7 are located in front of Temple III. Stela 24 and Altar 7 were the next to last monuments constructed at Tikal. The altar displays a woven mat (a symbol of authority) on both sides and a deity head resting in a bowl. The bowl contains a personification of the God of the Eccentric Flint and paper strips used in the bloodletting ceremony. A part of the self-sacrifice bloodletting involved allowing the blood to be caught and absorbed by strips of bark paper held in a bowl.

Both the stela and the altar appear to have been dedicated in 9.19.0.0.0 (A.D. 810). However, no name glyphs on the stela are recognizable.

Illustration 158.   Stela 24 and Altar 7, Tikal.

151

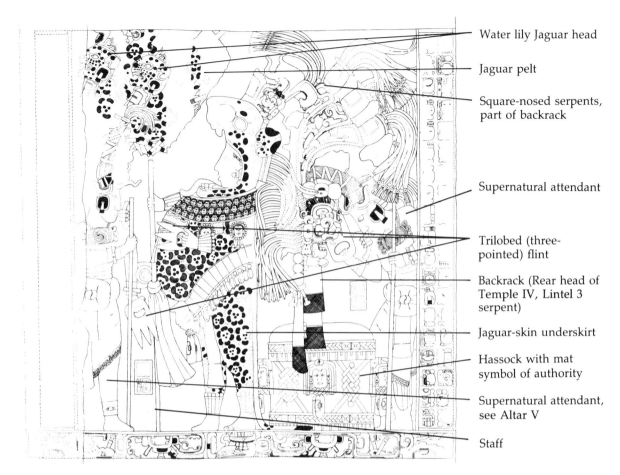

Water lily Jaguar head

Jaguar pelt

Square-nosed serpents, part of backrack

Supernatural attendant

Trilobed (three-pointed) flint

Backrack (Rear head of Temple IV, Lintel 3 serpent)

Jaguar-skin underskirt

Hassock with mat symbol of authority

Supernatural attendant, see Altar V

Staff

Illustration 159. Temple III, Lintel 2, Tikal. From W. R. Coe, *Tikal.* p. 76; iconography interpreted by Schele.

Lintel of Temple III

Lintel 2 of Temple III depicts a standing figure with a distended stomach, dressed in a jaguar costume. Flora Clancy has concluded that the central figure is a pregnant woman, basing her argument on the pregnant appearance plus the figure's small hands and feet. Comparing this lintel with Altar 5, she concludes that Chitam is referring back to the times of Ah Cacaw in order to display dynastic evidence of Chitam's right to rule. Jones has a different view. He suggests that the person depicted on this lintel may be Chitam (Ruler C) or his brother. The two figures flanking the jaguar character are the same figures seen on Altar 5.

The suggested date of the lintel is between 9.18.0.0.0 (A.D. 790) and 9.19.0.0.0 (A.D. 810) (Clancy 1980: 195).

Illustration 160.   Temple III, Lintel 2.

Stela 16 and Complex N

Stela 16 and Altar 5, monuments to Ah Cacaw, are a part of Complex N located just to the east of Temple IV. This stela and altar were once a part of a twin-pyramid complex. Each twin-pyramid complex was composed of a very low platform on which were located two four-stairway pyramids on an east-west axis, a stela and altar in an open enclosure on the north side, and a nine-doorway range-type building on the south side. The configuration is similar to complex Q.

Stela 16 was erected by Ah Cacaw in celebration of katun ending 9.14.0.0.0 (A.D. 711) The specific date can be read on the upper left portion of the stela. At Tikal in the Late Classic period, only the Calendar Round date (in this case, 6 Ahau 13 Muan) was given, from which the Long Count date was understood. The exact date of this stela is 9.14.0.0.0 6 Ahau 13 Muan, or December 5, A.D. 711. The lower two glyphs on the right, which Schele reads "3 Katun Batab," indicate that Ah Cacaw, at the time the stela is dated, was in his third twenty-year period as *batab* or ruler.

Ah Cacaw stands with feet splayed and his head in profile facing right. He holds a three-knot bloodletting staff with the Bloodletting God attached to the three bars. He is the first and foremost of the Late Classic Tikal rulers; this may have been the first stela he erected. Coggins has calculated that he was fifty-seven years of age at the time, which would indicate that he was in his teens when he became king. At the time he erected this stela, he had ruled more than forty years (two katuns) and was in his third katun.

The iconography of Stela 16 shows the effort by Ah Cacaw to unite the stylistic tradition begun by Kan Chitam and Jaguar Paw Skull with the more widespread tradition of the Maya. He holds the bloodletting staff introduced by Kan Chitam and wears traditional Maya dress. A copal (incense) bag suspended from his right arm displays the goggle-eyed Mexican god, Tlaloc, which probably indicates bloodletting.

The symbolic imagery of Ah Cacaw's costume, beginning from the top of the stela, in-

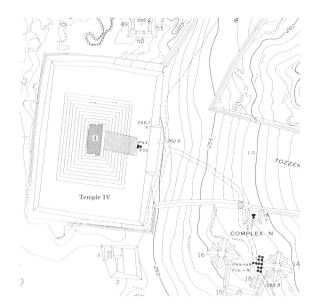

Illustration 161.   Temple IV and Complex N. From *Tikal Reports, No. 11.*

Illustration 162.   Glyph T 504 (Akbal).

cludes a feathered headdress with cropped and tied ends. The top of the headdress is an *akbal* (a day-name glyph, T 504). The *akbal,* in turn, rests on a Sun God face which has large eyes, a mirror in the forehead, and a hummingbird in front. Below is a skull, behind which rests a Venus-star sign.

He wears a half mask of the square-nosed serpent, which is engaged to the side flanges of the headdress. His earplug has a bone end and jade counterweights.

Over his shoulders he wears a small jade cape. On his chest are two pectorals, the upper one with a face in the center of a double tripartite bar. Below that pectoral and attached to it is another double-ended bar with bone ends. His belt displays faces of Ahau with mat markings designating him as "lord of the mat" or ruler. Below the Ahaus are celts and cloth strips.

He wears a skirt decorated with crossed bones

Illustration 163.   Stela 16 and Altar 5, Tikal.

and shield-like objects with serpents around the rims and a scroll in the center. On the fringe of the skirt are round objects, which may represent death eyes.

Suspended in front of the loincloth is the mat symbol of authority, below which is a serpent monster, then a strip with a double bead and bell motif. On each kneelet there is a face; below the kneelet on each leg is a complex set of deity monsters extending down to Ah Cacaw's sandals. Behind him the feathers of the backrack radiate from shoulder to buttock. This combination of headdress, pectoral, skirt, and belt is a costume specifically associated with period-ending rites at Tikal. It can also be seen on Stelae 19, 21, and 22.

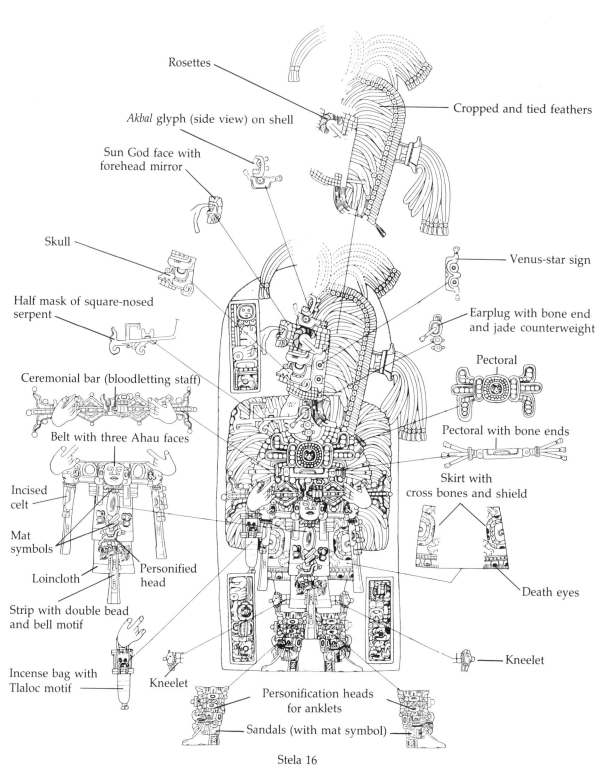

Rosettes

Akbal glyph (side view) on shell

Sun God face with forehead mirror

Skull

Half mask of square-nosed serpent

Ceremonial bar (bloodletting staff)

Belt with three Ahau faces

Incised celt

Mat symbols

Loincloth

Personified head

Strip with double bead and bell motif

Incense bag with Tlaloc motif

Kneelet

Cropped and tied feathers

Venus-star sign

Earplug with bone end and jade counterweight

Pectoral

Pectoral with bone ends

Skirt with cross bones and shield

Death eyes

Kneelet

Personification heads for anklets

Sandals (with mat symbol)

Stela 16

Illustration 164.   Stela 16, Tikal. After drawing by W. R. Coe, *American Antiquity*, Jan. 1977, Fig. 13; iconography interpreted by Schele.

Illustration 165.   Stela 16, Tikal.

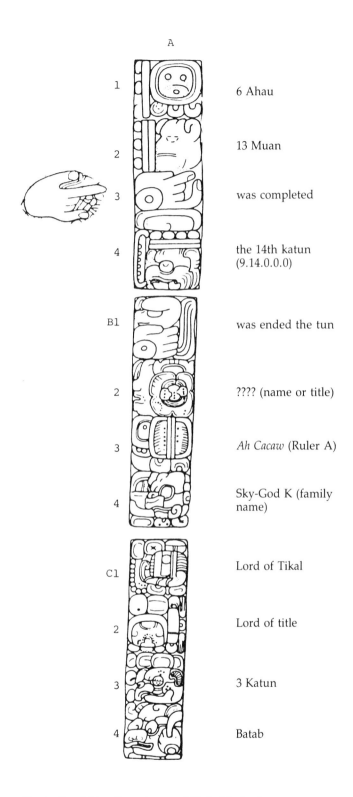

A

1   6 Ahau

2   13 Muan

3   was completed

4   the 14th katun
        (9.14.0.0.0)

B1   was ended the tun

2   ???? (name or title)

3   *Ah Cacaw* (Ruler A)

4   Sky-God K (family
        name)

C1   Lord of Tikal

2   Lord of title

3   3 Katun

4   Batab

Illustration 166.   Paraphrase of Stela 16 glyphs,
stela date December 5, A.D. 711. Drawing by W. R.
Coe, Linda Schele, *Maya Hieroglyphic Writing
Workshop,* p. 52.

Altar 5, Complex N

Next to Stela 16 is Altar 5, which is also dated 9.14.0.0.0 (A.D. 711). It has a large diameter, some five and a half feet, and is of the same material and style as Stela 16. Two figures face each other, separated by a skull on a pile of bones. The text seems to refer to a woman whose relation to Ah Cacaw is not specified. Some scholars have suggested that Altar 5 might represent Ah Cacaw's wife or mother, and that it was designed to substantiate Ruler B's credentials for rulership. However, Schele believes it more likely deals with the 9.14.0.0.0 (A.D. 711) katun-ending celebration.

The clothing of the figures is marked with sacrificial symbols such as the three knots, the bloodletting disk and bow, paper and cloth capes spattered with blood symbols, and the sacrificial flint knife. The costumes worn by the figures on the altar are the same as those worn by the supernaturals who flank the jaguar figure on Lintel 2 of Temple III (See Ill. 159). Both have katun-ending iconography.

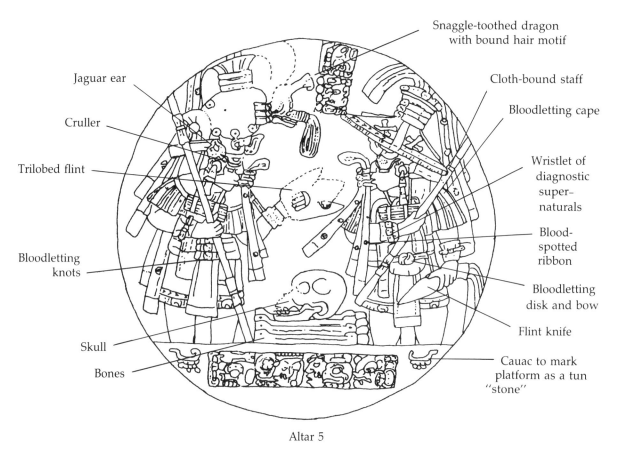

Snaggle-toothed dragon
with bound hair motif

Jaguar ear

Cruller

Trilobed flint

Bloodletting
knots

Skull

Bones

Cloth-bound staff

Bloodletting cape

Wristlet of
diagnostic
super-
naturals

Blood-
spotted
ribbon

Bloodletting
disk and bow

Flint knife

Cauac to mark
platform as a tun
"stone"

Altar 5

Illustration 167.   Altar 5, Tikal. Drawing by M.
Remmert (after W. R. Coe); iconography interpreted
by Schele.

Illustration 168.   Altar 5, Tikal.

Illustration 169.   Temple IV, from the trail near
Temple III.

162

Illustration 170.   Temple IV, aerial view from the east.

Temple IV

Temple IV was completed during the reign of Ruler B, who may be buried under it. The lintels of Temple IV are similar to those of Temple I. Because Ah Cacaw was buried under Temple I, many have assumed that Ruler B is buried in a tomb under Temple IV. William Coe, however, suggests that Ruler B was buried in Burial 196, that elaborate burial found in unexcavated Pryamid 73, located just south of Temple II. Six dates appear on the lintels, which are now in Basel, Switzerland; they all were carved after the death of Ah Cacaw in about A.D. 733. Estimates on the date of completion of Temple IV vary from A.D. 741 to A.D. 751 or later. Coe favors A.D. 741. The radiocarbon dates of the lintels averaged A.D. 720, ± sixty years.

This huge pyramid is located in the west portion of the ruins facing east. It measures some 212 feet to the top of its roof comb, and has been called the "highest standing aboriginal New World structure" (Coe 1967: 80). Some 250,000 cubic yards of rubble were incorporated in its construction. Massive and ponderous, it was constructed away from the center of Tikal. In contrast, Ah Cacaw's Temple I, which is slender and artistically appealing, is located at the meeting point of the causeways.

Illustration 171.   Palace of Windows (west).

Palace of Windows (Bat Palace, 5C-13)

Between Temple III and Temple IV on the south side of the trail is a large range-type building. This Late Classic structure has a double range below and a single range of vaulted rooms above, with low windows to the west toward Temple IV. Many of the vaults are stepped, some of the rooms contain large benches, and some Maya graffiti are still visible on the walls. The Palace of Windows is probably part of a residence complex, which extended to the east of the palace.

Illustration 172.   Palace of Windows (south).

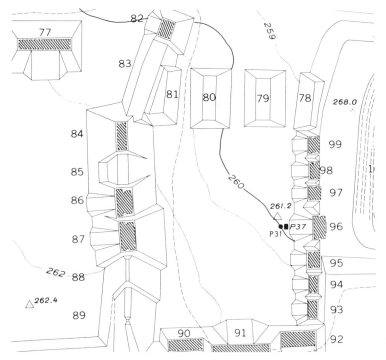

Illustration 173. Plan of Plaza of Seven Temples. From *Tikal Reports, No. 11.*

Plaza of the Seven Temples

Across the north side of the Plaza of the Seven Temples were three ball courts, side by side; along the east side of the plaza were seven temples from which the plaza takes its name. The central temple on the east side is Structure 5D-96, which is flanked by three temples on the north and three temples on the south. Visible on Structure 5D-96 is a wide medial molding. These temples have not been excavated. The University of Pennsylvania project dug trenches across this plaza and found that the whole area, which included the Lost World Pyramid Plaza to the west, had been paved from Preclassic times on, and was repaved a number of times in the Early Classic period, probably in association with the great Lost World Pyramid.

The temples on the west side of the Plaza of the Seven Temples faced west and were a part of the Lost World Temple Complex.

Illustration 174. Structure 5D96, detail of frieze.

Structure 5D-91 (Plaza of the Seven Temples)

The only restored structure in the area of the Plaza of the Seven Temples is 5D-91, located on the south side of the plaza. The jungle view of the south side and the view from the uncleared plaza to the north show Structure 5D-91 to be a long range-type building with three portals, which provide passage completely through the building. The building forms a long gallery divided into several rooms.

166

Illustration 175.   Structure 5D96, Plaza of the
Seven Temples (east side).

Illustration 176.   Structure 5D91, view from the
plaza.

Illustration 177.   Lost World Pyramid (west face).

Lost World Pyramid (5C-54)

A path leads south from Temple IV on the west side of the Palace of the Windows to the area of the Lost World Pyramid. In the early 1980s, this pyramid, located just west of the Plaza of the Seven Temples, was stripped and stabilized.

The Lost World Pyramid (5C-54) is much older than the temples in the Great Plaza. It is a Late Preclassic construction built before A.D. 300. It is a truncated pyramid, which was nearly a hundred feet high. In its final phase, it had four stairways, each with huge masks alongside.

This structure was not designed as an ancestor memorial as were the temples in the North Acropolis and Temples I, II, III, IV, and VI. It was a part of a calendric celebration ceremony complex, of which a row of temples immediately to the east, now covered by later temples, was a part. It was part of an astronomical assemblage and performed the same function as the Group E Complex at Uaxactún. Marvin Cohodas says that the common people participated in the calendric celebrations; they were not reserved for the elite as the ceremonies at the Great Plaza may have been.

Tunneling under the pyramid has demonstrated that the Lost World Pyramid was rebuilt in its final form in the Late Preclassic period. T. Patrick Culbert says that an earlier wall may date to as early as 500 B.C. (Culbert 1977: 39).

168

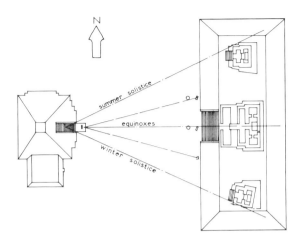

Illustration 179. Lost World Pyramid (center) and
Pyramid 5C49 (left foreground).

Illustration 178. Group E, Uaxactún. From
Andrews, *Maya Cities*, p. 71.

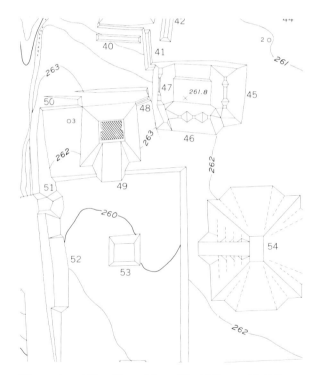

Illustration 180. Plat of Lost World Pyramid (5C-
54) and Pyramid 5C-49. From *Tikal Reports, No. 11*.

Illustration 181. Pyramid 5C-49.

Temple 5C-49 (Lost World Pyramid Plaza)

Temple 5C-49, an Early Classic temple-pyramid just north of the Lost World Pyramid, is being restored. Jones points out that this structure is similar to Structure 5D-22 (the north center temple-pyramid in the North Acropolis) in that just under the visible surface lies an earlier surface, which was renovated by applying a very thin coating of veneer masonry. A talud-tablero terrace is visible next to the stairway.

Temple 5C-49 was stripped of its mantle of trees in preparation for restoration by the government of Guatemala in late 1979 or early 1980. Unfortunately, that year had very heavy rains, which undermined the roof comb and caused it to collapse and scatter its masonry down the side of the pyramid.

Illustration 182.   Group G.

Group G (Palace of Vertical Grooves)

Group G, known as the Palace of Vertical Grooves, is southeast of the Great Plaza and is reached by a road, which branches off the Mendez Causeway to the southwest for a few hundred yards. This area, restored in 1980, contains a major group of palace-type range buildings.

There is a vaulted interior passageway from the east side of the complex which turns at a right angle and enters the court. The excavated portion of Group G (5E-60) is U-shaped and oriented with the base of the U to the east. The interior portion of the complex is a plaza.

Stairways on all sides enter the plaza. On the north and east sides, stairways enter a vaulted portal, which passes through the building. The buildings are faced with closely filled engaged pilasters, which extend to the medial mouldings.

The Group G construction now visible was built over earlier structures. The latest construction covered a perfectly preserved buried room. The stuccoed room contained much graffiti and a painting with a glyph related to Ruler B. If Ruler B was alive during the earlier period, the later construction must have been during or after his reign—sometime after A.D. 734.

Arthur Miller suggests that this residential area may have been a palace area used on occasion by one or more of the Late Classic rulers or their families.

Under the existing structures at Group G were a series of structures. Some had very thin walls and no vaulted roofs. Also present were structures of wattle-and-daub construction, whose walls were constructed of vertical poles interwoven with flexible twigs and small branches and filled with plaster.

This simple construction, thought to date from

171

Illustration 183.   Group G tunnel entrance.

between the Early Classic and the Late Classic periods, suggests that Tikal underwent hard times for two centuries, beginning about A.D. 500. This hypothesis may explain the apparent slackening of cultural activity at Tikal between the reigns of Curl Head (A.D. 528) and Ah Cacaw (A.D. 682).

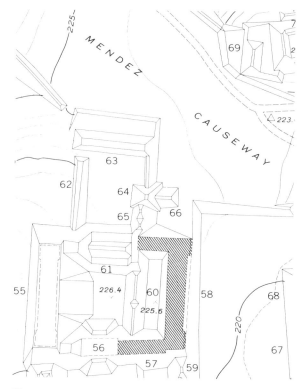

Illustration 184.   Plat of Group G (Plaza of the Palace of Vertical Grooves). From *Tikal Reports, No. 11.*

Illustration 185.   Group G portal.

Illustration 186.   Plat of North Zone and Complex
P. From *Tikal Reports, No. 11.*

North Zone Complex P and Stela 20

The North Zone, or Morley's Group H, comprises several unexcavated structures (Structures 3D-40 through 3D-46, built around A.D. 700). The road from Temple IV follows the Maudslay Causeway and terminates at Twin-pyramid Complex P. To the east is the unexcavated mound of Temple 3D-43.

Ruler B erected Stela 20 and Altar 8 in 9.16.0.0.0 (A.D. 751). Stela 20 is the third stela he erected—the others were Stela 21 at the Temple of the Inscriptions and Stela 5 in the Great Plaza. Ruler B was the son of the great Ah Cacaw, who appears on Stela 16, and the father of Chitam, who is depicted on Stela 22 in Twin-pyramid Complex Q. Stela 20 is part of Ruler B's first twin-pyramid complex. Clemency Coggins suggests that, in addition to the celebration of the 9.16.0.0.0

katun, it may also celebrate the thirteenth katun anniversary of 9.3.0.0.0 honoring Jaguar Paw Skull, who appears on Stela 7.

Stela 20 suggests an alternative possibility. Jones points out that "statements on St.5 that Ruler B is the 27th ruler in succession and on St.22 that Ruler C is the 29th (Riese 1979) alert us to the alternative possibility that another ruler is represented and named here: the missing 28th in succession" (Jones 1982: 46).

This stela contains some of the iconography that manifests the Maya requisites of rulership—divine origin, royal ancestry, and ritual sacrifice. The iconography on Stela 20 has some features of the Oval Palace Tablet of Pacal and Lady Zac-Kuk of Palenque, pictured in *Maya Ruins of Mexico in Color* (Ferguson and Royce 1977).

Ruler B wears what Schele calls the "Drum Major Headdress," a cylinder-shaped hat with

174

Illustration 187.   Stela 20 and Altar 8, Tikal.

a plume of feathers. He is standing in front of a double-headed jaguar throne. God K (GII), a symbol of royal lineage, appears on top of the headdress. GIII, the Jaguar God of the underworld, appears on his pectoral. The serpent-hair motif at the front of his headdress also appears on the figures on Altar 5; and the three knots of bloodletting are mounted on the side of his headdress. All of the elements that demonstrate the credentials for rulership are present on this stela.

On the ruler's left arm is a shield, and in his left hand he carries an incense bag. Two celts hang from his belt in front, and Oliva shells dangle around his waist. In his right hand, he holds a shaft, to which three axe heads are affixed. The Sun God faces to the right on his backrack, below which hang several celts. A Venus-star sign is mounted on his serpent half mask.

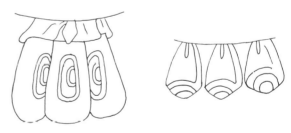

Illustration 188.   Celts and Oliva shells.

175

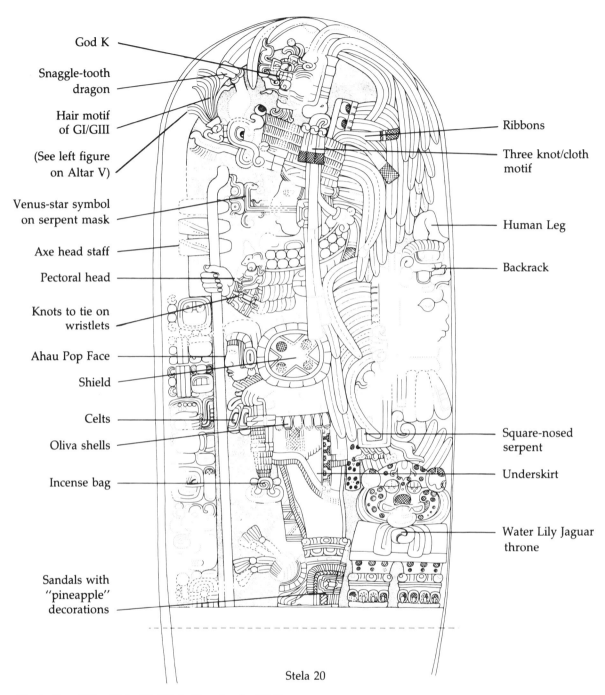

God K

Snaggle-tooth
dragon

Hair motif
of GI/GIII

(See left figure
on Altar V)

Venus-star symbol
on serpent mask

Axe head staff

Pectoral head

Knots to tie on
wristlets

Ahau Pop Face

Shield

Celts

Oliva shells

Incense bag

Sandals with
"pineapple"
decorations

Ribbons

Three knot/cloth
motif

Human Leg

Backrack

Square-nosed
serpent

Underskirt

Water Lily Jaguar
throne

Stela 20

Illustration 189. Stela 20, Tikal. Drawing by W. R.
Coe, from *American Antiquity*, Jan. 1977, p. 50;
iconography interpreted by Schele.

176

Illustration 190.   Stela 20, Tikal.

Glyphs: Upper left, a general verb.
    The other three name the captive. ——————

Toad or iguana headdress ——————

Rope ——————

Paper ear ornaments (symbol of captive) ——————

Necklace ——————

Tikal emblem glyph ——————

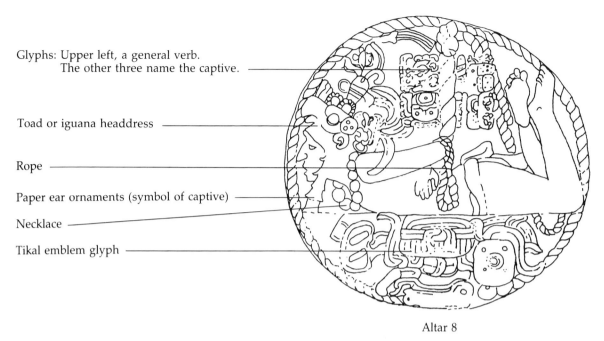

Altar 8

Illustration 191.   Altar 8, Tikal. Drawing by M.
Remmert (after W. R. Coe); iconography interpreted
by Schele.

Altar 8

Altar 8 is an excellent rendition of the belly-down
captive tied with his arms behind his back and
his head and feet raised. The Tikal emblem glyph
is in the center directly below the captive. The
pedestal is designed to represent the captive on
an altar on the terrace of a temple. The glyphs
are the name phrase of the captive.

Illustration 192.   Altar 8, Tikal.

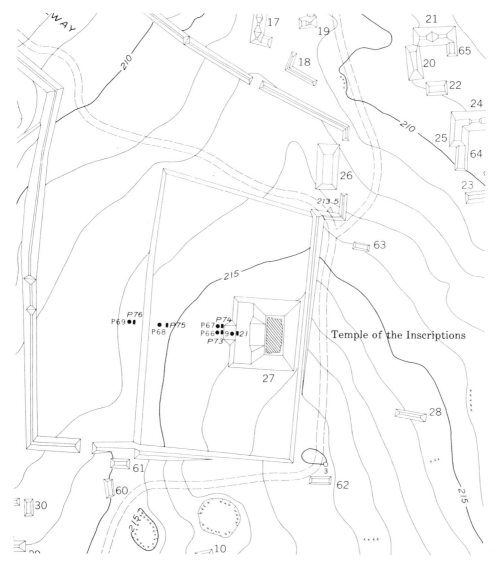

Illustration 193. Plat of Temple of Inscriptions from *Tikal
Reports, No. 11*, Map Temple of Inscriptions.

Temple of the Inscriptions (Temple VI, 6F-27)

The Temple of the Inscriptions, or Temple VI, is located slightly more than one-half mile south of the entrance to the Tikal ruins, on a trail branching south just inside the entrance.

This pyramid-temple (Structure 6F-27) was Ruler B's inauguration monument. Jones feels that it was completed at about the same time as Stela 21 (A.D. 736), but that it was later renovated. A roof comb was added and carved with glyphs. The back room of the Temple of the In-

scriptions was blocked off after it was built, probably to sustain the new roof comb.

The question of sequence arises because the dedication date on the roof comb is some thirty years later (9.16.15.0.0, A.D. 766) than the date on Stela 21 set in front of the pyramid-temple. Jones concludes that the original pyramid and temple, as well as Stela 21, were all part of Ruler B's inauguration monument. Later, he specu-lates, Ruler B's son, Ruler Chitam, erected the roof comb and had it carved.

The east side of the roof comb is a gigantic signboard of glyphs, which make up a geneal-

Illustration 194 Temple of the Inscriptions (west side).

ogical inscription similar in tone and form to the inscriptions found in the Temple of the Inscriptions at Palenque. The roof-comb glyphs refer to Tikal rulers beginning some 1,200 years before the Christian era. Early dates deciphered by Jones are 1139 B.C., 457 B.C., and 156 B.C. Later dates extend through Early Classic times, then refer to Late Classic rulers. Ruler B is referred to on the roof comb, not as the ruler, but as the father of the ruler (either Chitam or another son).

Another interesting facet of the question of which ruler built the Temple of the Inscriptions, and when, is that Ruler B was Tikal's twenty-seventh ruler and Chitam, his son, was the twenty-ninth ruler: this sequence indicates the existence of an unknown ruler, who may have been a brother or another son of Ruler B. Could Ruler 28 have remodeled the temple and engraved the glyphs on the roof comb? Jones does not believe Ruler B, Chitam, or anyone else is buried under the Temple of the Inscriptions.

Illustration 195.   Temple of the Inscriptions (east side).

Illustration 196.   Stela 21 and Altar 9, Tikal.

Stela 21 (Temple of the Inscriptions)

Ruler B appears on Stela 21, which celebrates the end of the fifth tun of Katun 15 or 9.15.5.0.0 (A.D. 736) Although the stela is badly eroded at the top, it depicts the ruler standing in profile and holding the Tikal staff introduced on Stelae 9 and 13 by Kan Chitam. The rite shown is "scattering," which is recorded in the last glyph of the text as a picture of a hand scattering small round objects. This "scattering" rite is connected in the text with the accession of Ruler B (written as "he was seated as *batab*"), which occurred 570 days (or about a year and a half) earlier. The drops shown falling from Ruler B's hand have generally been thought to be copal balls, seeds, or water, but Schele now believes that the "scattering" rites—not only at Tikal, but at all Maya sites—represented bloodletting in the form of

penis perforation. The drops are blood. The stela is located on the west side, in front of the Temple of the Inscriptions, erected in its original form by Ruler B.

Stela 21 indicates Ruler B's inaugural date as 9.15.3.6.8, 3 Lamat 6 Pax (December 10, A.D. 734). The readable glyphs on Stela 21 begin with the Tikal emblem glyph on the upper left. Three blocks down on the right is "3 Lamat," followed below on the left by "6 Pax," which computes to be 9.15.3.6.8. Following "6 Pax" to the right is the seating glyph of Ruler B as *batab* or ruler, followed on the right by the scattering gesture (see Jones 1977: 34).

Altar 9 has a bound belly-down captive carved on its top. Bound captives shown in sculpture were common in the Early Classic, and the practice was revived in the Late Classic by Ruler B.

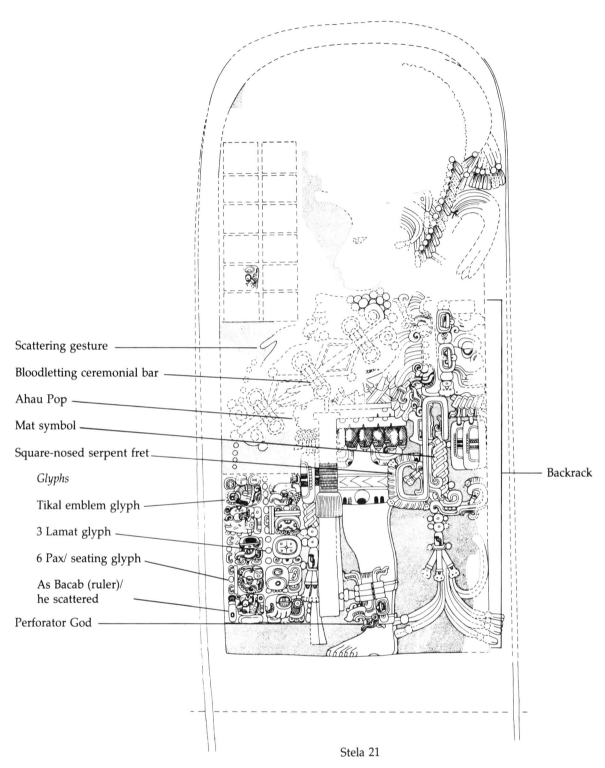

Scattering gesture

Bloodletting ceremonial bar

Ahau Pop

Mat symbol

Square-nosed serpent fret

Glyphs

Tikal emblem glyph

3 Lamat glyph

6 Pax/ seating glyph

As Bacab (ruler)/
he scattered

Perforator God

Backrack

Stela 21

Illustration 197.   Stela 21, Tikal. Drawing by W. R.
Coe, *American Antiquity,* Jan. 1977, p. 30;
iconography interpreted by Schele.

Illustration 198.   Stela 21, Tikal.

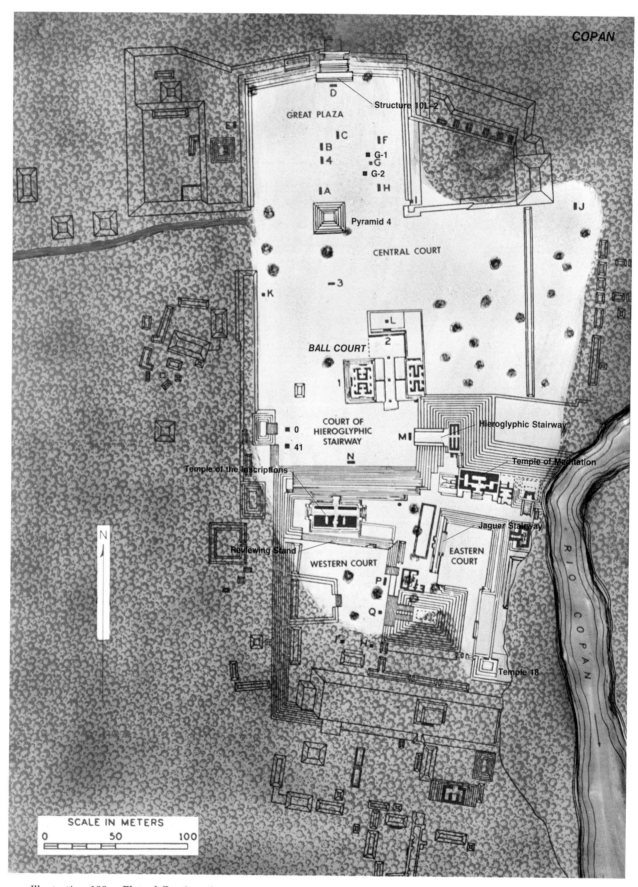

Illustration 199.   Plat of Copán ruins.

Copán

Introduction

Copán is located in the southeastern Maya lowland zone. The excavated ruins cover about forty acres and contain the acropolis and five plazas. The visible buildings are Late Classic—that is, the monuments and buildings were erected between A.D. 600 and 800.

Stela E (ca. A.D. 650) and Stela P (A.D. 623) are the earliest monuments now located in the ruins. Both were reset in their present location by the Maya after being moved from other areas. The same is true of Stela 2 dated 9.11.0.0.0 (A.D. 652), on the north side of the ball court, and Stela 3, dated 9.11.0.0.0 (A.D. 652), located in the middle of the Central Court. Earlier dated monuments have been found in the Copán area, between the excavated ruins and the modern town of Copán Ruinas.

Some archaeologists have suggested that Copán was settled in the Early Classic period by Maya from the central Petén area around Tikal and Uaxactún. The visible ruins at Copán are Late Classic. However, there is evidence both of a long architectural sequence which extends back to Early Classic times and of Early Classic or even Preclassic occupation in the area where the village of Copán is now situated. Little archaeological work has been done there, so information about Copán's earliest levels of occupation is scarce.

Copán was near the ancient trade route from the Pacific south coast to the mouth of the Motagua River at the modern city of Puerto Barrios.

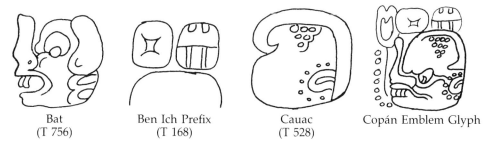

Bat	Ben Ich Prefix	Cauac	Copán Emblem Glyph
(T 756)	(T 168)	(T 528)	

Illustration 200. Glyphs that make up the Copán emblem glyph.

Copán was nearer to the early site of Kaminaljuyú than the Petén sites of Tikal and Uaxactún. Future excavations may show that the tide of Maya culture went through Copán to the Petén, rather than the other way around. Copán's highly individualistic sculptural style does not appear to be something borrowed and modified. Although the images of Copán's sculpture are shared by other sites in the Maya mainstream, the way in which these images are presented is very much a Copán trait.

The Copán emblem glyph has been interpreted by David Kelley to mean "Place of the Clouds." The glyph is composed of the head of a bat, into which are placed the Maya sign for "rain and storm" known as Cauac. David Kelley has pointed out that the Chol Maya word for both "bat" and "cloud" is *zutz*. The "rain" signs are placed in the Copán bat, apparently to indicate the meaning of "cloud" instead of "bat"; thus, in Classic times, Copán was known as *zutz*, "Place of the Clouds."

Copán is located on the Rio Copán, just inside Honduras near the Guatemala border. The river flows westward from the ruins through an area of low mountains until it joins the Motagua River in Guatemala. The river valley in which the Copán ruins are located is about eight miles east-west and two to two and one-half miles north-south. The elevation of the valley floor is about 2,000 feet.

Work by Gordon Willey, Richard Leventhal, and William Fash has demonstrated that the main center was surrounded by complexes of mounds, which probably functioned as living areas for elite families.

The site organization of Late Classic Copán and Quiriguá differs from Late Classic Tikal. Tikal's basic plan is radial; that is to say, the city fanned out from the center area (the Great Plaza and the East Plaza) along the great ceremonial ways. Copán, on the other hand, is built south to north with an artificially elevated ceremonial assemblage on the south and a large lower-level plaza containing public structures, such as ball courts, radial pyramids, and autonomous stelae, to the north. This kind of arrangement is in a line or in sequence, so we refer to the Copán site plan as being "sequential"—a Maya site-planning concept developed by Marvin Cohodas.

Copán's great man-made acropolis is an architectural assemblage incorporating four major temples and associated structures located at the south end of a large public plaza. The acropolis was initially constructed to restrict accessibility by the public. The area seems to have been where important dynastic, administrative, and ceremonial activities were conducted.

Little evidence exists that the acropolis was a residential area, as there are no palace-type buildings. But recent evidence appears to indicate that Platform 3, located in the north of the Great Plaza and northeast of the Central Court, did support elite residential structures.

The rulers of Copán and their retinue may have lived just outside the main center, while administering the city from the center and the acropolis. Leventhal postulates that elite families had one residence at the main site of Copán and another in the suburbs.

To the northeast, and technically outside of

Illustration 201.   Copán reconstruction.

the limits of the archaeological park, lie the groups of low mounds which form the Sepulturas Group. Groups of mounds are clustered around small courtyards. These clusters seem to constitute courtyard groups or compounds, which may reflect the social organization of the families who lived there. According the William Sanders, who directed excavations at Copán during 1980 and 1981, these clusters of mounds may have been suburban residential areas of the noble families. The more important nobles had compounds, which boasted more elaborate architectural features—cut stone, vaulted rooms, hieroglyphic decoration—while families of lower prestige or status had less elaborated architecture—uncut river cobble construction, thatched roofs, and no hieroglyphic decoration.

An example of a compound that may have housed a family with close kinship ties to the rulers of Copán can be seen in a structure that contains an elaborately decorated hieroglyphic bench. The presence of a raised, paved causeway (*sacbe*) leading to the site center from the Sepulturas Group attests to the probable importance of the inhabitants of this area of the suburbs of ancient Copán.

Such families as lived in the Sepulturas Group probably controlled the land and the food production and were the wealthy landed gentry. Other elite families may have controlled the commerce in such items as obsidian from Guatemala, jade from the Middle Motagua drainage, polychrome pottery of local or foreign manufacture, and perishable goods. The organization of Copán society seems to have been analogous to medieval Europe's feudal system.

To the north of the acropolis, including the ball court, Central Court, and Great Plaza, were public areas for entertainment, ceremonies, and markets. The Copán site plan manifests the social and religious dichotomy of the Classic Maya. The elite conducted their social and religious ac-

Illustrations 202 and 203. Copán ruins from the
northwest. A view of the Central Court, Ball Court,
Hieroglyphic Stairway, and the Rio Copán in the
background.

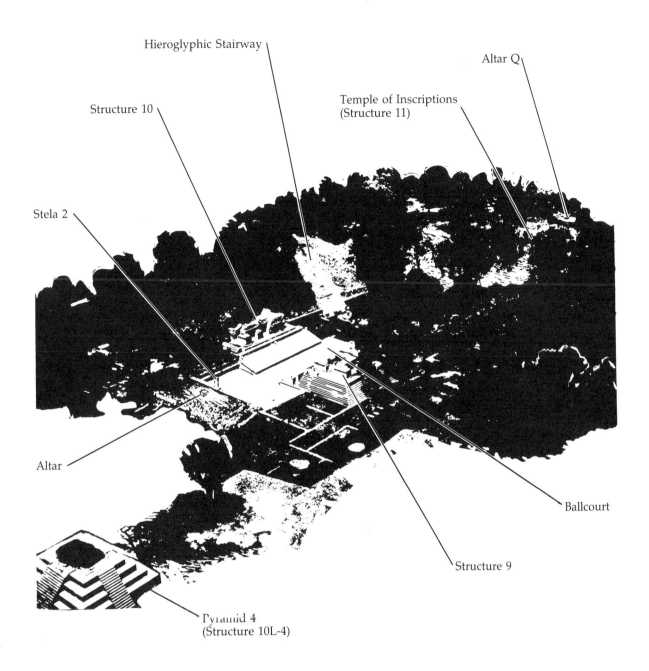

Hieroglyphic Stairway

Altar Q

Structure 10

Temple of Inscriptions
(Structure 11)

Stela 2

Altar

Ballcourt

Structure 9

Pyramid 4
(Structure 10L-4)

Illustrations 204 and 205.   Copán ruins from the
south.

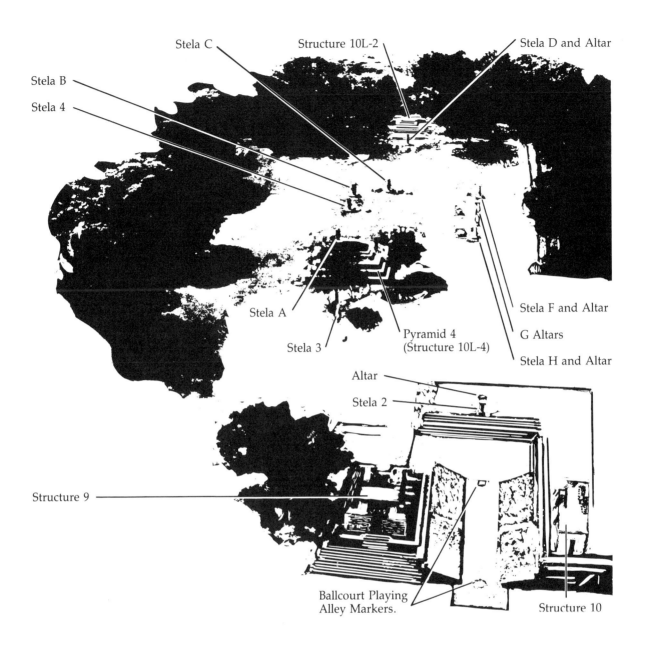

Stela B

Stela 4

Stela C

Structure 10L-2

Stela D and Altar

Stela A

Stela 3

Pyramid 4
(Structure 10L-4)

Stela F and Altar

G Altars

Stela H and Altar

Altar

Stela 2

Structure 9

Ballcourt Playing
Alley Markers.

Structure 10

193

tivities in the acropolis area, while ceremonies with general public participation were located in the plaza areas.

The identification and sequence of rulers at Copán is beginning to unfold. Claude F. Baudez and Berthold Riese have identified the following kings.

began a great period of construction, which saw the building of the Temple of the Inscriptions (Temple 11), the Temple of Meditation (Temple 22), and Temple 18.

Baudez suggests that Temple 18, dated A.D. 800, might have been Rising Sun's burial place. Rising Sun is depicted in Temple 18's iconog-

Ruler 12	Smoke-Jaguar	Prior to A.D. 700
Ruler 13	18 Rabbit	ca. A.D. 700
Ruler 14	Unknown	
Ruler 15	Cuc	
Ruler 16	Madrugada (Rising Sun)	Possibly A.D. 763 to A.D. 801

Baudez of the Musée de l'Homme, Paris, directed the Honduran government's *Proyecto Argueológico Copán* from 1977 to 1980, and Riese was the epigrapher for the project.

The difficulty in identifying and sequencing the rulers of Copán stems from the absence of event glyphs coupled with names and dates. There are a number of dates on the stelae, but these are not connected with glyphs referring to accession, death, or ceremonies. Also key monuments are missing. Apparently the rulers before 18 Rabbit destroyed or buried the stelae that referred to prior rulers. The presence of the *hel* glyph reveals that there were sixteen kings of Copán.

Eighteen Rabbit, the most prominent Copán ruler, became king around A.D. 700. Baudez feels that Stela B commemorates his accession. Eighteen Rabbit commissioned all of the Great Plaza stelae, except Stela I, which is in the niche on the east side, and possibly Stela C. Eighteen Rabbit entered into conflict with Quiriguá in A.D. 737. As a result, he was either killed or captured and held prisoner by Cauac Sky of Quiriguá. Most likely he was sacrificed. Eighteen Rabbit was followed by Ruler 14, and Cuc, Ruler 15, who is credited with building the Hieroglyphic Stairway.

Madrugada (Rising Sun), the sixteenth and last known ruler, took over about twenty-six years after the Quiriguá incident in A.D. 737. His reign

raphy, and he was a ruler of Copán either before or during its construction. The Long Count date carved in the temple's first room, 9.18.10.17.18 (A.D. 801), is the latest date found so far in the main group at Copán.

No one knows how much longer Copán flourished—perhaps a generation—but Copán began to collapse along with the rest of the Classic Maya sites around 10.0.0.0.0 (A.D. 830).

Illustration 206.   Great Plaza Stela clockwise from the left: C, F, H, and A and Pyramid 4.

Great Plaza

The Great Plaza may properly be considered 18 Rabbit's showcase. It is a large plaza—300 by 360 feet, with tiers of steps or possibly seats on three sides. It is studded with stelae erected by 18 Rabbit.

The south side is bounded by a recently restored radial pyramid (Structure 4), which had no temple on its top. With its free-standing stelae and radial pyramid bounded by gallery-type stairs, the Great Plaza fits the public-assemblage concept suggested by Marvin Cohodas. He believes the area was designed for the common people to use for public ceremonies.

The Copán Project made an electrical resistivity survey in the Great Plaza to locate buried structures and features, after which the project excavated in the plaza. Aerial photographs reveal that the trenches that were dug appear as

Illustration 207.   Glyph T 757 (Jog).

Illustration 208.   18 Rabbit name glyph.

195

Illustration 209.   Great Plaza from Structure 10L-2, Stela D, foreground.

geometric lines. The excavations produced evidence of a long architectural sequence, beginning with the Middle Classic, divided into nineteen phases (Baudez 1980).

Eighteen Rabbit is also referred to as 18 Jog. Glyph T757 is generally referred to as "Jog" in the literature on Copán, since Thompson thought it combined characteristics of a jaguar (Thompson 1962: 350) and a dog (Kelley 1976: 118). Proskouriakoff (1968) proved that the animal head was that of a rodent of some sort. In *The Mirror,*

the Rabbit, and the Bundle: "Accession" Expressions from the Classic Maya Inscriptions (1983), Schele suggests that the model for the glyph was the short-eared tropical-forest rabbit. According to her reading of the glyphs, this Copán ruler was named 18 Rabbit.

Illustration 210.   Great Plaza. Monuments clockwise from the extreme left: Stela H, Pyramid 4, Stelae A, 4, C, B, F, and the G Altars.

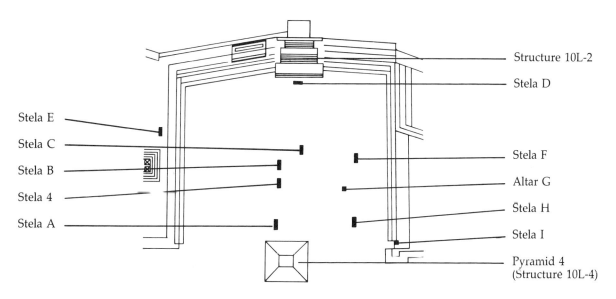

Illustration 211.   Great Plaza, Copán.

197

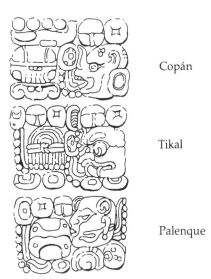

Copán

Tikal

Palenque

Illustration 212.   Emblem Glyphs of identified Maya sites which appear on Stela A, Copán: Copán, Tikal, Palenque.

Stela A

Erected by 18 Rabbit, Stela A is located in the Great Plaza just north of Pyramid 4. The style is Copán Late Classic or the "Great Period," according to Morley. This stela portrait of 18 Rabbit has a larger than normal head, perhaps as an emphasis on the face of the ruler in relation to the body.

He holds a double-headed serpent bar with Sun Gods emerging from each side. His headdress contains the mat symbol of royalty and is topped by a head variant of Ahau, marking him as lord or ruler. His belt is adorned with sky bands and Ahau Pop (lord of the mat or throne) faces. Two perforator or bloodletting bags containing stingray spines hang from the belt. Beneath the belt is a string of Oliva shells. Over the center of the loincloth are three celts with symbols showing their reflective surfaces. With all these dangling appendages, imagine the jangling as he walked!

Behind each leg, a paper-decorated bloodletting three-knot staff and a shield are carved, and another double-headed serpent peeks out from behind his ankles. His anklets represent the three-knot Perforator God with a scroll ⟨ᵒ⟩ eye. He wears the same bloodletting iconography on his wrists. On the north side of the stela, fol-

Illustration 213.   Stela A (east side), Copán.

lowing the introductory glyph, the Initial Series date, 9.14.19.8.0, can be read from the top. Calculations considering the additional dates on the stela give the dedication date as 9.15.0.0.0 (A.D. 731). On the south side, four glyphs from the top, are emblem glyphs of four Maya sites. Three are identified as Copán, Tikal, and Palenque; the fourth is unknown.

198

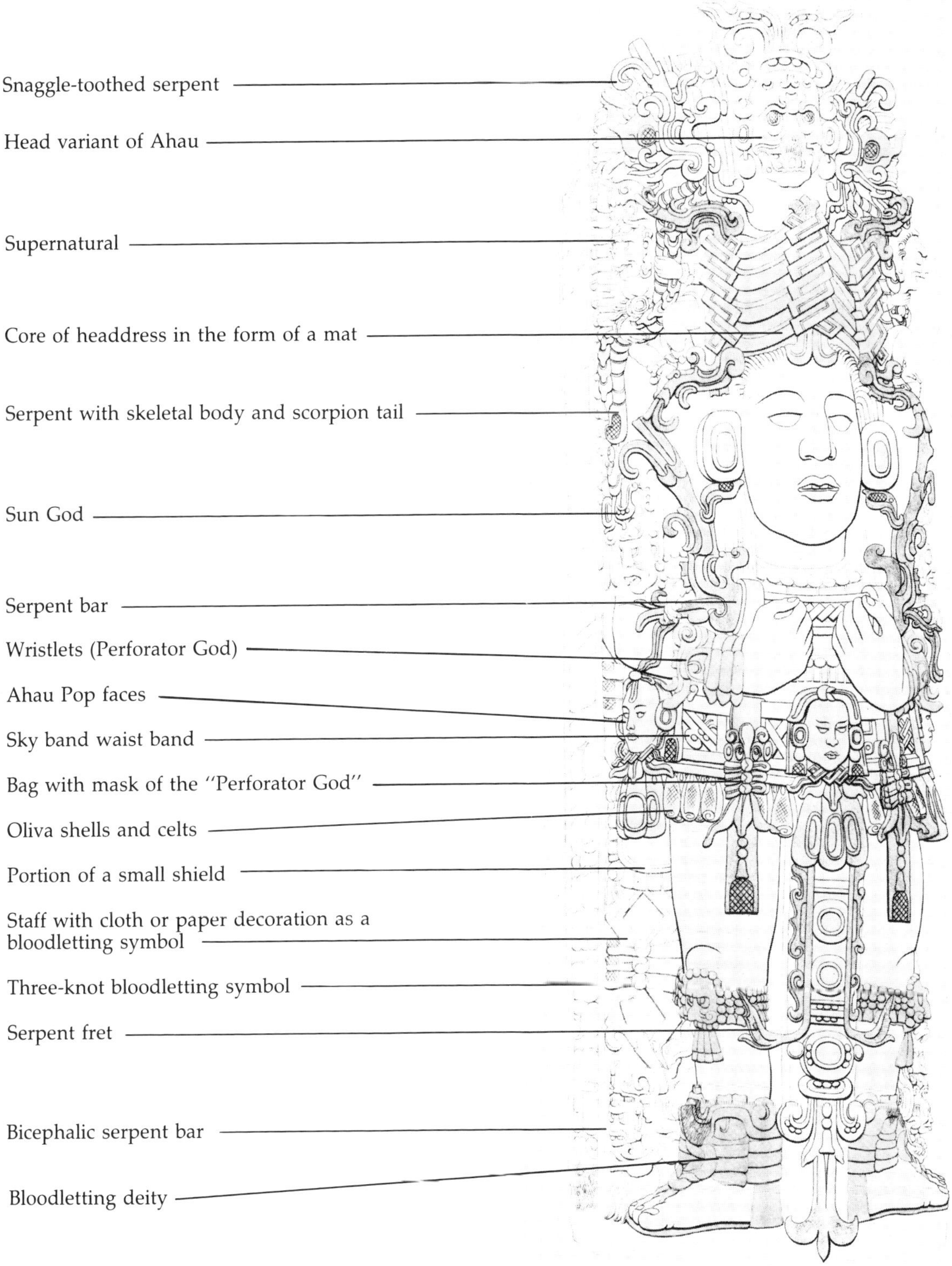

Snaggle-toothed serpent

Head variant of Ahau

Supernatural

Core of headdress in the form of a mat

Serpent with skeletal body and scorpion tail

Sun God

Serpent bar

Wristlets (Perforator God)

Ahau Pop faces

Sky band waist band

Bag with mask of the "Perforator God"

Oliva shells and celts

Portion of a small shield

Staff with cloth or paper decoration as a
bloodletting symbol

Three-knot bloodletting symbol

Serpent fret

Bicephalic serpent bar

Bloodletting deity

Illustration 214.   Stela A, Copán, 18 Rabbit.
Drawing by A. P. Maudslay, 1889–1902, *Biologia
Centrali-Americana*, vol. 1, Illustration 26;
iconography interpreted by Schele.

Illustration 215.   Stela A, Copán (winter view, south side).

Illustration 216.   Stela A, Copán (north side), Pyramid 4 in the background.

Stela A is a portrait stela on which the ruler is shown in the traditional position. His feet are in a 180-degree configuration, and he holds the double-headed serpent bar with his arms in what has been referred to as the "crab claw" position. The crab claw is an archaic characteristic of stelae at Maya sites other than in the Copán and Quiriguá area, where this posture continued throughout the Classic period. Small creatures with solar symbols entwined with a serpent flank the headdress.

200

Stela 4

Three stelae (A, 4, and B), each dedicated to 18 Rabbit and each with the date 9.15.0.0.0 (A.D. 731), form a line just north of the newly restored Pyramid 4. Riese dates Stela 4 at 9.14.15.0.0.

Although Stela 4 is contemporary with Stelae A and B, Schele feels that it was carved by a different artist. Both Stelae 4 and F are carved in very deep relief with the figure carved fully in the round; Stelae A and B are much less rounded in their treatment. The Stela 4 stone headdress is cantilevered over the face, and the head is in proportion to the body. The feet are cut away from the stone on a less oblique angle than on Stelae A and B, and the legs are completely freed from the shaft of the stela.

Schele has suggested that these two distinctive but contemporary art styles might represent rival sculptural schools—one more traditional (Stelae A, B, C, D. H, and N) and the other more innovative (Stelae 4, F, and M). The innovative style developed into the brilliant three-dimensional architectural sculpture of Madrugada's reign.

Eighteen Rabbit holds a serpent bar on Stela 4. Because of the sculpture in the round, the bar had to be turned on the sides.

Illustration 217.   Stela 4, Copán (east side).

201

Illustration 218.   Stela 4, Copán (west side).

Illustration 219.   Stela 4, Copán (north side).

202

Stela B

Stela B, located in the center of the Great Plaza, is another of the Great Plaza monuments erected by 18 Rabbit (Ill. 221), who acceded to the throne of Copán around A.D. 700. Stela B and Stela A manifest the same school of carving, and both bear the katun ending date 9.15.0.0.0 (A.D. 731). Baudez considers Stela B to be his accession monument.

Eighteen Rabbit wears a ceremonial beard, which may have been a Classic Maya emblem or symbol of prestige. He wears a turban overlaid by the shell diadem characteristic of GI, and he wears the shell beard of GIII. The double-headed serpent bar with anthropomorphic heads and sky symbols is standard iconography for the period, as are the large earplugs mounted on flanges of the headdress.

In his headdress are two macaws (which some people have argued to be Southeast Asian elephants). On the stela are numerous little faces and figures, perhaps *aluxob* (the Maya equivalent of leprechauns) or ancestral figures. Around his hips, the figure wears a girdle with hanging celts, Oliva shells, and a stingray spine bag marked by the face of the Perforator God. Lower down on his loincloth are the Sun God and serpent frets. Bloodletting symbols are a part of his sandals. Eighteen Rabbit is standing in the mouth of a Cauac Monster with the upper jaw above him, and the teeth of the lower jaw visible behind his ankle. The muzzle of the Cauac Monster appears just above its teeth. *Aluxob* sit in the eyes of this monster at the top of the stela.

Illustration 220.   Stela B, Copán (north side).

Illustration 221.   "18 Rabbit, Lord of Copán," bottom of south side of Stela B.

203

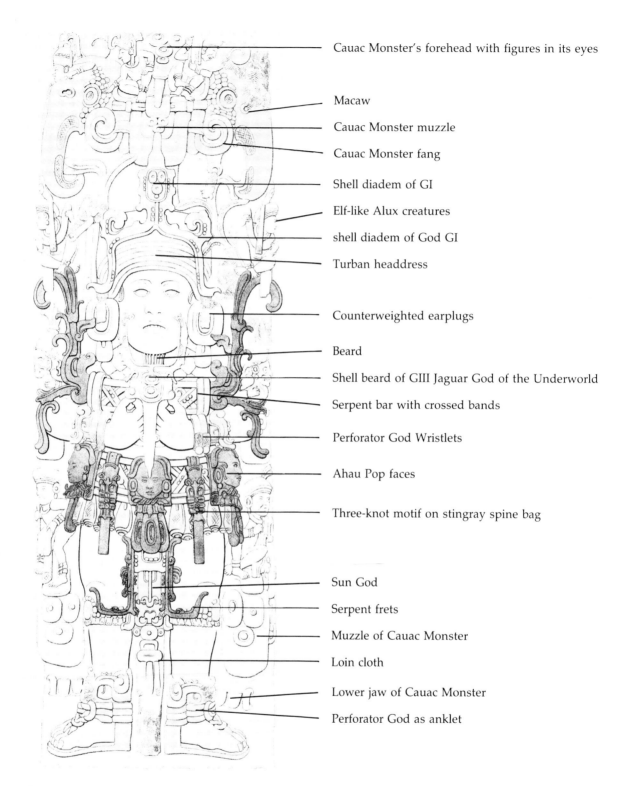

Cauac Monster's forehead with figures in its eyes

Macaw

Cauac Monster muzzle

Cauac Monster fang

Shell diadem of GI

Elf-like Alux creatures

shell diadem of God GI

Turban headdress

Counterweighted earplugs

Beard

Shell beard of GIII Jaguar God of the Underworld

Serpent bar with crossed bands

Perforator God Wristlets

Ahau Pop faces

Three-knot motif on stingray spine bag

Sun God

Serpent frets

Muzzle of Cauac Monster

Loin cloth

Lower jaw of Cauac Monster

Perforator God as anklet

Illustration 222. Stela B, Copán, east side.
Drawing by Maudsley, *Biologia Centrali-Americana,*
vol. 1, Illustration 34. Iconography by Schele.

Illustration 223.   Stela B, Copán (east side).

Stela B (Back Side)

The back (west) side of Stela B is a Cauac monster mask, identified as Cauac by the clusters of circles. The eyes and mouth are inset with glyphs, and a bone nose plug pierces the nostril, with more Cauac symbols below. At the top is a figure seated tailor fashion, wearing a headdress which shows the three-knot bloodletting iconography.

On the north side of the stela following the Initial Series Introducing Glyph (ISIG) is the Long Count date 9.15.0.0.0 4 Ahau 13 Yax (A.D. 731).

Illustration 224.   Stela B, Copán (west side).

206

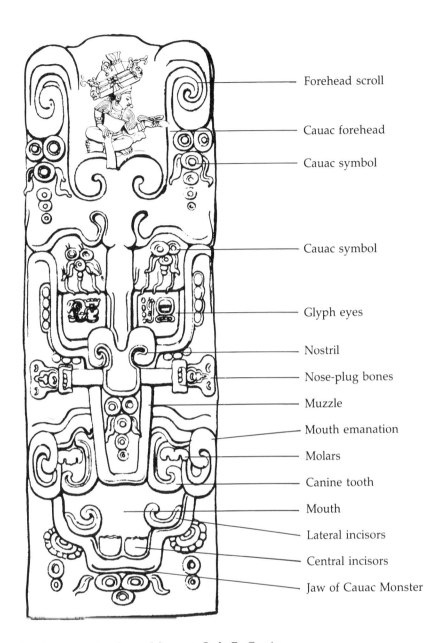

Forehead scroll

Cauac forehead

Cauac symbol

Cauac symbol

Glyph eyes

Nostril

Nose-plug bones

Muzzle

Mouth emanation

Molars

Canine tooth

Mouth

Lateral incisors

Central incisors

Jaw of Cauac Monster

Illustration 225. Cauac Monster, Stela B, Copán, west side. From Francis Robicsek, *Copán, Home of the Mayan Gods*, p. 75. Iconography interpreted by Schele.

Stela C

Because it lay buried prior to its restoration, Stela C, a double-portrait, still retains traces of original red paint. It is located just north and east of Stela B.

Scholars disagree over the date of this stela. In 1920, Morley looked at Stelae C, H, F, and 4, all of which are in the Great Plaza. Based upon the dates and style, he concluded that all four stelae were erected around 9.17.12.0.0 (A.D. 782). Schele has concluded that these four stelae, including Stela C, were erected by 18 Rabbit much earlier, within ten years before or after 9.15.0.0.0 (A.D. 731). Baudez says, "I would offer the hypothesis that Stela C was erected by Rising Sun [Madrugada] in 782 to commemorate the succession of 18 Rabbit to the late Smoke-Jaguar, an event which had been celebrated at the end of the 15th *katun*" (Baudez 1983: 2).

The east side bears the face of 18 Rabbit as a young man. He holds the double-headed serpent bar. The open jaws of the serpent extend up the stela past the large flanged earplugs. His headdress is composed of two masks with the square eyes of the Sun God, with a third mask on top of others. On his arms are wristlets with bloodletting iconography. An alligator head overlaps his loincloth.

On the west side of the stela, facing the Great Turtle, the lord is depicted as older and wearing a beard. He too holds a double-headed serpent bar, but the emerging Sun Gods are shown to be very aged. Attached to his waistband are the Jaguar God of the underworld, crossed bands, and Oliva shells in front and the God of (the month) Pax at the sides. The loincloth portrays the Sun God wearing a water-lily pad to mark him as connected with the Western underworld. In the headdress are the Monkey Sun God and a jaguar mask, around which are some small figures. Baudez feels Stela C portrays Smoke-Jaguar as the old and dying king and 18 Rabbit as the young succeeding ruler. The old ruler is likened to the setting sun when he dies, and the young acceeding ruler epitomizes the rising sun.

All the stelae in the Great Plaza north of Pyramid 4 were done in the Late Classic period, around 9.14.10.0.0 (A.D. 721) and later. They differ in design from the earlier stelae at Copán (Stelae 1, 2, 3, P, E, and I) and represent what Tatiana Proskouriakoff calls the "Ornate Phase" at Copán. The artists were concentrating on sculpture in the round, as shown by the deep undercut relief. Proskouriakoff points out that the earlier monuments were designed on perpendicular planes. "A drawing of the front or the side of such a stela involved virtually no foreshortening. The artist could design the monument by sketching or blocking it out directly on the surface of the stone, establishing his principal planes and then rounding the forms" (Proskouriakoff 1950: 129).

The late stelae (such as Stelae A, B, and C) could not have been designed in the same simple way as the earlier stelae, so Proskouriakoff suggests that they may have been modeled in clay or plaster before these volumetric three-dimensional figures were carved.

Bicephalic-zoomorphic Turtle: The Great Two-headed Turtle Altar stands in front of the ruler as an old man on Stela C (west face). Although the shell is that of an old turtle, the heads and feet are not. The feet have claws similar to those of a jaguar. The north head is skeletal with fangs, and the south head has a serrated row of teeth.

Illustration 226.   Stela C and Great Turtle, Copán
(west side).

Illustration 227.   Great Turtle, Copán (south head).

Illustration 228.   Great Turtle, Copán (north head).

210

Illustration 229.   Stela C, Copán (east side).

Stela D

Stela D is the northernmost stela in the Great Plaza. The stelae of the Great Plaza may have been carved for 18 Rabbit by two different artists—one more conservative than the other. Stela D appears to be one of those carved by the old master, as were Stelae A and B. Stela D, dated 9.15.5.0.0 (five years after Stelae A and B), celebrates the hotun (five-year) ending following 9.15.0.0.0.

The ruler on Stela D is wearing a Sun God mask over his face. The attributes of the Sun God are the large square eyes, a mirror in the forehead, and a pompadour hairdo with the hair brushed up from the forehead. He wears a beard and carries a double-headed serpent bar. His loincloth belt contains the royal mat symbol and sky bands, below which hang Oliva shells and celts with reflection indicators.

The loincloth apron depicts the Bloodletting God with his three knots, his anklets, and part of his headdress just above his head. Above that is a two-headed serpent with God K—with the characteristic flair in his forehead—in the open jaws on each side.

The back of Stela D shows a series of full-figure glyphs, which are uncommon in Maya art. They are found only at Copán, Quiriguá, Palenque, and on a lintel at Yaxchilán, a site on the Usamacinta River in Chiapas, Mexico. The full-figure glyphs give the date of the stela, 9.15.5.0.0 (A.D. 736).

Illustration 230.   Stela D, Copán (south side).

212

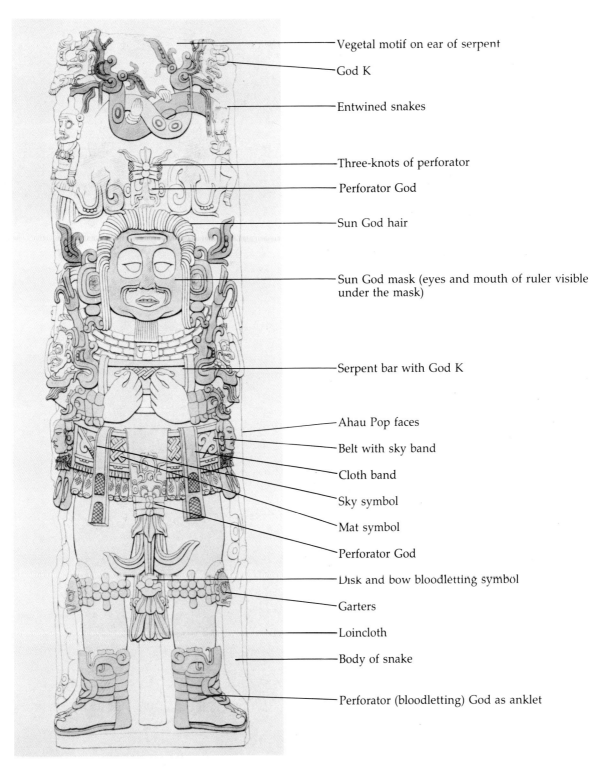

Vegetal motif on ear of serpent

God K

Entwined snakes

Three-knots of perforator

Perforator God

Sun God hair

Sun God mask (eyes and mouth of ruler visible under the mask)

Serpent bar with God K

Ahau Pop faces

Belt with sky band

Cloth band

Sky symbol

Mat symbol

Perforator God

Disk and bow bloodletting symbol

Garters

Loincloth

Body of snake

Perforator (bloodletting) God as anklet

Illustration 231.   Stela D, Copán, south side. Drawing by Maudslay, *Biologia Centrali-Americana*, vol. 1, Illustration 45; iconography interpreted by Schele.

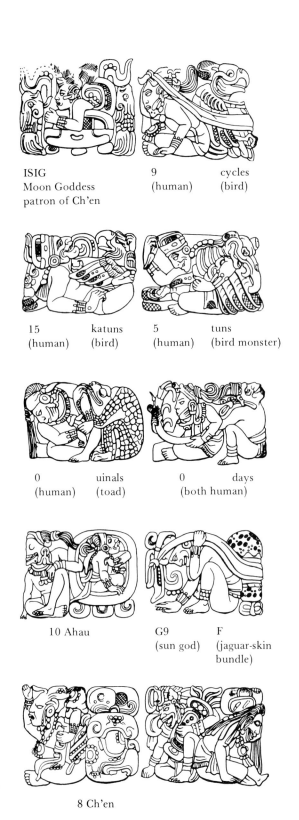

ISIG
Moon Goddess
patron of Ch'en

9
(human)

cycles
(bird)

15
(human)

katuns
(bird)

5
(human)

tuns
(bird monster)

0
(human)

uinals
(toad)

0
(both human)

days

10 Ahau

G9
(sun god)

F
(jaguar-skin
bundle)

8 Ch'en

Illustration 232.   Stela D, Copán, full-figure glyphs.
From D. H. Kelley, 1976, *Deciphering Maya Script*, p.
24.

Illustration 233.   Stela D, Copán (north side).

Illustration 234. Bottle drawing showing a ball player and a rabbit as the ball. Photograph courtesy of Linda Schele.

Illustration 235. "18 Ball," ideogram for 18 Rabbit.

Illustration 236. "18 Ball."

"18 Ball"

Perhaps the most intriguing aspect of the glyph panel is the interpretation given the second glyph from the bottom left column by Schele and Lounsbury. At that point, the artisan found a flaw in the shaft, consisting of a ball of hard stone, which could not be carved. The flaw posed a dilemma because it rested at the point where the "rabbit" of 18 Rabbit's name should have been carved. The Copán artisan solved the problem with a brilliant visual pun based on an earlier version of a story in the *Popol Vuh*.

In the story of the Hero Twins of the Popol Vuh, one of the twins, Hunahpú, had lost his head by the bite of a bat, and his brother, Xbalanqué, faced the problem of retrieving the lost head. He had to get the lords of the underworld away from the ball court. During the ball game, Xbalanqué kicked the ball into the brush; he then persuaded a rabbit to imitate the lost ball, leading the lords of death into a futile chase long enough to retrieve the head and bring Hunahpú back to life. The Copán scribe used this story to solve the problem of the stela flaw; he exposed the round ball of the flaw, and thus represented the "rabbit" as the "ball." A similar scene on a small bottle shows a ballplayer striking a ball represented as a rabbit.

215

Illustration 237. Stela D Altar.

Illustration 238. Structure 10L-2, north end of the Great Plaza. Stela D and altar in the foreground.

Stela D Altar

Stela D Altar has two heads. The north head, the Cauac Monster, can be identified by the dots in and around its eye. The south head has skeletal teeth. In front of the altar is the grave of Dr. John Owens, who died while working at Copán on April 1, 1893, having requested before his death that he be buried there.

Structure 10L-2

Just behind Stela D, in the middle of the steps that limit the plaza to the north, is Structure 10L-2-1st, which consists of a stairway covering two earlier structures. Two hieroglyphic steps were incorporated into the stairway. The stairway was built at about the same time that Stela D was erected (A.D. 736). Baudez says this building was probably in use for some 225 years. The function was primarily ceremonial, although in its final phase it may have been used as a residence.

Stela E

Stela E is an Early Classic stela, which was originally erected at another, possibly older, site in the Copán Valley. It is now located in the center of the upper terrace on the west side of the Main Plaza. Morley dates this stela at 9.9.2.17.0, 10 Ahau 8 Uo (A.D. 616). Riese, however, places it after A.D. 647.

Proskouriakoff considers this to be an Early Classic stela because the ruler holds a flaccid double-headed serpent bar. The figure wears large asymmetrical earplugs and has the crab-claw arm position. On the loincloth apron appears the three-knot bloodletting symbol. The sandals have overlapping straps. The stela itself has more slender proportions than those of a later vintage.

Illustration 239.   Stela E, Copán.

Stela F

Stela F is dated 9.14.10.0.0. It is the earliest of 18 Rabbit's stelae, and Schele feels it was done by the same artist that carved Stela 4.

Stela F and Stela 4 are very similar in execution. Both have deep undercutting. The thighs and legs are carved fully in the round, with the back of the knee released from the stela shaft. The back of Stela F is treated as the rear of a backrack, so that it looks like a Copán ruler would have looked from the rear. Glyphs are recorded in cartouches formed by entwined rope lining the concave feather-fringed rear. The undercuts heighten the relief texture by creating deep shadows, particularly in the face.

The second and third glyphs on the back are 5 Ahau 3 Mac which, read in this context, correspond to 9.14.10.0.0. The "end of Katun 15" below the 3 Mac glyph, followed by a "half period" glyph and a "count" glyph, lead to the date 9.15.0.0.0 (Morley 1920: 354). Baudez, however, places it ten years earlier.

Stela F Altar

The altar associated with Stela F represents a giant bloodletting god with bloodletting knots in its forehead, squint eyes, front teeth, and fangs.

Illustration 240.   Stela F and altar, Copán.

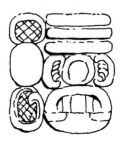

Illustration 241. Stela F, Copán, glyphs indicating 9.15.0.0.0: 5 Ahau, 3 Mac, end of Katun 15 (A.D. 731).

Illustration 243.   Stela F, Copán (north side).

Illustration 242.   Stela F, Copán (east side).

Jaguar paw

Bloodletting knots

Edge of eye

Squint Eye

Mouth emanation

Stela F Altar

Illustration 244.   Stela F Altar, Copán.

Illustration 245.   Altar G-1, Copán.

Illustration 246.   Altar G-2, Copán.

Altars G, G-1, and G-2

In the center, Altar G is the largest of these three similar altars. Altars G-1 and G-2 almost identical in size and shape, flank Altar G on the north and south. These three altars are located on the east side of the Great Court between Stelae F and H.

Altar G is a double-headed serpent with its heads reared into the air toward the east and west. Morley dates Altar G at 10 Ahau 8 Zac, 9.18.10.0.0 (A.D. 800), making it one of the latest dated monuments at Copán.

Altars G-1 and G-2 are double-headed serpents with open mouths and arched feathered backs. They have the traditional serpent spots. Clearly readable on G-2 (erected on the south side of Altar G) is "4 Ahau 13 Ceh," which may date G-2 as 9.18.5.0.0 (A.D. 795). G-1 (on the north side of Altar G) displays what appears to be "7 Ahau 18 Pop," which may be 9.16.15.0.0 (A.D. 766). G-1 may have been erected to celebrate the katun ending 9.17.0.0.0 (A.D. 771). Schele is not yet convinced of these dates. She feels these altars may have been constructed at a much earlier time.

223

Illustration 247. Altar G, Copán.

Stela H

The figure on Stela H wears a skirt and has generally been considered a woman, the wife of 18 Rabbit, who was possibly from Palenque; now, however, many authorities believe that Stela H is 18 Rabbit wearing bloodletting regalia. No period-ending date appears on Stela H, but it was most likely done by the same master who carved Stela A and Stela B, and celebrates the 9.15.0.0.0 (A.D. 731) katun ending.

According to Schele, Stela H celebrates an event before the 9.15.0.0.0 katun ending. The event (or rite) on Stela H occurs sixty days prior to the first event on Stela A, which, in turn, is followed sixty days later by a repetition of the same rite. These three rites are probably bloodletting rites. This interrelationship indicates that Stelae A and H were probably erected as a pair.

A quadripartite mask on the back of Stela H shows a bloodletting lancet in the form of a stingray spine; in the headdress is a disk with a knot bloodletting motif. Eighteen Rabbit, not a woman, is named in the text; thus, Schele and others now believe that Stela H represents the male ruler in a female role associated with the bloodletting ritual.

The bloodletting ritual, as described in the *Popol Vuh*, is characterized as an act of "nourishing" and "sustaining" the gods. Man was placed on earth by the gods to be a "nourisher" of the gods by the giving of blood. Man was directed:

> Now give thanks further,
> and now order
> The piercing of your ears,
> The cutting of your elbows.
> Sacrifice, then.
> That is your appreciation before god
> (Edmonson 1971: 5620).

The term used for the word *nourishing* in the *Popol Vuh* is also used for the act of nursing in the Quiché language. "Nursing" and "nourishing" are female functions: therefore, in at least some of the bloodletting rituals of the Classic period, male rulers wore regalia associated with females to signal their roles as nourishers of the gods. Blood could be taken from any part of the body, but surviving pictures of this ritual indi-

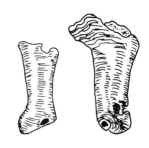

Illustration 248.   Legs from a gold figurine, Stela H vault, Copán.

cate the the tongue and penis were the favored locations.

Stela H was erected over a cruciform vault. In the dirt fill of the vault, archaeologists found a pair of legs made of a gold-copper alloy, which belonged to a small hollow figurine. The rest of the figurine was not located, and many now believe that the gold was not interred by the ancient Maya but was placed in the vault at a later time. Thompson suggests that it was a Panamanian gold figurine deposited there in recent times, perhaps by the Chortí Maya. These Indians are known to have returned to the Copán ceremonial center to burn copal incense, much as the Quiché Maya have done for years on market day on the steps of the Catholic church at Chicicastenango, Guatemala.

The Classic Maya had no metal tools and no gold. In addition to this bit of gold from Copán, a small golden bell shaped in the form of a human head was found at Palenque, but not enough gold has been found to be of any significance. Metal objects from the Postclassic period are also rare. A few objects have been dredged from the Chichén Itzá Well of Sacrifice.

It was the gold of the Aztecs of the Mexican highlands and of the Incas of South America, not the gold of the Maya, that fired the blood of the invading Spaniards.

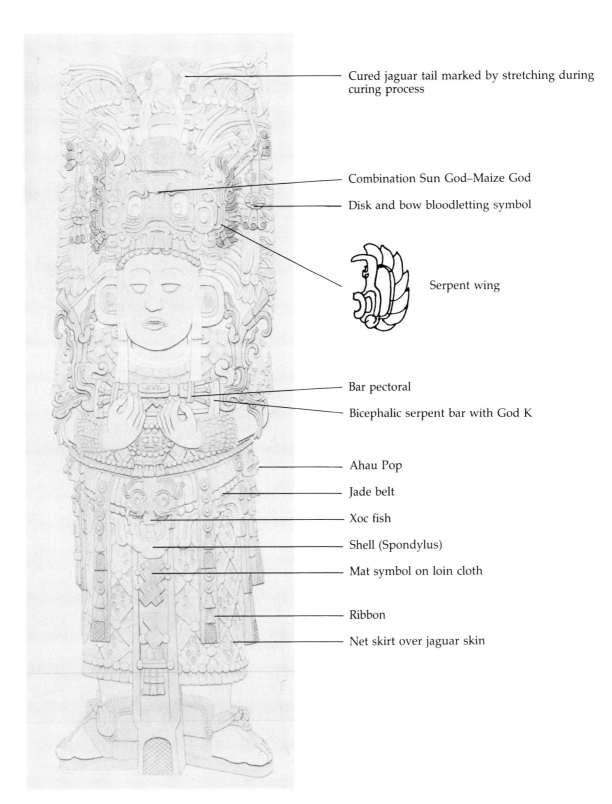

Cured jaguar tail marked by stretching during curing process

Combination Sun God–Maize God

Disk and bow bloodletting symbol

Serpent wing

Bar pectoral

Bicephalic serpent bar with God K

Ahau Pop

Jade belt

Xoc fish

Shell (Spondylus)

Mat symbol on loin cloth

Ribbon

Net skirt over jaguar skin

Illustration 249.   Stela H, Copán, west side.
Drawing by Maudslay, *Biologia Centrali-Americana*,
vol. 1, Illustration 56; iconography interpreted by
Schele.

Illustration 250.   Stela H and altar, Copán.

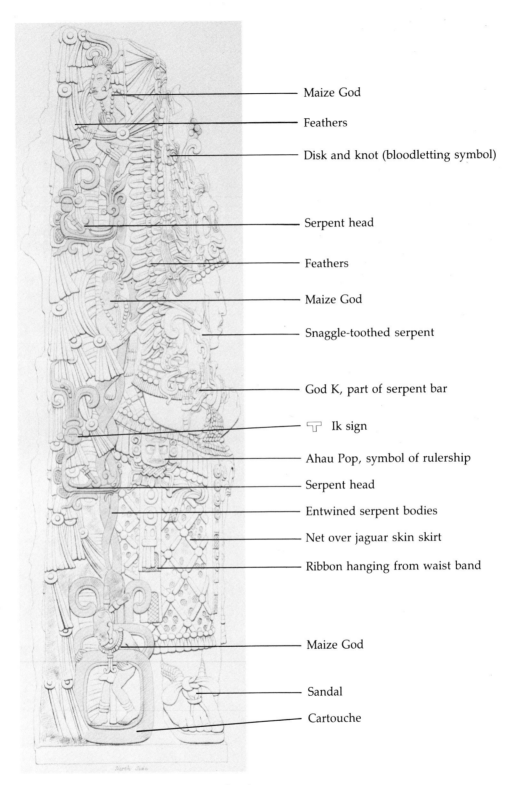

Maize God

Feathers

Disk and knot (bloodletting symbol)

Serpent head

Feathers

Maize God

Snaggle-toothed serpent

God K, part of serpent bar

⊤ Ik sign

Ahau Pop, symbol of rulership

Serpent head

Entwined serpent bodies

Net over jaguar skin skirt

Ribbon hanging from waist band

Maize God

Sandal

Cartouche

Illustration 251.   Stela H, Copán, north side.
Drawing by Maudslay, *Biologia Centrali-Americana*,
vol. 1, Illustration 59; iconography interpreted by
Schele.

Illustration 252.   Stela H, Copán (north side).

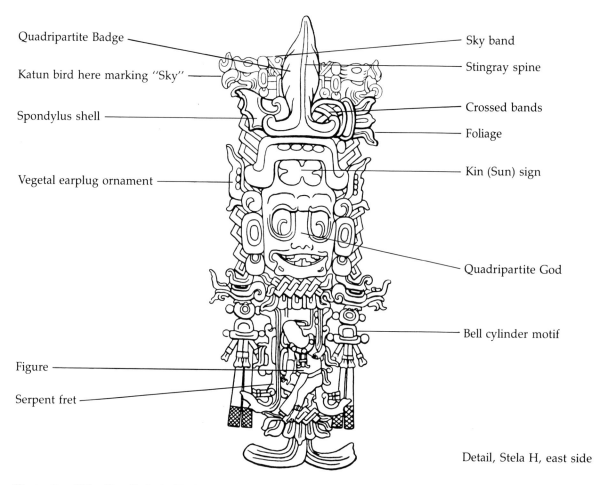

Quadripartite Badge

Katun bird here marking "Sky"

Spondylus shell

Vegetal earplug ornament

Figure

Serpent fret

Sky band

Stingray spine

Crossed bands

Foliage

Kin (Sun) sign

Quadripartite God

Bell cylinder motif

Detail, Stela H, east side

Illustration 253. Detail, Stela H, Copán, east side.
From Robicsek, *Copán*, p. 87. Iconography
interpreted by Schele.

230

Illustration 254.   Stela H, Copán (east side).

Stela I

Stela I is located in a niche in the terrace on the east side of the Great Plaza, almost directly east of Stela H. Stela I was commissioned by 18 Rabbit's immediate predecessor, Smoke-Jaguar. Baudez and Riese date Stela I at A.D. 692 and speculate that the figure on the stela might be an ancient ruler, Ornate Ahau, mentioned in the stela inscription with the date 8.6.0.0.0 (A.D. 160). Morley and Proskouriakoff date this stela at 9.12.5.0.0 (A.D. 676), although the actual Long Count date on the back of the stela is 9.12.3.14.0, 5 Ahau 8 Uo (A.D. 675), which is the date given by Nuñez Chinchilla. This date is important because the style and location of this stela predate the Great Plaza; therefore, the construction of the plaza can be dated after Stela I.

The style of Stela I is earlier than that of other stelae on the Great Plaza. The ruler holds a serpent bar in the stiff "crab claw" position, and it is far more two-dimensional than the later stelae. The ruler wears a mask of the god known as GI of the Palenque Triad of Gods. Michael Coe says:

> The features which serve to identify GI are (1) a large "god-eye," (2) Roman nose, (3) "egg-tooth" or filed front teeth in the upper jaw, (4) barbel-like whiskers or perhaps a fish barbel itself at the corner of the mouth, (5) a thorny oyster (*Spondylus*) shell over the ear, and (6) a peculiar belt with prominent bosses at the hips. His glyph is 1011. . . .
>
> I think that it may thus be concluded that GI of the Palenque Triad is a chthonic, underwater god with both fish and mollusk attributes, closely connected with death by decapitation, and with the dance accompanying human sacrifice. (M. Coe 1975: 14).

GI also is connected with accession of rulers. On the top of the ruler's headdress is the Quadripartite God, who also appears on the rear of Stela H. Floyd Lounsbury has identified GI as the Classic period version of Hunahpú of the Hero Twins.

GIII, the Jaguar God of the underworld, an-

Illustration 255.   Stela I, Copán.

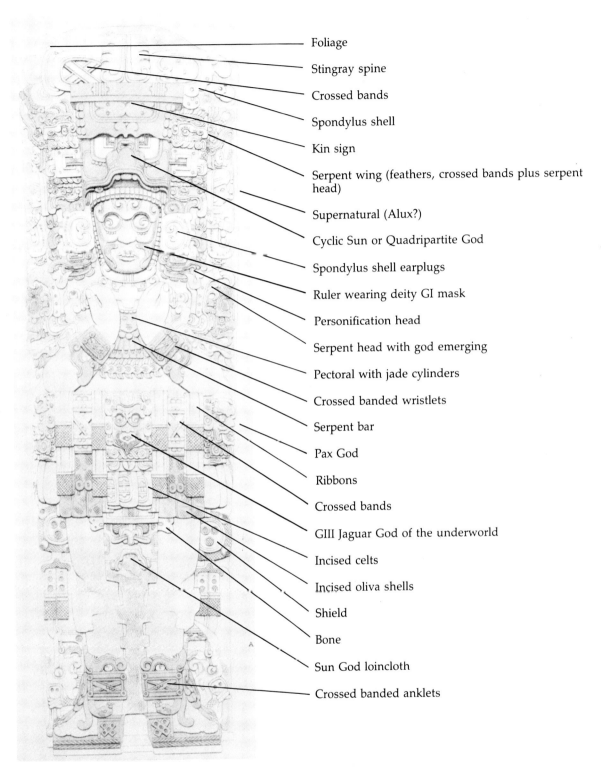

Foliage

Stingray spine

Crossed bands

Spondylus shell

Kin sign

Serpent wing (feathers, crossed bands plus serpent head)

Supernatural (Alux?)

Cyclic Sun or Quadripartite God

Spondylus shell earplugs

Ruler wearing deity GI mask

Personification head

Serpent head with god emerging

Pectoral with jade cylinders

Crossed banded wristlets

Serpent bar

Pax God

Ribbons

Crossed bands

GIII Jaguar God of the underworld

Incised celts

Incised oliva shells

Shield

Bone

Sun God loincloth

Crossed banded anklets

Illustration 256.   Stela I, Copán. Drawing by Maudslay, *Biologia Centrali-Americana*, vol. 1, plate 63. Iconography interpreted by Schele.

other god of the Palenque Triad, appears on the front of the belt. Lounsbury has concluded that GIII is Xbalanqué, the other twin. Both of these gods were very important to the ritual and regalia of rulers in the Classic period. In the myth of the *Popol Vuh*, Hunahpú and Xbalanqué, the Hero Twins, overcame death, a feat that the Maya lords hoped to emulate.

Illustration 257.   Glyph T 1011 (GI).

Illustration 258. Pyramid 4, Copán (Structure 10L-4). Stelae clockwise from center: A, 4, B, C, and H.

Pyramid 4 (Structure 10L-4)

Pyramid 4, in the middle of the Great Plaza at Copán, was excavated and restored in 1980, under the direction of Charles Cheek. The excavation uncovered four stages of construction. The fourth stage, visible in the aerial view, shown in Illustration 258, is the last stage of construction (10L-4-1st) done in Late Classic times, which coincides with the date of Stela A (9.15.0.0.0 or A.D. 731). The final phase of construction consisted of the remodeling of the fourth terrace and the addition of a small fifth terrace.

The earliest construction phase was probably in the Late Middle Classic. The second phase (10L-4-3rd) was a three-terrace pyramid with two stairways, one on the north and the other on the south, and a superstructure with a bench or altar on the north side of the third terrace. Some steps lead to the altar. In the construction of the pyramid, fragments of four stelae were used. The next to last reconstruction (10L-4-2nd) added stairways on the east and west and transformed the superstructure into a fourth terrace, on which there may have been a small platform. This remodeling was done in the Late Classic period.

Claude Baudez says two Early Classic stelae were buried in the fill on the north side of Pyramid 4. One of these, Stela 35, "is the earliest monument ever found at Copán and it is stylistically dated at the very end of baktun 8 (around A.D. 400). The large fragment does not bear any inscription but depicts two identical standing human figures very reminiscent of the drawing on the Leyden plaque (Baudez 1980).

Pyramid 4 was neither a funerary monument nor a residence. It fits Marvin Cohodas's concept of a public structure located in a public area, which, he suggests, was or could have been utilized by commoners in ceremonial activity.

Stela J

Stela J is located on the east side of the ruins of Copán in the northeast corner of the Central Court. It is a squarish, pilaster-type monument (eight feet, four inches high), with glyphs on all four sides and no portrait figures. The inscription on the west side is displayed over a stylized Cauac Monster. The Cauac Monster is identified by the circle clusters like bunches of grapes at the center top and bottom.

The most unusual aspect of this stela is the diagonal organization of the glyphs on the east face. This design imitates a woven mat, one of the symbols of power and authority of rulers; but the diagonal arrangement of the glyphs makes them very difficult to decipher. Spinden and Morley both struggled with this organization and did not agree.

Morley and Proskouriakoff set the date of Stela J at 9.13.10.0.0 (A.D. 702).

Illustration 259.   Stela J, Copán (west side).

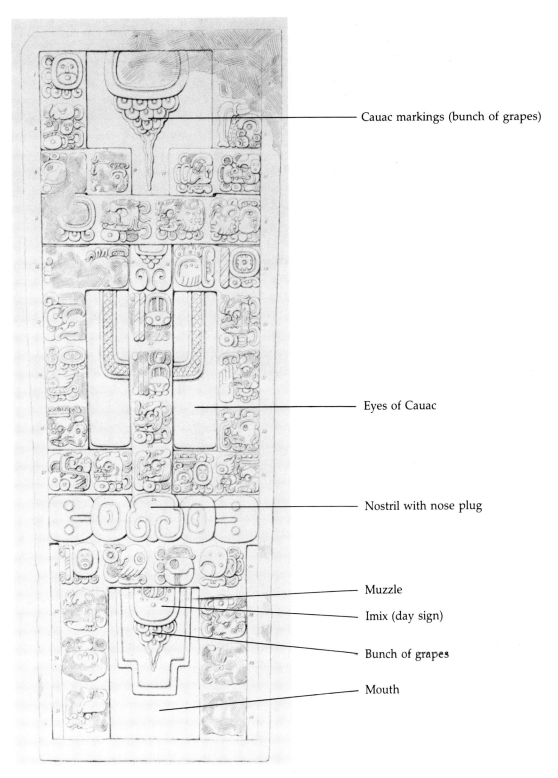

Cauac markings (bunch of grapes)

Eyes of Cauac

Nostril with nose plug

Muzzle

Imix (day sign)

Bunch of grapes

Mouth

Illustration 260.   Stela J, Copán, back side.
Drawing by Maudslay, *Biologia Centrali-Americana*,
vol. 1, plate 68; iconography interpreted by Schele.

Illustration 261.   Stela J, Copán (east side).

238

Stela 1

Stela 1 sits on the west side of the ball court on the steps of Structure 9. Its date is 9.11.15.0.0 (A.D. 667). This monument marked a departure from earlier monuments (Stelae 2, 3, P, and E) and sets a pattern for the later monuments that we have seen. For the first time, the turbanlike headdress is shown on a stela.

The Copán monuments have no direct stylistic connection with those at Tikal or at other Petén sites. An indigenous spark of genius must have created this new form. Other Maya sites had stucco relief in the round or nearly so, but of the major Maya cities, only Copán created these magnificent figures in stone.

Illustration 262.   Stela 1 and altar, Copán.

239

Illustration 263. Stela 1, Copán, standing on the
west side of Ball Court Building 9.

Illustration 264.   Copán ruins from the northwest.
A view of the Great Plaza, Central Court, Ball
Court, Hieroglyphic Stairway, and the Rio Copán in
the background.

Ball Court

The ball court faced north and south with Building 9 on the west side and Building 10 on the east. Stela 2 is at the north end, and Stela M and its altar are in the foreground on the south. Built over two earlier courts, this court is the third and latest ball court at Copán.

The glyphs indicate a date of 9.17.4.0.0 (A.D. 775) for the court, indicating that it was remodeled late in the Late Classic period, during the reign of Madrugada. The second court was built shortly after A.D. 700; the first court was constructed early in the third century.

The ball court is eighty-six feet by twenty-three feet and has three uninscribed markers in place along the central axis of the playing alley and three tenoned macaw heads on each side of the court at the top of the inclined benches. In the Copán village museum are the three markers from 18 Rabbit's court bearing his name in hieroglyphs. The markers depict the large ball with a solar emblem, as well as the player's regalia showing chest protectors (probably of basketry) up to the armpits, and a single knee-pad and single sandal. The player on the right hits the ball with a rabbit head, which seems to relate to the story of Hunahpú and Xbalanqué's ball game with the underworld deities in the *Popol Vuh*, which was discussed in connection with "18 Ball" on Stela D.

At the base of the 18 Rabbit marker, shown in Illustration 268, is a portion of the Quadripartite Badge (all but the stingray spine), which indicates sacrifice and bloodletting.

The corbeled arches in Building 10 on the east side of the ball court are tenoned stepped vaults, with the steps diminishing in size as they ascend. The architecture utilizes negative batter—outward sloping—wall construction. Negative batter makes the shadows deeper—the architects at Copán understood the effects of light and dark.

The ball game at Copán probably had a ceremonial function involving the solstices and equinoxes. In addition to the ceremonial aspect of the ball game (if we can draw from the Aztec ball game at the time of the Spanish Conquest), the sport was also played by amateurs and professionals alike for fun or for high stakes. Some evidence reveals the game was used to settle disputes and to determine wagers.

Cohodas considers that the Maya ball court was a symbol of the earth's surface, which functions as a passageway from which the sun may enter into or exit from the underworld, and that the movement of the ball along the north-south axis of the playing area is a symbol of the sun's annual journey. The three markers found in the center of the court represent the *axis mundi*, which pierces the surface of the earth and links the three levels of the Maya cosmos: the celestial world, the surface of the earth, and the underworld. The three macaw heads on each side serve

Illustration 265. Ball Court from the north; Building 9 on the right and Building 10 on the left. Hieroglyphic Stairway in the background.

also as a symbolic representation of the *axis mundi*, as does Stela 2, which was erected directly to the north in line with the playing area markers. Cohodas also suggests that the vaulted passageways in Buildings 9 and 10, which are aligned east-west across the ball court, may indicate that the game was played on equinox days when the sun rises due east and sets due west. Modern pragmatists suggest, however, that most ball courts were aligned north and south to keep the sun out of the players' eyes.

Illustration 266.   Ball Court from the south. Stela
M in the foreground and Stela 2 on the Raised
Platform to the north.

Illustration 267.   Ball Court, Copán. Reconstruction
drawing by Proskouriakoff, *An Album of Maya
Architecture*, p. 41.

Illustration 268.   18 Rabbit's ball-court marker.
From Proskouriakoff, *An Album of Maya Architecture*,
p. 39.

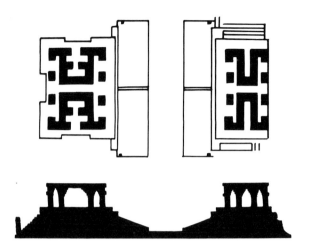

Illustration 269.   Plan of Buildings 9 and 10, Ball
Court, Copán. From Robicsek, *Copán*, p. 99.

Illustration 270.   Macaw, Ball Court Marker.

Illustration 271.   Ball Court Building 10, corbeled arch.

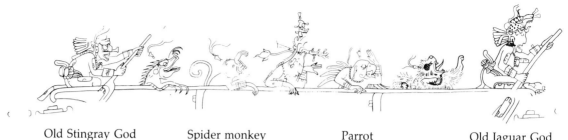

Old Stingray God   Spider monkey   Parrot   Old Jaguar God

Iguana   Dead lord   Kankin dog

Water symbol   Té sign for wood

Illustration 272. Paddler Gods (Tikal, Burial 116) conducting a dead lord to the underworld. From Kelley, *Deciphering Maya Script*, p. 234; Iconography interpreted by Schele.

Stela 2

Stela 2 faces the ball court from the platform to the north. This stela displays the early style, with feet splayed at a 180-degree angle, little undercutting, and a limp double-headed serpent bar. Morley dates it 9.11.0.0.0 (A.D. 652). Stela 2 is dated at about the same time as the double-portrait Stela 3 and portrays the same ruler. Schele identifies the heads emerging from the serpent bar as the Paddler Gods from the Tikal Burial 116 bone.

The stylistic and iconographic tradition established at Tikal during the reign of Stormy Sky, who became ruler in A.D. 426, is (again following Schele) the main emphasis of the monuments at Copán, Quiriguá, Caracol, and Palenque; but this tradition was abandoned at Tikal by the time of Kan Chitam (ca. 475), and never again became prominent at Tikal or in the central Petén.

Illustration 273. Stela 2, Copán.

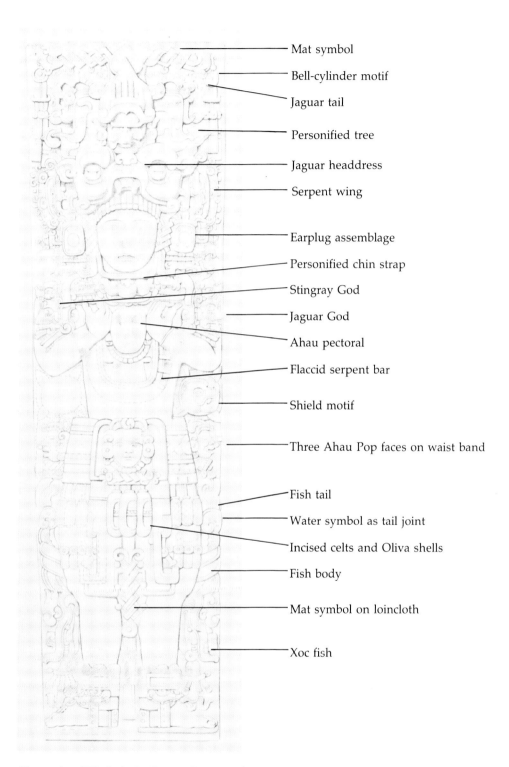

Mat symbol

Bell-cylinder motif

Jaguar tail

Personified tree

Jaguar headdress

Serpent wing

Earplug assemblage

Personified chin strap

Stingray God

Jaguar God

Ahau pectoral

Flaccid serpent bar

Shield motif

Three Ahau Pop faces on waist band

Fish tail

Water symbol as tail joint

Incised celts and Oliva shells

Fish body

Mat symbol on loincloth

Xoc fish

Illustration 274. Stela 2, Copán. Drawing by
Maudslay, *Biologia Centrali-Americana*, vol. 1, plate
101; iconography interpreted by Schele.

Stela 3

Just south of Structure 4, in the middle of the Central Court of Copán, is Stela 3. Stela 3 is Middle Classic, dated 9.11.0.0.0 (A.D. 652).

Stela 3 has double portraits of the same ruler who appears on Stela 2, and is done in the same early style as Tikal's Stelae 1 and 2. Schele suggests it is a double portrait with figures on each side, which may represent a cosmography of the underworld and the celestial world.

Illustration 275.   Stela 3, Copán (south side).

248

Illustration 276.   Stela 3 (north side), Ball Court
Building 9 and Temple of the Inscriptions Stairway
in background.

Court of the Hieroglyphic Stairway

The Court of the Hieroglyphic Stairway, aligned east and west, is bounded on the east by the Hieroglyphic Stairway leading to Temple 26. Both Temple 26 (unrestored) and the stairway were completed in 9.16.5.0.0 (A.D. 756). During the next fifteen years, the Eastern Court and Western Court of the acropolis were laid out and Temple 11, with its huge stairway on the south side of the court, was constructed. The ball court's Buildings 9 and 10 and the playing alley bound the Hieroglyphic Stairway Court on the north; Temple 7 is on the west.

The construction of the Court of the Hieroglyphic Stairway, the Eastern and Western Courts, between A.D. 756 and 770

> was the greatest and probably also the final period of architectural activity at Copán.
>
> Possibly the site continued to be occupied for a number of years after the closing of building operations, but since the later monuments show no falling off in style, we are forced to conclude that the city was abandoned at its zenith, and before decline and decay had made themselves felt to any appreciable extent (Morley 1920: 9).

In 1920, however, Morley did not know about Structure 18, the now restored beautiful temple located in the southeast corner of the acropolis. It displays a restored Long Count Date of 9.18.10.17.18 (A.D. 801), a generation after A.D. 770.

Illustration 277.   Court of Hieroglyphic Stairway,
Pyramid 4 and Central Court in the foreground and
Río Copán in background.

Illustration 278. Hieroglyphic Stairway.

Hieroglyphic Stairway

Sylvanus G. Morley, one of the greatest of all Mayanists, said in 1920, "the inscription on the Hieroglyphic Stairway of Mound 26 at Copán is the longest in the *Corpus Inscriptionum Mayarum*, containing as many as 2500 individual glyphs, truly encyclopedic as compared with all other known texts" (Morley 1920: 237). This stairway is one of the great ancient architectural monuments of the world, but, unfortunately, it is not so valuable as a historical document because the stairway collapsed, and most of the glyph blocks were found in a huge pile at the base of the stairway. Only ten complete steps and a portion of five more were in place. The Peabody Museum project restored the stairway, but the fallen glyphs were replaced at random, producing an unintelligible jigsaw puzzle of unrelated glyph

blocks. Baudez believes the stairway was constructed by Ruler 15, Cuc, and constituted a litany concerning Copán's rulers.

The glyphic inscriptions that appear on the Temple of the Inscriptions at Palenque have been interpreted by Schele, and those on the roof comb of the Temple of the Inscriptions at Tikal are being interpreted by Jones. Both of these temples have a recitation of the names of the rulers' progenitors—actual and mythological. We can assume, therefore, that the legend on the Heiroglyphic Stairway at Copán probably contained a recitation of the names of the king's ancestors, with reference to past events and a projection into the future. Thus far, thirty dates have been deciphered, extending for two hundred years from A.D. 544 to 744.

The *alfardas* (balustrades), over nine feet wide, are carved with birds and serpents. In the center

252

Illustration 279. Hieroglyphic Stairway, Copán. Reconstruction drawing by Proskouriakoff, *An Album of Maya Architecture*, p. 37.

Illustration 280. Court of the Hieroglyphic Stairway, Stela M and altar.

of the stairway are five pedestals, which supported statues of seated personages, probably portraits of ancestral rulers of Copán. Only the topmost figure is in place. It is a standing figure joined to the front elevation of Structure 26. It is impossible to be sure who the statues represented, but they were probably ancestors of the ruler. Bound captives and reclining God Ks are also carved on the riser of the stairs in the upper half.

Illustration 281.   Hieroglyphic Stairway, North
Alfarda (balustrade).

Illustration 282. Figure at top of Stairway.

Illustration 283. Stela M Altar, Copán (north head).

Stela M and Stela M Altar

Stela M and its altar are part of the Hieroglyphic Stairway complex. The Stairway, Stela M, and Building 26 were probably dedicated about 9.16.5.0.0 (A.D. 756).

The continuity of events relating to Copán's relationship with Quiriguá, to the northeast on the Motagua River, remains problematic. Quiriguá has long been assumed to have been closely connected to Copán because of the proximity and the similarity of the art, architecture, and urban plan.

Trouble between Copán and Quiriguá began about A.D. 737, and Quiriguá seems to have been the victor. At Quiriguá shortly before, in A.D. 724, Cauac Sky (Two-Legged Sky) came to power. He may have been the son of Copán's 18 Rabbit, and his wife may have come from Palenque. For several years after 9.15.6.14.6 (A.D. 738), a hiatus seems to have occurred at Copán. Schele thinks that 18 Rabbit may have been captured by Cauac Sky and held a prisoner, intended for sacrifice, for many years.

It may be that Ruler 14 could not accede until after 18 Rabbit's death. The date 9.15.6.14.6, 6 Cimi 4 Zec (April 29, A.D. 738) must have been very important because it is inscribed at Copán and appears several times at Quiriguá on Stelae E, F, and J, and on Zoomorph G. It was likely a day that lived in infamy for the people of Copán.

After the apparent hiatus, a great burst of building took place, beginning with Ruler 15, Cuc, who built the Hieroglyphic Stairway. Temple 11, the fabulous Temple 22 on the Eastern Court of the acropolis (which became his dynastic focal point), and Temple 18 were built by Madrugada.

The ruler, depicted on the west side of Stela M, holds a double-headed serpent bar; he wears a belt with crossed bands, from which hang Oliva shells and celts; the Sun God is shown on his loincloth. His feet are splayed at a 45-degree angle. The face and headdress are badly eroded, but Ruler Cuc seems to be depicted as the Sun God.

Stela M is now badly damaged but in its original state it must have been one of the most

Illustration 284.   Stela M Altar, Copán (south side).

beautiful in Copán. Its style follows the tradition of three-dimensional deep carving established with Stelae F and 4.

The altar of this stela is a three-dimensional rendering of the Maya Celestial Monster. The main element is the body of an iguana or crocodilian monster from whose mouth God N, an underworld god, emerges. The quadripartite Sun Monster is attached to the rear of the body, and the body torso carries a relief face of the Cauac Monster. The Cauac Monster may reflect storms and lightning, or may simply mark this version of the Celestial Monster engaged in the underworld half of his daily journey.

Illustration 285.   Stela M, Copán.

Stela N

Ruler Madrugada appears on Stela N in the Court of the Hieroglyphic Stairway. Stela N, his double-portrait stela, was erected at the base of the stairway leading to Temple 11 on the south side of the Court of the Hieroglyphic Stairway. There is a single row of glyphs on each side. On the east side of the top glyph is the Initial Series Introductory Glyph followed by glyphs showing 9.16.10.0.0 (A.D. 761).

Although the figure on the north side (who is variously called Madrugada, Lord Sunrise, New Sky Horizon, New Sky, or Rising Sun) is stiff, the secondary motifs are alive with decoration and regalia. The ruler wears a jade collar and holds a rigid serpent bar with God K heads emerging from each of the serpent's mouths. In the headdress is the Water Lily Monster, on top of which sits a tiny humanoid figure. The top of the stela is embellished with a tied-feather motif.

Around Madrugada's waist dangle Oliva shells and celts. On his loincloth apron is the Sun God, flanked by two square-nosed serpents. At the side of the stela, a fish nibbles at a blossom from the water lily, and various figures cavort between the intertwined bodies of square-nosed serpents. *Xoc* fish heads emerge from behind the Water Lily Monster.

Illustration 286. Xoc fish.

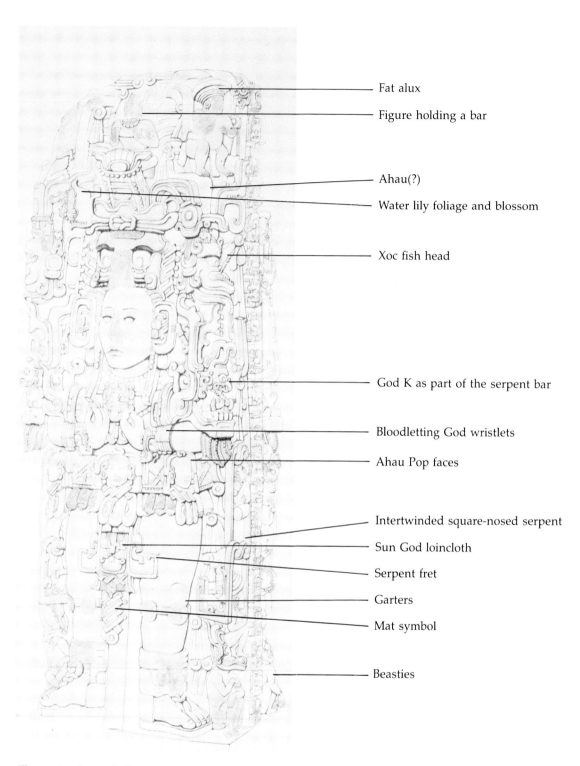

Fat alux

Figure holding a bar

Ahau(?)

Water lily foliage and blossom

Xoc fish head

God K as part of the serpent bar

Bloodletting God wristlets

Ahau Pop faces

Intertwinded square-nosed serpent

Sun God loincloth

Serpent fret

Garters

Mat symbol

Beasties

Illustration 287.   Stela N, Copán, north side.
Drawing by Maudslay, *Biologia Centrali-Americana*,
vol. 1, plate 77; iconography interpreted by Schele.

Illustration 288.   Stela N, Copán (north side).

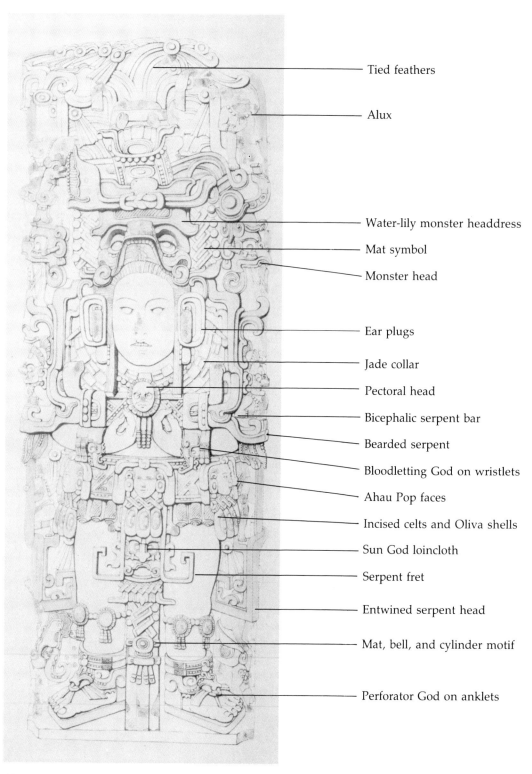

Tied feathers

Alux

Water-lily monster headdress

Mat symbol

Monster head

Ear plugs

Jade collar

Pectoral head

Bicephalic serpent bar

Bearded serpent

Bloodletting God on wristlets

Ahau Pop faces

Incised celts and Oliva shells

Sun God loincloth

Serpent fret

Entwined serpent head

Mat, bell, and cylinder motif

Perforator God on anklets

Illustration 289.   Stela N, Copán, south side.
Drawing by Maudslay, *Biologia Centrali-Americana*,
vol. 1, plate 82; iconography interpreted by Schele.

Illustration 290.   Stela N, Copán (south side).

Initial Series Introductory Glyph

9 Baktun

16 Katun

10 Tun

0 Uinal

0 Kin

Illustration 291.   Stela N, Copán, date 9.16.10.0.0
(A.D. 761).

Illustration 292.   Stela N, Copán (east side).

Illustration 293.   Stela N Altar, Copán.

Stela N Altar

The Stela N Altar is a three-dimensional representation of the Xoc Fish Monster combined with
the Cuauc Monster. The top edge of the altar is
carved in the form of a mat-throne. Madrugada
probably sat or stood on this altar, which is set
in the shadow of his portrait stela.

Illustration 294.   Altar O, Copán.

Altar O

Altar O is a large monument located in front of
Mound 7 on the west side of the Court of the
Hieroglyphic Stairway across from the Hieroglyphic Stairway. The west side of the altar shows
a single serpent with attached feather, scales,
belly plates, and double disks. The east side (toward the court) shows two intertwined serpents
with the ends of their tails at the top of the loops;
arms, perhaps of iguanas, emerge from below
the jaws of each head. On the rear end (north),
a toad and a fish are carved; on the front (south)
end, two figures and a fish are carved. This is a
Late Classic sculpture, dating from around A.D.
800.

Illustration 295.   Altar 41, Copán.

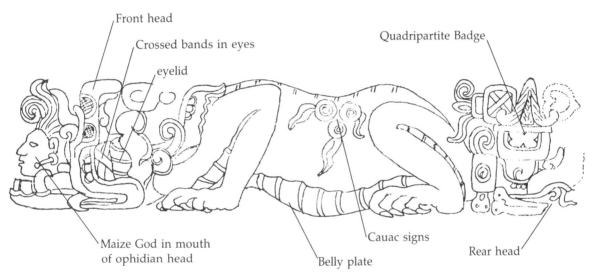

Illustration 296.   Altar 41, Copán, reptilian bicephalic monster. Drawing by Marvin Cohodas; iconography interpreted by Schele.

Altar 41 (Altar D¹ or CPN 82)

To the south of Altar O, Altar 41 has been repaired and placed on a pedestal. It is a rectangular stone block with sculpted sides with Madrugada depicted on the west side. The monument probably was carved later than A.D. 757.

A reptilian creature, with the Cauac "bunch of grapes" sign on its ribs and an ophidian head with the Maize God coming from its mouth, is depicted facing south. On the north side is a Celestial Moster with a Quadripartite God on its head. The iconography may symbolize the struggle between the rainy and dry seasons at Copán.

Illustration 297.   Temple of the Inscriptions and Acropolis Stairway, Ball Court Structure 9 in foreground.

Temple of the Inscriptions (Temple 11)

The Temple of the Inscriptions divides the ball court area from the acropolis. A pathway leads around the west side of Temple 11 from the Court of the Hieroglyphic Stairway to the Western Court of the acropolis. The temple, built upon a rubble substructure some ninety feet high, provided access control for the entire acropolis.

The Temple of the Inscriptions was constructed by Madrugada and dedicated in 9.16.12.5.7 (A.D. 763). This temple was probably Madrugada's accession monument. The northern face of the Copán acropolis is composed of a great stairway that rises to the level of the temple. At the top, the stairway divides into three sections. The central stairway leads to the door of Temple 11.

The interior of the temple forms a cross with entrances on four sides. The west and south elevations are mirror images of the north and east. This temple was not designed to be an entrance to the Western Court or an exit to the Great Plaza; in effect it was designed internally as two structures—one facing north and the other south.

Each of the entrances is decorated with two glyph panels. The exterior of the temple was filled with large sculptures carved in the round. At the northeast corner of the temple is the great head of God N, one of the chief gods of the underworld. This sculpture, known as the "Old Man of Copán," has become a hallmark of Copán. The alligator heads in the Western Court were originally part of the exterior decoration of the south side of the temple. The Temple of the Inscriptions has an interior stairway, which indicates that it had either a second story or an observation platform on the top.

266

Illustration 298. Temple of the Inscriptions,
Reviewing Stand to the right and Court of the
Hieroglyphic Stairway to the left.

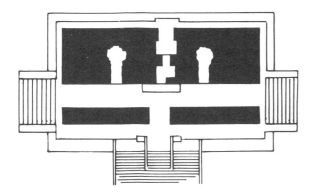

Illustration 299. Floor plan, Temple of the
Inscriptions, Copán. From Robicsek, *Copán*, Fig. 97.

267

Temple 11 is built on a four-door plan, with a long east-west corridor, a shaft sunken in the central chamber, and stairways leading upward. The three levels of the temple may symbolize the three levels of the Maya cosmos—the underworld, the earth, and the celestial world. Death and rebirth symbolism are represented by the colossal images that once decorated the four corners of the temple: two elderly *bacabs* associated with death imagery, and two reptiles associated with water and rebirth.

An excavation tunnel into the pyramid of Temple 11 enters on the north side near Stela N. The excavation was done by archaeologists to determine whether earlier structures existed under Temple 11. Several superimposed structures, with stairways containing hieroglyphic texts, were found.

Jesús Nuñez Chinchilla reports that another tunnel, designated Tunnel No. 2, was dug into the pyramid of Temple 26, which surmounts the Hieroglyphic Stairway. "Very primitive structures were found which perfectly demonstrates the change of materials employed in the different construction systems used by the Copán Mayas. A wall decorated with rough stucco masks, which evokes the Palenque decorations, was also found in this tunnel" (Nuñez C.1975: 90).

Illustration 300. Old Man of Copán (God N).

Illustration 301. Alligator Head.

Illustration 302.   Reviewing Stand.

Reviewing Stand, Western Court

The south elevations of the Temple of the Inscriptions and the Reviewing Stand have been partially restored. This construction forms the lower south portion of Temple 11 and faces the Western Court. The Reviewing Stand is composed of six steps (or possibly tiers of seats) to a terrace, upon which eight niches have been constructed. Two of the doorways lead to small rooms. Near the center of the row of glyphs is 13 Ahau 18 Cumku, which Morley uses to fix the date of this construction at 9.17.0.0.0 13 Ahau 18 Cumku (A.D. 771).

At each end of the reviewing stand is a kneeling humanoid or monkey figure. The figure on the west end holds a torch with an Ik sign, which has wind, sun, and life connotations.

On the terrace are three large stone conch shells. Above the terrace was a two-story temple, shown in Proskouriakoff's reconstruction drawing (Ill. 306). She says the temple

> appears to be an almost solid mass of masonry, crossed by two

Illustration 303.   13 Ahau 18 Cumku, A.D. 771.

perpendicular passages, which form the only room space in the building. Its especially massive construction and two interior stairways leading up from the longitudinal passage hint at a second story, of which however, there are no traces. In this drawing a second story has been restored, whereas in the general view of the Acropolis the possibility is considered that the interior stairways led up to an open roof (Proskouriakoff 1963: 48).

Illustration 304.   Reviewing Stand (southwest view).

Illustration 305.   Ik figure.

270

Illustration 306.   Reviewing stand, Western Court,
Copán. Reconstruction drawing by Proskouriakoff,
An Album of Maya Architecture, p. 49.

Illustration 307.   Monkey figure.

Illustration 308.   Plaque (possibly the Fire God).

Western Court Plaques

In the Western Court to the south of the Reviewing Stand are three flat sculptures or horizontal plaques. A cross-legged, barefoot, long-
nosed deity, who is possibly the Fire God, is
portrayed. The figure wears a pectoral on his
chest, armlets, and earplugs. In each hand he
holds an object; the object in his right hand appears to be a ball. Near his bare left foot appears
to be a skull. The deity lies upon and is partially
enveloped by foliage or smoke.

Illustration 309. Pyramid 16 with Stela P to the left and Altar Q to the right.

Western Court and Pyramid 16

Illustrations 309 and 310 show two views of the Western Court. On the left is the west face of Pyramid 16, which was topped by a small temple excavated by Maudslay in 1885. He found a headless stone figure and a few small objects in the single chamber.

At the base of Pyramid 16 is the well-known Altar Q and a row of skulls. On the right is a view of the southern end of the Western Court. In the center background is the unrestored Mound 14, and in the right background are the rubble remains of Mound 13. On the right side of Mound 14 is Altar I', and on the left (east) side is Altar H', which marks the entrance to the path around Pyramid 16 to the Eastern Court of Copán.

These photographs show Copán in winter, the dry season in the mountains of Honduras. The landscape no longer reflects the lush green of the tropical summer, but rather it displays the beige and brown colors of winter.

Illustration 310. Western Court (winter), Altar Q in the foreground.

273

Stela P

Stela P bears the Early Classic date 9.9.10.0.0 (A.D. 623) and now stands on the east side of the Western Court by the stairway leading to Terrace 25 and the Eastern Court. With the exception of Stela E, which is on the west side of the Great Plaza. It is the oldest stela in the main Copán ruins. Stela P was carved long before that portion of the Acropolis was constructed. It was reset there in Late Classic times when the Western Court was constructed, about 9.15.0.0.0 (A.D. 731).

The Copán rulers commissioned stelae to be carved showing a frontal view rather than the profile. This method allowed the display of all the regalia; however, it presented more of a problem in the portrayal of the face, particularly the lips and nose. Copán artists handled this difficult problem of sculpture with skill and finesse by using deep relief in the facial area. The artist who carved Stela P adhered to the tradition of stelae carving in which the figure conforms to the narrow shape of the stone shaft; later figures were sculpted from much larger blocks of stone, which gave the artist greater latitude in carving the monument.

In the ruler's arms is a flaccid serpent bar, from which emerges the Jaguar God on the right side and the Stingray God on the left. According to Schele, these are the same deities that appear as paddlers on the underworld canoe on an incised bone at Tikal (pictured in Ill. 272 in connection with the discussion of Stela 2). On the ruler's kilt are Ahau heads combined with mat symbols to identify the figure as "Ahau Pop, lord of the mat." The symbolism designates him as ruler or king.

Square-nosed serpents and hanging celts cover a jaguar skin undergarment. The headdress rests on a "cylinder and bead" headband, and the headdress itself is composed of four stacked heads with the Jester God on the top.

Illustration 311.   Stela P, Copán.

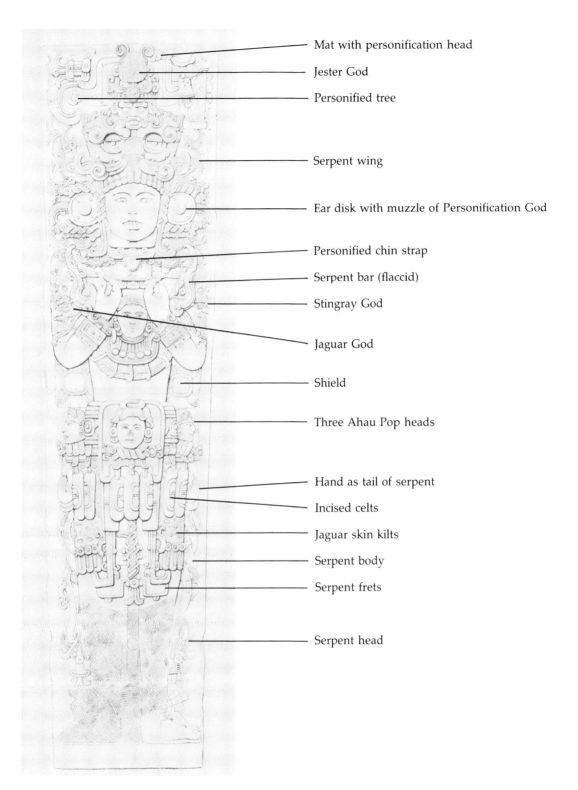

Mat with personification head

Jester God

Personified tree

Serpent wing

Ear disk with muzzle of Personification God

Personified chin strap

Serpent bar (flaccid)

Stingray God

Jaguar God

Shield

Three Ahau Pop heads

Hand as tail of serpent

Incised celts

Jaguar skin kilts

Serpent body

Serpent frets

Serpent head

Illustration 312.   Stela P, Copán. Drawing by Maudslay, *Biologia Centrali-Americana,* vol. 1, plate 87; iconography interpreted by Schele.

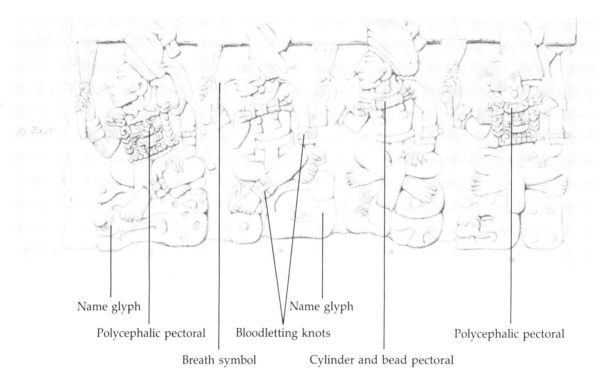

Name glyph

Polycephalic pectoral

Breath symbol

Name glyph

Bloodletting knots

Cylinder and bead pectoral

Polycephalic pectoral

Illustration 313. Lords of Copán, Altar Q, east side. Drawing by Maudslay, *Biologia Centrali-Americana,* vol. 1, plate 92; iconography interpreted by Schele.

Altar Q

For years, scholars assumed that Altar Q was erected to commemorate the computation of the exact 365-day year. Some suggested that this altar depicts a conference of representatives from various Maya sites gathered at Copán to establish a Mesoamerican calendar. From this concept, together with its magnificent sculpture, Copán has gained the reputation of being the "Athens of Mesoamerica"—"the intellectual capitol and spiritual guide of the Great Mayan Civilization" (Nuñez C. 1975: 81).

The date of Altar Q puts it in an interesting historical perspective for visitors from the United States; it is dated 9.17.5.3.4 (A.D. 776), exactly 1,000 years before the Declaration of Independence.

Recent analyses no longer support the conference interpretation. According to Kubler and Schele, the altar is really a portrait gallery—probably of ancestors—erected by Madrugada.

No indication of any non-Copán person appears on the monument.

The altar is thirty inches high and about fifty-six inches square. It has four seated figures on each of four sides and thirty-six glyphs on the top. Each figure wears a turban, which is a Copán-type headdress, and each carries a baton or scepter. Each figure wears a pectoral, which may indicate nobility. The iconography varies from figure to figure. Tlaloc, the Sun God, the Jaguar God of the underworld, the Cauac Monster, and the three-knot bloodletting symbols are represented, but they are probably utilized to portray the relationship of the ancestors with the deities or their attributes. Some of the figures sit upon their name glyphs.

Illustration 314.   Altar Q, Copán.

Illustration 315. Eastern Court, Temple of Meditation.

Eastern Court

The Eastern Court is bounded on the east side by a steep embankment, nearly a hundred feet high, cut by the Copán River.

In Classic times, buildings stood on the east side of the court, but they have been destroyed over the centuries by erosion from the Copán River. The number of buildings destroyed can never be known. From ground level on the east side of the acropolis, one can see the great sub-structure upon which the entire acropolis—all the construction south of the Court of the Hi-eroglyphic Stairway—stands. This entire sub-structure is man-made with stone, earth, and rubble fill. It was built to a height some one hundred feet above the level of the plazas to the

Illustration 316. Eastern Court, east side, Stone Head.

278

Illustration 317.   Eastern Court, south side, and Temple 18.

north and more than six hundred fifty feet along the river front; it may be built over older pyramids and buildings. The acropolis has not been excavated, so the style, type, and period of earlier construction is not yet known. In 1935, the Carnegie Institution expedition changed the course of the Copán River to prevent further destruction of the acropolis.

On the north side is Temple 22, the focal point of the Eastern Court; on the west is the Jaguar Stairway. The entrance to the Eastern Court is from the south, with Pyramid 16 on the west and Structure 18 on the east. On the east side are two huge stone heads and a headless jaguar altar. On Terrace 25, west of the Venus Altar, is another stone head. On the south end of the passage leading to the Eastern Court is Temple 18 (restored in 1980), which was erected about 9.18.10.0.0 (A.D. 800).

Illustration 318.   Jaguar Throne.

Illustration 319.   Eastern Court, east side, Stone Head.

Illustration 320.   Stone head, Terrace 25.

Illustration 321. Jaguar Stairway.

Jaguar Stairway, East Court

On the west side of the East Court is the Jaguar Stairway with three sculptures. On the north and south sides of the first flight of stairs are two upright jaguars—carved rampant—each with one paw on its hip, and each carved in high relief. The round recesses on the bodies held obsidian inlay "spots."

At the top of the stairs is the Venus Altar. The deity portrayed is the Jaguar God of the underworld and Number 7, whose attributes are big squarish eyes, a tau tooth, pompadour hairdo, a jaguar ear, and a cruller design around his eyes. He is GIII of the Palenque Triad of Gods and Xbalanqué of the Hero Twins. On each side

of his head are star signs. The Venus Altar may be a combination of Venus and the night sun.

The astronomy of the Classic Maya was substantially limited to horizon observations. For centuries they kept precise records of horizon points and dates of solar, lunar, and celestial risings and settings, and they were aware that the planet Venus was both a morning and an evening star. The window of the Temple of Meditations is assumed to have been utilized in calculating the cycles of Venus and for other west horizon observations.

In the center of the East Court are three inscribed stone slabs, but the inscriptions are illegible.

281

Illustration 322.   Jaguar.

Illustration 323.   Venus Altar.

Illustration 324.   The Jaguar Stairway and Temple
of Meditation, Copán. Reconstruction drawing by
Proskouriakoff, *An Album of Maya Architecture*, p. 45.

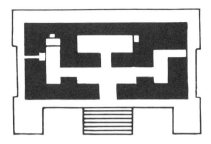

Illustration 325. Floor plan, Temple of Meditation (Structure 22), Copán. From Robicsek, *Copán*, p. 121.

Temple of Meditation (Structure 22)

The Temple of Meditation (Structure 22) was the *chef d'oeuvre* of Madrugada's buildings and probably his dynastic focal point. Morley dates this building at 9.17.0.0.0 (A.D. 771). The front portion of the building is gone. Originally, as shown in Tatiana Proskouriakoff's drawings of the Eastern Court, a highly decorated facade faced the Eastern Court. Two flights of stairs terminated in a single doorway. The entire facade of the building was covered by a Cauac Monster with two fangs, which are still visible flanking the outside door. The Cauac mask was of stone fitted in mosaic fashion. At other Maya sites, much of the sculpture was done in stucco, which has long since been destroyed; at Copán it was done in stone, and thus preserved. In addition, the sculpture surrounding the inner door is still in place.

Reflecting Maya cosmology, the floor of the entrance divides the earth from the underworld. The Maya concept of the cosmos separated it into three parts: heavens, earth, and underworld. The skulls at each end and the intervening skulls and glyphs refer to the underworld.

Above floor level at each end are Bacabs. Each Bacab holds one head of a celestial crocodilian monster, which arches over the door representing the daily passage of the sun. The S-shaped motifs with small figures entwined represent the sun's movement throughout the year, counterclockwise in summer and clockwise in winter.

On the east side of the frieze just above the serpent head being held by the Bacab is the perforator (stingray spine), with crossed bands and

Illustration 326. Temple of Meditation, north end of the Eastern Court.

shell—bloodletting symbols—and a Sun Monster attached to the rear. And on the west side are two celestial Venus-star signs. The Bacabs on the east and west sides of the door are shown kneeling. The marks on the cheeks of each buttock of the Bacab represent the muzzle of the Cauac Monster.

On the west end of the Temple of Meditations is a window—a somewhat unique feature in temple, but not residential, construction. The Temple of the Seven Dolls at Dzibilchaltún in Yucatán also has a window, and there are windows at Palenque. The window was probably designed for the observation of Venus cycles and other horizon manifestations of celestial movement. On the southwest corner of Structure 22 is a Cauac mask. The center of the mask is missing except for the long nose. The long nose was for some time thought always to represent Chaac, the rain god; now, that is not so clear. This mask has the circular elements in the supraorbital plate of the mask, which is the indicator of the Cauac Monster.

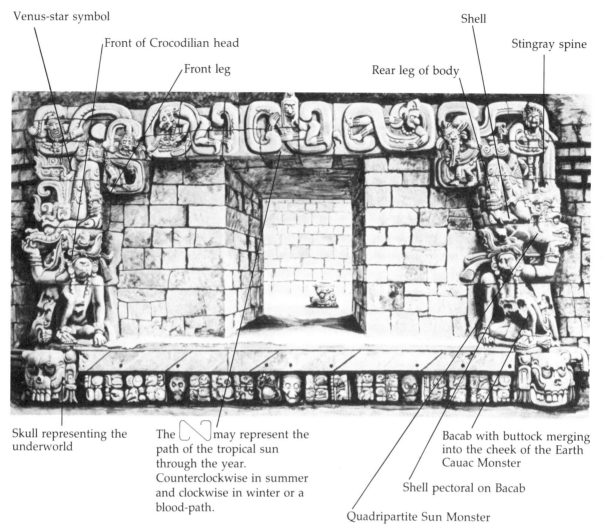

Venus-star symbol

Front of Crocodilian head

Front leg

Shell

Stingray spine

Rear leg of body

Skull representing the underworld

The [symbol] may represent the path of the tropical sun through the year. Counterclockwise in summer and clockwise in winter or a blood-path.

Bacab with buttock merging into the cheek of the Earth Cauac Monster

Shell pectoral on Bacab

Quadripartite Sun Monster

Illustration 327. Inner doorway, Temple of Meditation, Copán. Drawing by Maudslay, *Biologia Centrali-Americana*, vol. 1, plate 12; iconography interpreted by Schele.

Illustration 328.   Temple of Meditation, inner door (detail).

Illustration 329.   Temple of Meditation, inner door (detail).

Illustration 330.   Temple of Meditation, inner door (detail).

285

Illustration 331.   Stairway to the Temple of
Meditation.

Illustration 332.   Left: Venus-star symbol. Right:
Cauac Monster indicators.

Illustration 333.   Entrance to Temple of Meditation.

Temple 18 and Tomb 1

Structure 10L-18 (dated A.D. 800) was restored in 1980 under the direction of Marshall Becker of the Copán Project. It is located on the southeast corner of the acropolis, south of the Eastern Court, east of Pyramid 16, and attached to Platform 17.

The two-room Temple 18 was a true funerary temple. Beneath it on the south side is a rectangular vaulted chamber, which is a well-preserved example of funerary architecture. When the tomb was discovered in the nineteenth century, it contained human bones with vestiges of lime. The niches and floor contained a number of ceramic vessels and a small jade bead. But the tomb itself was emptied not long after the original royal burial, still during Late Classic times.

Much evidence indicates that Temple 18 is Madrugada's funerary monument. Baudez says, "I offer the hypothesis that the person buried in Temple 18 was King Madrugada himself, for he is represented on the temple's jambs with his names and titles; besides, it seems that Stela 11, which depicts the dead Madrugada, was associated with the temple" (Baudez 1980).

The decoration of the temple was done either during the lifetime of Madrugada or after his death. He is depicted as a great warrior and the one responsible for the crops and his people's subsistence. The interior terrace displays beautifully preserved masks, alternately portraying the Sun God and the Cauac Monster. According to Baudez, "The purpose of the decoration is to show the ruler surrounded with cosmic images in order to define his role in the universe." The iconography displays mainly the "Earth Mother" theme and its fertility. The temple's sculptures do not present a dead Madrugada, and there are no symbols of death or of the underworld.

The Long Count date carved around a niche in the temple's first room is 9.18.10.17.18 (A.D. 801), which makes this structure the latest so far reported.

Illustration 334.   Temple 18, aerial view from the northeast.

Illustration 335.   Temple 18.

Illustration 336.   Temple 18 northwest pilaster with
Long Count glyphs in background.

289

Illustration 337.   Temple 18, Long Count glyphs:
9.18.10.17.18 (A.D. 801).

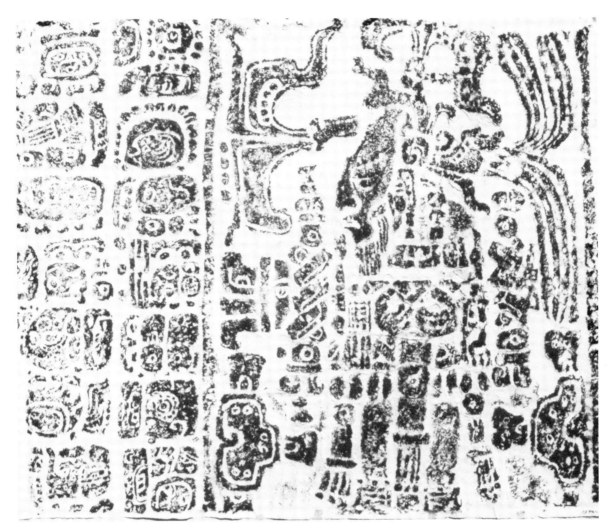

Illustration 338.   Stela 11, Copán. From Merle
Greene, et al., *Maya Sculpture,* plate 174.

Illustration 339.   Sun God and Cauac masks.

Illustration 340.   Temple Pilaster, Long Count
glyphs in background.

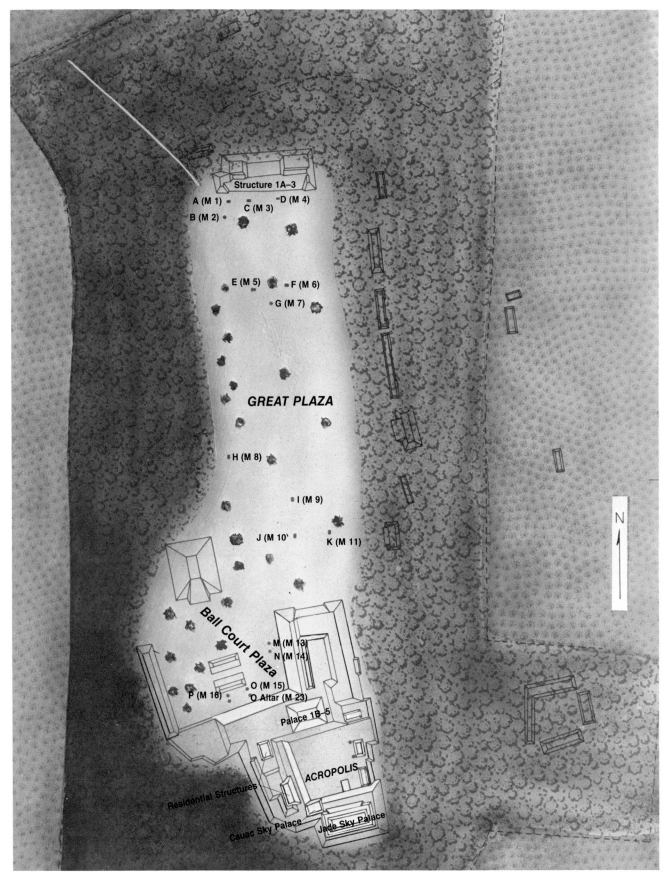

Illustration 341.   Plat of Quiriguá.

Quiriguá

Introduction

The Quiriguá National Park in eastern Guatemala contains the major Quiriguá Classic Maya ruins. It is a small area of primeval forest surrounded by fields of bananas. On the south is the Motagua River, and on the north across the valley is a low range of mountains.

This lowland Maya site has been seriously studied and investigated intermittently since the late nineteenth century. The most recent effort has been the Quiriguá Project undertaken by the University Museum, University of Pennsylvania, and the Ministry of Education of the Government of Guatemala. Research was directed by William R. Coe and Robert J. Sharer of Pennsylvania; the architectural restoration program was headed by Luis Lujan Muñoz and Marcelino

González C. of the Instituto de Antropología e Historia, Guatemala City.

Robert Sharer reports that an occupation floor discovered near the park appears to date from the Late Preclassic (ca 300 B.C.–A.D. 200), but that the best clue to the beginnings of Quiriguá are from Group A, located on a ridge north of the valley. Here were found some monuments dated to around A.D. 475 to 495).

Alfred P. Maudslay made the first scientific study of Quiriguá beginning in 1881. It was published in 1889–1902 in his five-volume study *Biologia Centrali-Americana,* or *Contributions to the Knowledge of the Fauna and Flora of Mexico and Central America*. Maudslay designated the monuments alphabetically. S. G. Morley followed Maudslay's system. The University of Pennsylvania project has reorganized the identification system by designating the monuments numerically. This volume includes both the numerical and the alphabetical designations.

The visible ruins at Quiriguá cover a period of some three hundred years from A.D. 550 to 850. So far, the earliest dated monument discovered in the park is Altar L (ca. A.D. 672), but it has been removed. The earliest monument (Altar M, Monument 13) remaining on display in the park is dated 9.15.0.0.0 (A.D. 731), and the latest dated monument (Jade Sky's Palace, Structure 1B-1 frieze) is 9.19.0.0.0 (A.D. 810).

Rulers of Quiriguá during the Late Classic period have been identified by Robert J. Sharer (1978: 69):

Ruler	Date of Accession	Length of Reign
Cauac Sky	A.D. 724	60 years
Sky Xul	A.D. 784	11 years
Imix Dog	A.D. 795	less than 5 years
Scroll Sky	A.D. 800	5 years
Jade Sky	A.D. 805	more than 5 years

Scroll Sky and Jade Sky may have been the same ruler.

The Late Classic period was dominated by Cauac Sky's sixty-year rule. He acceded to power on 9.14.13.4.17 (A.D. 724) and ruled until his death on 9.17.14.13.0 (A.D. 785). Prior to Cauac Sky's rule, Quiriguá had close connections with and was probably dominated by nearby Copán. Some scholars have suggested that Cauac Sky came from Copán and, possibly, was the son of 18 Rabbit. On the other hand, evidence indicates that he or his family, the Sky dynasty, may have come from Belize or Tikal, or he may have had Quiriguá forebears.

Recently, a new monument (M 26) has been discovered at Quiriguá, which exhibits a wrap-around design that Jones feels is close to the early Tikal style. This design indicates early Quiriguá contact with Tikal.

In A.D. 737, a confrontation occured between Quiriguá and Copán. After that, Quiriguá, the victor, became independent of Copán and of all other Classic Maya sites. Quiriguá controlled trade

Illustration 342.   Left: Quiriguá emblem glyph, Stela A (M 1), Quiriguá. Right: Cauac Sky's name glyph.

along the Motagua River from the highlands to the Caribbean and continued to prosper for more than a hundred years.

Jones and Sharer divide the building at Quiriguá into four construction stages; the earliest, Stage 4, was begun about A.D. 550, and the latest, Stage 1, was completed about A.D. 830. A summary of the construction stages is as follows:

Construction Stage 4 (A.D. 550–720): Construction during this early period utilized river silt and cobble fills faced with large river cobbles. The acropolis at this stage comprised three small structures, which faced the acropolis plaza. An elite burial dated sometime before A.D. 700, containing a body with notched teeth inlaid with small jade disks and with a large jade bead in his mouth, was found on the acropolis, indicating that Quiriguá had an elite class at that time, and probably had a dynasty of local chieftains.

Construction Stage 3 (A.D. 720–40): A large ball court in Copán style was constructed on the west side of the acropolis, and Cauac Sky's palace (1B-2) was erected on the southwest corner. Rhyolite (a glassy volcanic rock similar to granite) blocks were used for building and facing. Altar M (M13), the "Alligator" or "Jaguar" located on the east side of the ball court plaza, was carved.

Construction Stage 2 (A.D. 740–810): Sandstone was used along with rhyolite for construction. The west-side ball court was covered by a great terrace, and a new ball court was built in the ball court plaza north of the acropolis. Two north-facing structures were built on the northwest corner of the acropolis overlooking the ball court plaza, as were Zoomorphs O and P and their altars.

Illustration 343. Ruins of Quiriguá from the south with the Montana del Mico Mountains to the north.

The Kinich Ahau wall, which displayed masks of the Sun God, was built just west of the acropolis plaza. Later, during this same period, the wall was covered, and residential structures 1B-3 and 1B-4 were constructed on the west side of the acropolis plaza. During this period, all of the zoomorphs, altars, and stelae still at the park were carved and erected, with the exception of Altars M and N.

Construction Stage 1 (A.D. 810–50): Building blocks of sandstone, rhyolite, and marble were used. Jade Sky's Palace (1B-1) was constructed of sandstone; it bears the last known date at Quiriguá, 9.19.0.0.0 (A.D. 810). The palace (1B-5) at the north end of the acropolis was constructed and decorated with stucco.

A new terrace on the acropolis with the great stairway now seen on the south side of the ball court plaza was constructed, covering the two structures built there; the stairways on the north,

south, and west of the acropolis plaza were reconstructed during this phase. The small platform in front of Jade Sky's Palace represents the last known construction at the acropolis.

Quiriguá's site plan is much the same as Copán's, with an artificially elevated acropolis to the south, which contained elite ceremonial and administrative structures. At Quiriguá, it also contained the ruler's residence, along with a large lower plaza to the north holding public structures, a ball court, and autonomous stelae. This kind of organization, where the construction goes from elevated (south) to ground level (north), is called a sequential site plan.

Classic Quiriguá continued to flourish after other Classic Maya sites were abandoned. Quiriguá continued after 10.0.0.0.0 (A.D. 830) until at least A.D. 850. Quiriguá shows some evidence of Postclassic culture. Copper items, green obsidian, a *chac mool* sculpture of the Chichén Itzá type, and plumbate pottery (a Postclassic pottery with a lead-like glaze finish) have been found at Quiriguá, all of which are associated with the Postclassic Maya. These items suggest that Quiriguá was occupied well into the ninth century and even beyond.

The ultimate demise of Quiriguá is summed up by Wendy Ashmore and Robert J. Sharer in their observation that Quiriguá is located close to the Motagua fault, which caused the earthquake of 1976. They write:

> The discovery at Quiriguá of a group of domestic pottery vessels and the skeleton of a child, all crushed under the fallen walls of Structure 1B-18 (on the east side of the Acropolis Plaza) may indicate that an earthquake during antiquity dealt the final blow to a lingering local population. By the sixteenth century arrival of the Spaniards, however, Quiriguá's place as a primary port town had been taken over by Nito, a site on the Rio Dulce near the Caribbean coast (Ashmore and Sharer 1978: 18)

Illustration 344. Kinich Ahau mask.

Illustration 345.   Quiriguá from the north with the
Motagua River and the Sierra de Espiritu Santo
Mountains to the south.

Illustration 346.   Great Plaza (south to north).

Great Plaza

The Great Plaza at Quiriguá began with a surface paved with cobblestones large enough to accomodate Stela H (M8) and Stela J (M 10) (A.D. 751–56). This plaza was greatly enlarged in Construction Stage 2 (A.D. 740-810) to its present size—an area 325 feet by 275 feet (about two acres) and more than four feet thick.

Ashmore and Sharer point out that

> the present "flat" appearance of the
> Great Plaza belies the fact that it is
> really composed of a series of
> platforms and discontinuous stone
> pavements, some associated with
> structures and others with
> monuments, but now all buried by the
> alluvial silt laid down during the last
> thousand years (Ashmore and Sharer
> 1978: 15).

Beginning with Stela H (M 8) in A.D. 751 and continuing every five years until A.D. 771, a monument was erected. Each stela was bigger and more imposing that its predecessor, until Stela E (M 5) was erected in A.D. 771.

Stela E (M 5), dedicated to Cauac Sky and dated A.D. 771, is the grandest of them all and the tallest stela erected by the Classic Maya. At the next hotun (five-year) ending, twin Stelae A (M 1) and C (M 3) were erected by Cauac Sky; then, in A.D. 780, Zoomorph B (M 2) was set in place. Five years later, Zoomorph G (M 7) was erected as Cauac Sky's funerary monument and Sky Xul's accession monument. Stela I (M 9) was erected in A.D. 800 by Scroll Sky, and the last stela set in the Great Plaza was Stela K (M 11), erected in A.D. 805 by Jade Sky.

Unexcavated Structure 1A-3 (formerly Substructure III) with its long east-west axis forms the north boundary to the Great Plaza. The short trail from the park entrance skirts its west side. It was a structure some 270 feet long, 66 feet

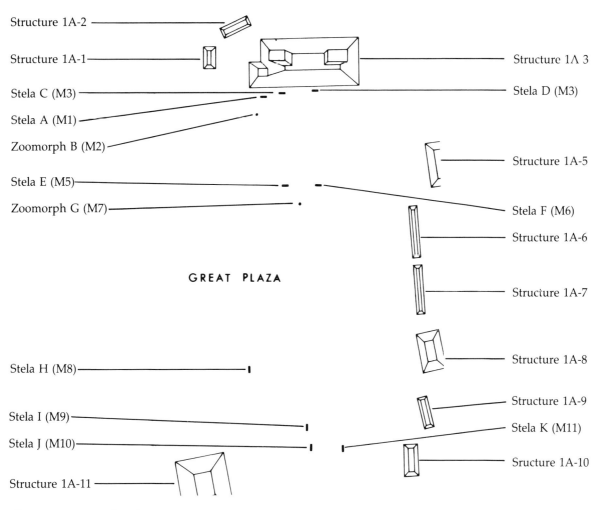

Structure 1A-2

Structure 1A-1

Stela C (M3)

Stela A (M1)

Zoomorph B (M2)

Stela E (M5)

Zoomorph G (M7)

Structure 1Λ 3

Stela D (M3)

Structure 1A-5

Stela F (M6)

Structure 1A-6

GREAT PLAZA

Structure 1A-7

Structure 1A-8

Stela H (M8)

Stela I (M9)

Stela J (M10)

Structure 1A-11

Structure 1A-9

Stela K (M11)

Sructure 1A-10

Illustration 347.   Plat of Quiriguá Great Plaza.

Quiriguá Monuments

Stela A (M 1)	9.17.5.0.0	A.D. 775
Stela C (M 3)	9.17.5.0.0	A.D. 775
Stela D (M 4)	9.16.15.0.0	A.D. 766
Zoomorph B (M 2)	9.17.10.0.0	A.D. 780
Stela E (M 5)	9.17.0.0.0	A.D. 771
Stela F (M 6)	9.16.10.0.0	A.D. 761
Zoomorph G (M 7)	9.17.15.0.0	A.D. 785
Stela H (M 8)	9.16.0.0.0	A.D. 751
Stela J (M 10)	9.16.5.0.0	A.D. 756
Stela I (M 9)	9.18.10.0.0	A.D. 800
Stela K (M 11)	9.18.15.0.0	A.D. 805
Zoomorph P (M 16)	9.18.5.0.0	A.D. 795
Zoomorph O (M 23)	9.18.0.0.0	A.D. 790
Altar M (M 13)	9.15.0.0.0	A.D. 731

(After Sharer 1978:57)

Illustration 348.   Great Plaza, north end.
Monuments from left to right: Zoomorph B, Stela
A, Great Stela E, Stela C, Zoomorph G, Stela D,
and Stela F in the shadows to the right.

wide, and 23 feet high. This structure epitomizes
the enormous time and effort involved in construction by a people with no beast of burden
or usable wheeled vehicle, but whose rulers had
the power and affluence to order construction
of such buildings. The sedimentary sandstone
was brought from over two miles north and the
marble from twelve and a half miles away. In
addition, a staggering amount of rubble had to
be moved on the backs of men to form the fill.

The Great Plaza was a public area. In those
times, the Motagua River ran close by and the
plaza may well have been a staging and trading
center for goods moving along the river between
the Guatemala highlands and the Caribbean.

Illustration 349.   Stela A (M 1), the face of Lord Cauac Sky.

Stela A (M 1)

The first stela one sees upon entering the ruins is Stela A at the northwest corner of the Great Plaza. Stela A, dated 9.17.5.0.0 (A.D. 775), was erected late in the reign of Lord Cauac (or Two-legged) Sky. The lord is shown on the south face

wearing a beard and holding the double-headed ceremonial bar. He has a Quadripartite Badge in his headdress. At his waist are crossed bands with dotted rain symbols and Oliva shells. Two square-nosed serpents are on each side of his loincloth. His feet are splayed 180 degrees.

Beneath the great Initial Series Introductory

Glyph at the top on the east side, the first five glyphs give the stela's date, 9.17.5.0.0. On the west side appears Cauac Sky's name glyph and a Copán emblem glyph located just above a Quiriguá emblem glyph.

The north side of the stela is difficult to make out, but it shows a profile of God GIII, the Jaguar God of the underworld. He is considered to be dancing, as one paw is raised slightly. To indicate dancing by this device was common in Maya iconography. God GIII is represented with claws for hands, paws for feet, and with a stone axe as the pupil of his eye.

Illustration 350.   Stela A (M 1), west side.

Cauac Sky name glyph

Copan emblem glyph

Quiriguá emblem glyph

Illustration 351. Stela A (M 1), Quiriguá, west side, glyphs. Drawing by Maudslay, *Biologia Centrali-Americana*, vol. 2, plate 7.

Illustration 352. Stela A (M 1), Quiriguá, north side. Drawing by Maudslay, *Biologia Centrali-Americana*, vol. 2, plate 8.

Illustration 353.   Stela A (M 1), east side.

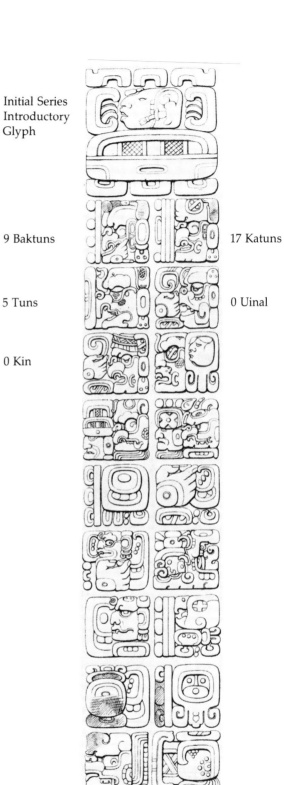

Initial Series
Introductory
Glyph

9 Baktuns   17 Katuns

5 Tuns   0 Uinal

0 Kin

Illustration 354.   Stela A (M 1), Quiriguá, east side, glyphs showing date 9.17.5.0.0 (A.D. 776). Drawing by Maudslay, *Biologia Centrali-Americana*, vol. 2, plate 7.

Stela C (M 3)

Stela C is, in effect, the twin of Stela A (M 1). They were erected in 9.17.5.0.0 (A.D. 775) by Lord Cauac Sky in celebration of the hotun ending. The hotun, a five-year period, is a quarter of a katun (twenty-year period). The two stelae are about the same size. Stela A is fourteen feet by four feet six inches by three feet two inches, and Stela C is thirteen feet one and one-half inches by three feet eleven and one-fourth inches by two feet nine inches; both are carved from blocks of brown sandstone.

Stelae A and C were the last erected by Cauac Sky. His personal name glyph appears on the west side of Stela C in the second row from the bottom. This ruler has been given the name Cauac Sky by Ashmore and Sharer because of the sky glyph with the Cauac sign. Kelley refers to the same glyph as "Two-Legged Sky" because of the sky glyph which appears to have two legs; Dütting calls it "Two-Armed Sky." None of these designations are either correct or incorrect; each is an attempt to provide an accurate descriptive term for the ruler's name glyph. The sky glyph may indicate that he was a member of the great Sky family.

The Quiriguá emblem glyph is visible on the same glyph panel of Stela C, seven rows from the bottom. The key element in the Quiriguá emblem glyph is the treelike shape, which is also the month glyph Kankin.

The Stela C glyphs show the year from which the Classic Maya calculated time, 13.0.0.0.0. 4 Ahau 8 Cumhu (August 11, 3114 B.C.), which to the Maya was the beginning of the last great cycle of time. The series begins at the top on the east side of the stela following the Initial Series Introductory Glyph. This is the same concept as the Gregorian system of measuring time from the birth of Christ. The text indicates the erection of the stela in 9.17.5.0.0, 3,888 years and 138 days after the beginning of the cycle.

This is derived as follows: Nine baktuns equals 1,296,000 days (9 × 144,000), seventeen katuns equals 122,400 days (17 × 7,200), five tuns equals 1,800 days (5 × 360), and there are zero uinals and zero kins; the total, therefore, is 1,420,200 days. Dividing by 365.2422, the number of days

Illustration 355.   Stela C (M 3), Quiriguá.

in a tropical year, yields 3,888.3787, or 3,888 years and 138 days.

On the back of Stela C is the Jaguar God of the underworld depicted dancing. He wears a pectoral and loincloth and has crossed bands in his mouth. He has an Ik sign in front of his nose, which may indicate a deity's breath.

Illustration 356.   T 559 (Kankin).

Illustration 357.   Quiriguá emblem glyph, Stela C (M 3), Quiriguá (after Maudslay.)

Illustration 358.   Cauac Sky's name glyph, Stela C (M 3), Quiriguá (after Maudslay).

Stela D (M 4)

Stela D is Cauac Sky's magnificent stela with full-figure glyphs on both sides. Stela D is the easternmost of the A, C, D row of stelae at the north end of the Great Plaza in front of Structure 1A-3. Cauac Sky appears on the north and south sides.

The south face is worn away, possibly by the action of a branch rubbing the face over the centuries. Because of the effacement of Stela D, it is difficult to make out the iconography. According to Morley, the ruler holds a manikin scepter in his right hand diagonally across his breast, and in his left hand he holds a small, round shield. On the north side, he holds the scepter in his left hand with God K's long nose pointing down (Morley 1935: 73), and he wears a large mosaic pectoral.

The extraordinary thing about Stela D is the set of full-figure glyphs, which dates the stela to the hotun ending 9.16.15.0.0 7 Ahau 18 Pop (A.D. 766). The glyphs on the eastern side are shown in sequence in Illustration 361.

Cauac Sky's personal name glyph is the fourth from the bottom on the left side. On the west side, the two-katun (forty-year) anniversary of Cauac Sky's accession is memorialized.

The glyphs following the Initial Series Introductory Glyph are the baktun (400-year cycle), katun (20-year cycle), tun (year), uinal (month), and kin (day). Those five periods and the numbers are represented by the complicated anthropomorphic and zoomorphic figures intertwined with each other. The glyphs of Stela D and Stela F represent the pinnacle of Quiriguá's artistic achievement. They were utilized when a message of paramount importance was intended, because their use enabled the scribe to portray meaning with wider latitude and greater subtlety than was possible by using ordinary hieroglyphs.

Illustration 359.   Stela D (M 4), Quiriguá.

Illustration 360.   Stela D (M 4), Quiriguá, glyphs.
(b)

310

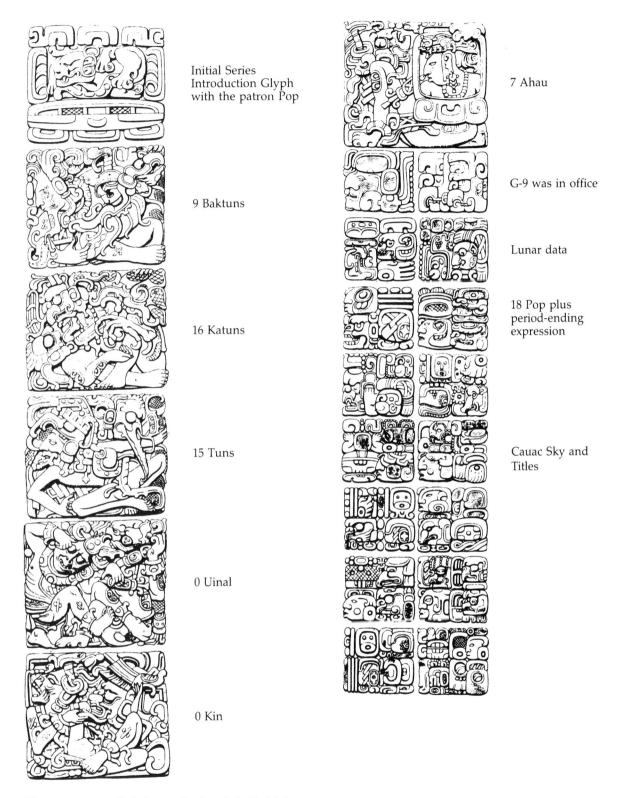

Initial Series Introduction Glyph with the patron Pop

9 Baktuns

16 Katuns

15 Tuns

0 Uinal

0 Kin

7 Ahau

G-9 was in office

Lunar data

18 Pop plus period-ending expression

Cauac Sky and Titles

Illustration 361.   Full-figure glyphs, Stela D (M 4), Quiriguá, east side. Drawing by Maudslay, *Biologia Centrali-Americana*, vol. 2, plate 26; iconography interpreted by Schele.

Zoomorph B (M 2)

Zoomorph B was erected by Cauac Sky in 9.17.10.0.0 (A.D. 780), about four years before his death. The zoomorph faces south, and the south face probably represents Cauac Sky emerging from a Celestial Monster with crossed bands in its eyes. The monster's fangs are just to the right and left of his elbows. A serpent with cartouches appears on each side of the ruler's face. A Sun God mask appears on his headdress.

The entire text and the date of this zoomorph are written in full-figure glyphs in which the personified forms of the glyphs cavort in the most imaginative display of the Maya scribe's skill and poetry as an artist. Morley says, "The inscriptions of Zoomorph B may, in all fairness, be said to be the most complex, the most involved, the most intricate text in the entire range of Maya inscriptions . . ." (Morley 1935: 97).

Illustration 362. Zoomorph B (M 2), Quiriguá,
Stela A in the background.

Stela E (M 5)

Stela E, facing south, bears the image of Lord Cauac Sky holding a manikin scepter and shield. It was erected to celebrate the katun 9.17.0.0.0 (A.D. 771). The east-side glyph column begins with the Initial Series Introductory Glyph, followed by 9.17.0.0.0.

The stela weighs some sixty-five tons, with a shaft length of thirty-five feet and a sculptured panel of twenty-six feet six inches. The stela fell without breaking in 1917 and was raised and reset in concrete by Strömsvik in 1934.

On the west side is Cauac Sky's inauguration date in Long Count: 9.14.13.4.17, 12 Caban 5 Kayab. This inscription contains an ancient error. As Morley says, "Somebody blundered in that long forgotten past, probably the sculptor who carved the monument. . . . The error, once having been carved upon stone, however, has thus endured throughout the centuries." The error is that the second glyph in the first column on the west side is 12, placed on the left of the tun (360-day) sign. The correct numeral should have been 13. So the date carved was 9.14.*12*.4.17 12 Caban 5 Kayab, "an impossible date in Maya chronology, just as impossible in fact as February 30th or June 31st would be in our own calendar" (Morley 1935: 81). Similar erroneous date inscriptions have been found at Palenque, in the codices, and at other locations.

In addition, Stela E on the west side, beginning ten groups from the top, after the Initial Series Introductory Glyph, refers to the "6 Cimi-4 Zec" (April 29, A.D. 738) date (see Stela J, Ill. 374, involving the capture of 18 Rabbit of Copán).

Stela E is the tallest stela erected at Quiriguá, and probably the tallest erected by the Maya. This stela was the culmination of the increasingly large structures at Quiriguá. The next katun markers were the twin stelae, A and C (Monuments 1 and 3), which are much smaller.

Illustration 363.   Stela E (M 5), Quiriguá. Stela E (M 5), Quiriguá, Cauac Sky.

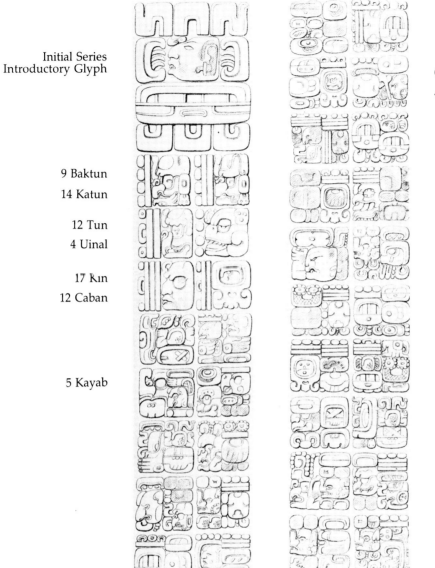

Initial Series
Introductory Glyph

9 Baktun
14 Katun

12 Tun
4 Uinal

17 Kin
12 Caban

5 Kayab

6 Cimi

4 Zek/War Club and Rabbit

Illustration 364.   Stela E (M 5), Quiriguá, west side, showing erroneous *twelve* glyph. Drawing by Maudslay, *Biologia Centrali-Americana*, vol. 2, plate 31.

Stela F (M 6)

Cauac Sky's Stela F was erected in 9.16.10.0.0 (A.D. 761), five years after Stela J (M 10) and ten years before its companion, Stela E (M 5). Stelae E and F stand together and are located near the center of the Great Plaza. They are the giants of the Quiriguá monuments—Stela F is twenty-four feet high and Stela E is twenty-six feet six inches high—and represent the zenith of great Classic Maya stelae.

On the south face of Stela F, the body of a bicephalic skeletal serpent rises from a left-side head on Lord Cauac Sky's waistband and crosses the top of the headdress, then goes down to join the right-side serpent head. He is not holding a ceremonial bar, but rests his hands on his chest in the same position as if he were holding the bar. On his shoulders are Sun God heads shown vertically for visual effect. On the north face he holds the God K Manikin scepter and sun shield.

In each figure, Cauac Sky wears a beard in the fashion of Stelae B, C, and D at Copán. At the base of the stela on the south side is represented the fleshed Deity GI, over which is a human figure, possibly an ancestor, wearing a Sun God headdress.

On the west side is Cauac Sky's accession date, 9.14.13.4.17 (A.D. 724). In this case, however, head variant numerals are used rather than bar and dot notations. Reference is also made to 18 Rabbit, Lord of Copán, and the date of his capture by Cauac Sky in A.D. 738.

Morley says that the glyphs on Stela F "are perhaps the most beautifully carved of any among the Maya inscriptions. The low relief is exquisitely rounded and the individual glyph blocks are all the same size, each a masterpiece of design" (Morley 1935: 71).

Illustration 365.   Stela F (M 6), Quiriguá.

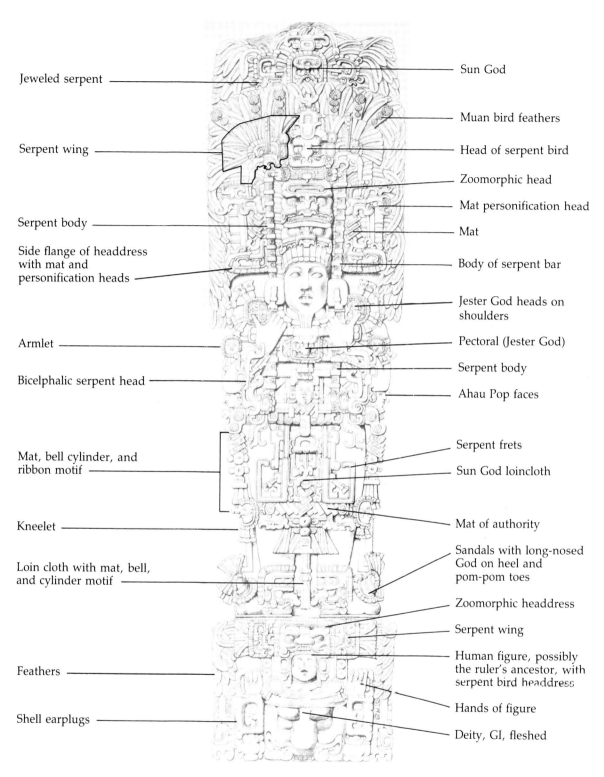

Jeweled serpent

Serpent wing

Serpent body

Side flange of headdress with mat and personification heads

Armlet

Bicelphalic serpent head

Mat, bell cylinder, and ribbon motif

Kneelet

Loin cloth with mat, bell, and cylinder motif

Feathers

Shell earplugs

Sun God

Muan bird feathers

Head of serpent bird

Zoomorphic head

Mat personification head

Mat

Body of serpent bar

Jester God heads on shoulders

Pectoral (Jester God)

Serpent body

Ahau Pop faces

Serpent frets

Sun God loincloth

Mat of authority

Sandals with long-nosed God on heel and pom-pom toes

Zoomorphic headdress

Serpent wing

Human figure, possibly the ruler's ancestor, with serpent bird headdress

Hands of figure

Deity, GI, fleshed

Illustration 366.   Stela F (M 6), Quiriguá, south face. Drawing by Maudslay, *Biologia Centrali-Americana*, vol. 2, plate 36; iconography interpreted by Schele.

317

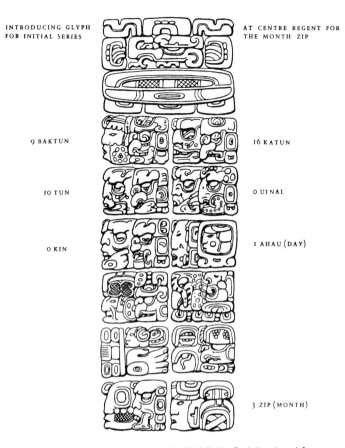

INTRODUCING GLYPH
FOR INITIAL SERIES

AT CENTRE REGENT FOR
THE MONTH ZIP

9 BAKTUN

16 KATUN

10 TUN

0 UINAL

0 KIN

1 AHAU (DAY)

3 ZIP (MONTH)

Illustration 367. Stela F (M 6), Quiriguá, with transcription of Initial Series and Supplementary Series dates. Stela F at Quiriguá uses face numerals; namely, those of the gods who preside over numbers. The reading here is

9 ×	144,000	1,296,000 days
16 ×	7,200	115,200 days
10 ×	360	3,600 days
0 ×	20	0 days
0 ×	1	0 days

From Kubler, George, 1975, *The Art and Architecture of Ancient America*, p. 126; drawing by Maudslay, *Biologia Centrali-Americana*, vol. 2, plate 46.

Illustration 368. Stela F (M 6), Quiriguá, Cauac Sky.

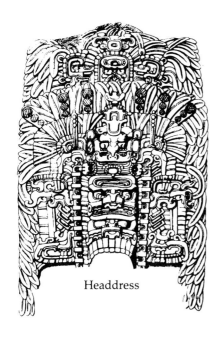

Headdress

Shoulder pads

Sun God pectoral

Waistband

Loincloth

Human figure pedestal

Sandals

G-I pedestal

Illustration 369. Stela F (M 6), Quiriguá, south face, exploded view, details. From drawing by Maudslay, *Biologia Centrali-Americana*, vol. 2, plate 36.

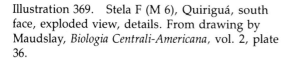

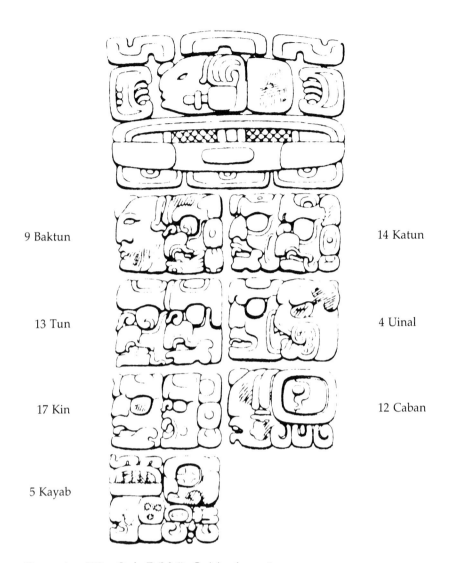

9 Baktun

14 Katun

13 Tun

4 Uinal

17 Kin

12 Caban

5 Kayab

Illustration 370.   Stela F (M 6), Quiriguá, west side, showing Cauac Sky's accession date.

Illustration 371.   Zoomorph G (M 7), Quiriguá.

Zoomorph G (M 7)

Zoomorph G, dated 9.17.15.0.0 (A.D. 785), bears a death clause in association with Cauac Sky, placing the date of his death one hundred days earlier at 9.17.14.13.0 (A.D. 785). Zoomorph G is Cauac Sky's funerary monument. It also refers to the A.D. 737 date of the capture of 18 Rabbit of Copán.

On the same monument appears the inscription 9.17.14.16.18—three uinals (twenty-day months) plus eighteen kins (days), a total of seventy-eight days later—which indicates the date of the accession to power of Sky Xul, who was probably the son of Cauac Sky.

The north face of the zoomorph has the attributes of a jaguar, including claws, teeth, and spots. The head and upper torso of a human figure is in the open mouth of this jaguar. From the south end emerges a head wearing a headdress with feathers and a mask.

Stela H (M 8)

West-facing Stela H is the oldest stela in the Quiriguá Park area; its date is 9.16.0.0.0 (A.D. 751). It is located on the west edge of the area near Mound 1A-11.

Lord Cauac Sky became king of Quiriguá on 9.14.13.4.17 12 Caban 5 Kayab, which we calculate to be December 29, A.D. 724. His first stela, Stela S (M 19), erected in A.D. 746, is in Group B, about one mile northwest of the Quiriguá ruins. The next stela he erected was Stela H, at the 9.16.0.0.0 katun ending.

Cauac Sky holds a double-headed ceremonial bar. God K appears at the right end of it holding a shield. The ruler wears an enormous feathered headdress. Around his waist is a belt with crossed bands and a series of hanging Oliva shells. He stands with his feet splayed at 180 degrees on a pedestal in the form of a Cauac Monster mask. The earplugs are of a unique cylinder form inside a sleeve. The Sun God appears on his loincloth between two long-nosed serpents. The glyph columns on the back, patterned after a woven mat, are rare and appear on Stela H and on Copán's Stela J.

The Sun God mask appears above Cauac Sky's forehead. The pupils of the eyes are unusual; they are neither scroll nor squint, the customary ways of depicting a deity's eyes, but have downward-directed pupils.

Illustration 372.   Stela H (M 8), Quiriguá, east side.

322

Illustration 373.   Stela H (M 8), Quiriguá, west side.

Stela J (M 10)

Stela J displays the figure of Cauac Sky on the west face, with glyph columns of the back (east side) and on the north and south. The stela is dated 9.16.5.0.0 (A.D. 756). It is sixteen feet six inches tall, made of brown sandstone, and weighs some thirty tons. Lord Cauac Sky is posed with his feet on an angle of 180 degrees, with the manikin scepter in one hand and a shield with the Jaguar God of the underworld in the other.

On the north side, six glyphs from the bottom, begins the 12 Caban 5 Kayab inscriptions, which indicate the accession date of Cauac Sky to be 9.14.13.4.7 (A.D. 724); at the bottom of the column are four glyphs which Dütting reads as "Honor is given to Two-Armed Sky [Cauac Sky] the precious offspring of Quiriguá."

On the south side of the stela, beginning at the top of the glyph column, Dütting reads an account of Cauac Sky's successful raid on Copán on 6 Cimi 4 Zec (9.15.6.14.6) (April 29, A.D. 738). According to Dütting, this raid resulted in the beheading of 18 Jog (Rabbit), "the precious offspring of the lords of Copán" (Dütting 1978: 209). Ashmore and Sharer are more conservative and say that in A.D. 737, "there was clearly some sort of hostile interaction in which Quiriguá was the victor. After that date XVIII Jog' is no longer mentioned in the inscriptions of Copán. In fact, there is a twenty-year gap in the hieroglyphic record at that site" (Ashmore and Sharer 1978: 10). Schele feels it is more likely that 18 Rabbit (Jog) may have been captured and held by Cauac Sky for a long time before his sacrificial death. Capture and sacrifice of rival rulers was a common practice. A panel has recently been discovered at Toniná (a site located south of Palenque) which reveals the capture of Kan-Xul of Palenque on 9.13.19.13.3 (A.D. 711).

The glyph which records the conflict between Cauac Sky and 18 Rabbit includes a war axe. We now know that this same glyph records conflicts between rulers of other sites, where the captured ruler was held for several days or longer for ritual torture and eventual death by sacrifice. The deciphering of several of the event glyphs associated with these conflicts indicates that the

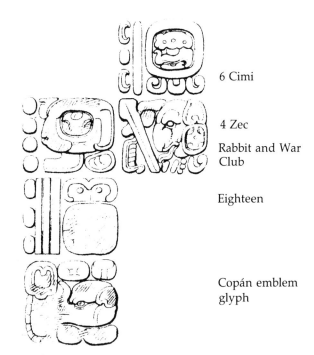

6 Cimi

4 Zec

Rabbit and War Club

Eighteen

Copán emblem glyph

Illustration 374.   Stela J, south side, depicting the capture (and possible sacrifice) of 18 Rabbit of Copán on May 3, A.D. 738. Drawing by Maudslay, *Biologia Centrali-Americana*, vol. 2, plate 6.

victors gained much honor and public recognition by sacrificing other powerful rulers. For this reason 18 Rabbit's capture is recorded on Stelae J, E, F, and Zoomorph G at Quiriguá, but only once at Copán. If Cauac Sky was indeed the son of 18 Rabbit, the conflict was interfamilial, as well as intersite.

324

Illustration 375. Stela J (M 10), Quiriguá, back side.

Illustration 376. Stela J (M 10), Quiriguá; photograph by Andrea Stone.

325

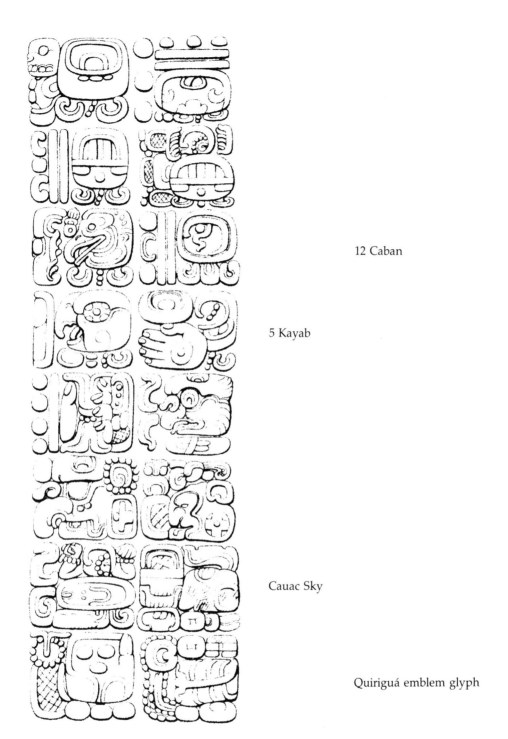

12 Caban

5 Kayab

Cauac Sky

Quiriguá emblem glyph

Illustration 377. Stela J, north side, showing accession of Cauac Sky in A.D. 724.

326

Stela I (M 9)

Stela I and Stela K (M 11) are much smaller than the stelae erected by Cauac Sky. Stela I is thirteen feet seven inches tall, and Stela K is eleven feet five inches. They are located in the southeast corner of the Great Plaza.

Stela I is dated 9.18.10.0.0 (A.D. 800), which may be the accession date of Ruler Scroll Sky. His name glyph is shown in Illustration 379. He may be a grandson or even a great grandson of Cauac Sky, but this hypothesis is by no means certain (Kelley 1962: 333).

The style of Stela I has changed from previous stelae. It faces west and no pedestal is depicted under the ruler's feet. Two Sun God masks make up the headdress. Scroll Sky holds a manikin scepter in one hand and a shield in the other. Oliva shells hang at his waist. The Sun God is on the loincloth between two square-nosed serpent frets. On the north and south sides are glyph columns. The north side has an Initial Series Introductory Glyph followed by the Initial Series date 9.18.10.0.0 (A.D. 800).

The back (east) side of Stela I represents Scroll Sky sitting tailor fashion in a niche on a Cauac Monster throne. The niche is framed on three sides by a sky band ending in two nearly identical heads, which Andrea Stone feels represents the *Muan* bird. Above and below the ruler are square-nosed serpents. The entire stela is enshrouded by more than two hundred feathers. Directly above the ruler's head is a bone on which balls are affixed, and above that is the mat symbol. Above the mat symbol is a head with three balls in its mouth, which possibly represent the Cauac Monster.

Illustration 378. Stela I (M 9), Quiriguá, west side.

Illustration 379. Scroll Sky's name glyph (Stela I). From Kelley, *Deciphering the Maya Script*, p. 225.

Illustration 380.   Stela I (M 9), Quiriguá, east side,
Stela H in the background.

328

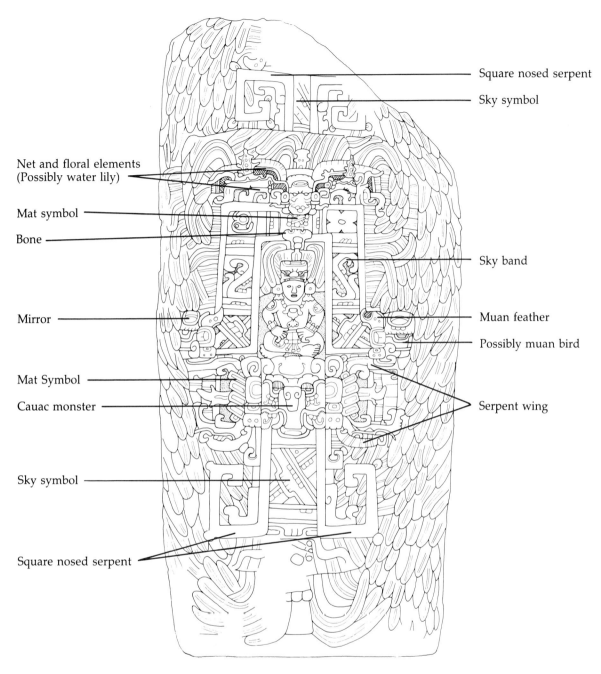

Square nosed serpent

Sky symbol

Net and floral elements
(Possibly water lily)

Mat symbol

Bone

Sky band

Mirror

Muan feather

Possibly muan bird

Mat Symbol

Cauac monster

Serpent wing

Sky symbol

Square nosed serpent

Illustration 381.   Stela I (M 9), Quiriguá, east side.
Drawing and iconography interpreted by Andrea
Stone.

Illustration 382. Jade Sky's name glyph. From Kelley, *Deciphering the Maya Script*, p. 224.

Stela K (M 11)

Stela K is the last stela erected at Quiriguá. Short and squat, it is far less imposing than the great shaft stelae erected by Cauac Sky. Maudslay, who found this stela in 1883, says, "It was always known to us as 'The Dwarf'" (Maudslay II, 15).

The date 9.18.15.0.0 (A.D. 805) is easily read on the north side following the Initial Series Introductory Glyph. This stela marks the accession of Ruler Jade Sky, the last known ruler of Quiriguá.

Although the shape of Stela K is different from earlier stelae at Quiriguá, the context is much the same. Jade Sky appears on the east face holding a double-headed ceremonial bar. His headdress consists of two Sun God masks and flowing feathers. He wears the standard crossed bands at his waist, and two square-nosed serpents are on each side of his loincloth.

On the west side, Jade Sky is depicted holding the God K manikin scepter and the Sun God shield. In his headdress is a Sun God mask. The other details of the iconography are similar to the drawing of Stela F.

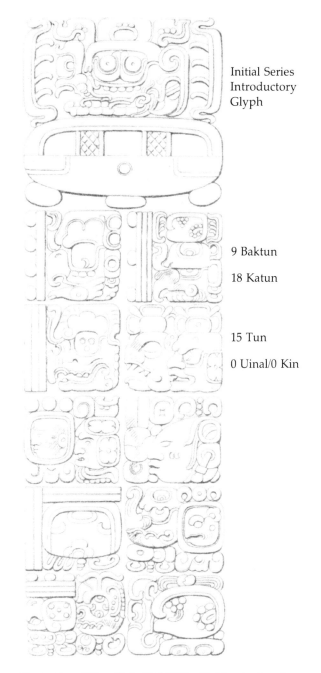

Initial Series Introductory Glyph

9 Baktun

18 Katun

15 Tun

0 Uinal/0 Kin

Illustration 383. Stela K (M 10), Quiriguá, showing accession of Jade Sky in 9.18.15.0.0 (A.D. 805).

330

Illustration 384.　Stela K (M 11), Quiriguá.

Illustration 385.   Southeast corner of the Ball Court Plaza.

Illustration 386.   Mound 1A-11 on north side of the Ball Court Plaza.

Ball Court Plaza

The small Quiriguá ball court has not been restored. Located in the center of a court at the south end of the Great Plaza, it is oriented east-west instead of the usual north-south.

Two parallel mounds lie south of the unexcavated mound, 1A-11 and west of the terrace 1B-17. The ball court is just to the north of Zoomorphs O and P and their altars (Monuments 16, 24, 15, and 23).

The ball court was constructed during Stage

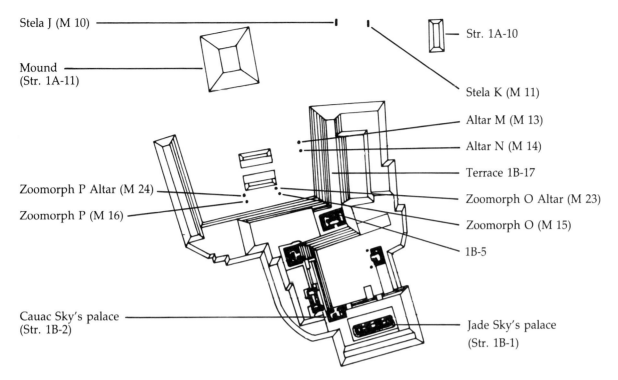

Stela J (M 10)

Str. 1A-10

Mound
(Str. 1A-11)

Stela K (M 11)

Altar M (M 13)

Altar N (M 14)

Terrace 1B-17

Zoomorph P Altar (M 24)

Zoomorph O Altar (M 23)

Zoomorph P (M 16)

Zoomorph O (M 15)

1B-5

Cauac Sky's palace
(Str. 1B-2)

Jade Sky's palace
(Str. 1B-1)

Illustration 387.   Plat of Ball Court Plaza.

Ball Court Plaza structures and monuments

Zoomorph P (M16)	A.D. 795
Zoomorph P Altar (M 24)	A.D. 795
Zoomorph O (M 23)	A.D. 790
Zoomorph O Altar (M 15)	A.D. 790
Altar M (M 13)	A.D. 731
Altar N (M 14)	
Ball Court (1B-7)	c. A.D. 740–810
Mound (1A-11)	
Stairways	c. A.D. 810–850

Illustration 388. Acropolis (left) and Ball Court Plaza (right).

2 (A.D. 740–810), the most active and ambitious period in Quiriguá's history. The west side of the acropolis was rebuilt with a terraced platform covering the old ball court, and the new one was rebuilt to the north in the ball court plaza (Sharer 1978: 57).

The plaza contains the earliest dated monument still in the Quiriguá National Park, Altar M, dated A.D. 731 (Altar L is earlier, but it has been removed) and one of the most remarkable of all Maya monuments, Zoomorph P, erected by Sky Xul in A.D. 795.

During Construction Stage 2, two single-room temples were built on the northwest corner of the acropolis, which faced the ball court plaza to the north. These temples were later covered and the grand staircase, which is now visible, was constructed on the south side of the court.

Illustration 389.   Ball Court plaza, Zoomorphs P
and O with Acropolis to the east. Ball Court
mounds to the left. Altars M and N just behind
workmen.

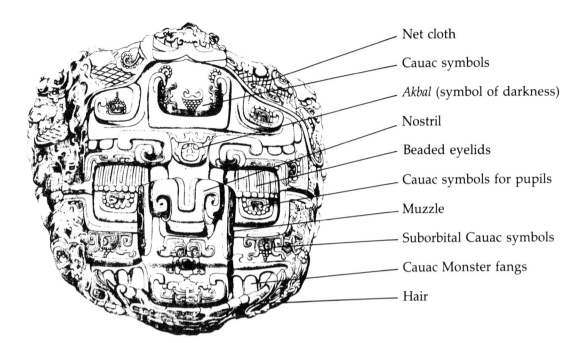

Net cloth

Cauac symbols

Akbal (symbol of darkness)

Nostril

Beaded eyelids

Cauac symbols for pupils

Muzzle

Suborbital Cauac symbols

Cauac Monster fangs

Hair

Illustration 390.   Zoomorph P (M 16), Quiriguá, top view. Drawing by Maudslay, *Biologia Centrali-Americana*, vol. 2, plate 58; iconography interpreted by Schele.

Zoomorph P (M 16)

Zoomorph P, "The Great Turtle," is Quiriguá's most famous monument. It is almost unbelievable that this great boulder could be so intricately and delicately carved by hand with stone tools. The monument is dated 9.18.5.0.0 4 Ahau 13 Ceh (A.D. 795). Sharer suggests that it was erected either at the end of the reign of Ruler Sky Xul or at the beginning of Imix Dog's reign. The indications are that Sky Xul died in A.D. 795 and that Imix Dog became king the same year.

The top of the boulder is all Cauac with circles in grapelike clusters on its forehead and supraorbital plates in its eyes and on its cheeks. It is also carved with the Cauac double-scroll muzzle and a full set of fangs.

Illustration 391.   Zoomorph P (M 16) and altar,
Quiriguá.

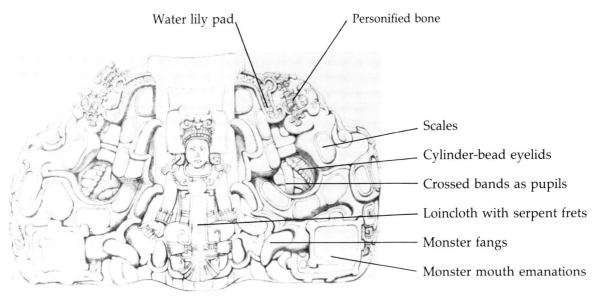

Water lily pad

Personified bone

Scales

Cylinder-bead eyelids

Crossed bands as pupils

Loincloth with serpent frets

Monster fangs

Monster mouth emanations

Figure sits in the mouth of the monster

Illustration 392. Zoomorph P, north face. Drawing by Maudslay, *Biologia Centrali-Americana,* vol. 2, plate 58; iconography interpreted by Schele.

Zoomorph P (North Face)

The ruler, either Sky Xul or Imix Dog, is portrayed on the north side of this great boulder, known as Zoomorph P. He sits cross-legged inside the open mouth of the monster. He is literally surrounded by the monster's fangs. The monster's eyes contain crossed bands and a cylinder and bead motif, which seem to be associated with the Cauac Monster at Quiriguá.

The ruler holds the serpent-footed God K manikin scepter in his right hand and a shield with a Sun God mask in his left hand. His loincloth overlaps his crossed legs. He wears Oliva shells and celts around his waist, cylinder and jade bead wristlets, a pectoral, and an elaborate headdress with Jester Gods on each side at the extreme top.

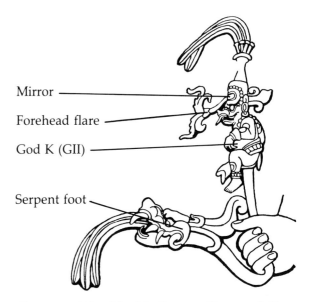

Mirror

Forehead flare

God K (GII)

Serpent foot

Illustration 393. Manikin Scepter, (Zoomorph P) (M 16), Quiriguá. Drawing by H. Spinden, *A Study of Maya Art, Memoirs,* p. 51.

Illustration 394.   Zoomorph P (M 16), Quiriguá,
north face.

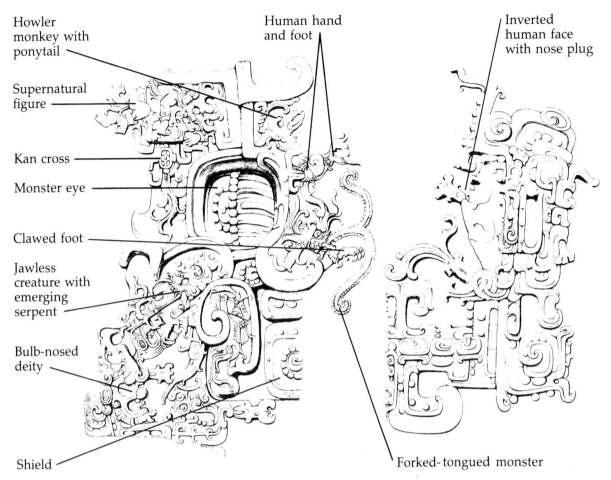

Howler monkey with ponytail

Supernatural figure

Kan cross

Monster eye

Clawed foot

Jawless creature with emerging serpent

Bulb-nosed deity

Shield

Human hand and foot

Inverted human face with nose plug

Forked-tongued monster

Illustration 395. Detail, Zoomorph P (M 16), Quiriguá, east side. Drawing by Maudslay, *Biologia Centrali-Americana*, vol. 2, plates 60, 61.

Zoomorph P (East Side)

The center of the east side of Zoomorph P (M 16) reveals a Quiriguá Cauac Monster eye with the cylinder and bead motif and water drops. On the right is an inverted serpent with the inverted face of a handsome young man emerging from its jaws. The inverted youthful head is connected to a deity mark of God C and vegetal scrolls.

Just above the eye to the right is a howler monkey with a ponytail hairdo just above a human arm and hand. This figure may be Hun Batz, one of the half brothers of the Hero Twins, who became a howler monkey, according to the *Popul Vuh*.

Illustration 396.   Zoomorph P (M 16), Quiriguá,
east side.

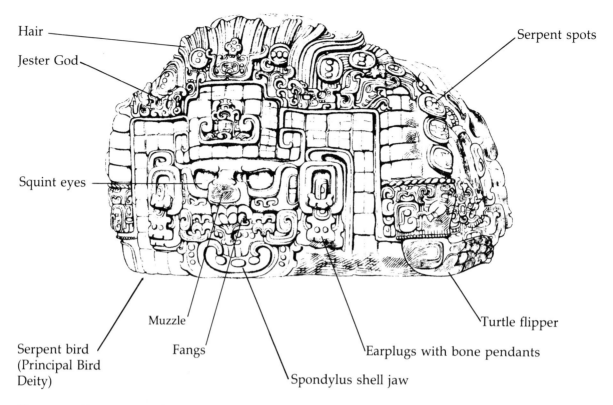

Hair

Jester God

Serpent spots

Squint eyes

Serpent bird
(Principal Bird
Deity)

Muzzle

Fangs

Spondylus shell jaw

Earplugs with bone pendants

Turtle flipper

Illustration 397. Zoomorph P (M 16), Quiriguá, south face. Drawing by Maudslay, *Biologia Centrali-Americana*, vol. 2, plate 58; iconography interpreted by Schele.

Zoomorph P (South Face)

Some suggest the south face of Zoomorph P is a skeletal Sun Monster. In the lower center is its fat muzzle, with the skeletal upper jaw and fangs just below. Instead of a lower jaw, there is a shell motif—a symbol of the Maya underworld. The earplugs have bone pendants. Andrea Stone feels the monster is the Principal Bird Deity which is identified by the crest of hair, squint eyes, and a long snout.

The face of the monster, including the inverted T-shaped emblem in the center forehead, is surrounded by glyph blocks. On the west side of the south face, beginning in the double column farthest to the left following the Initial Series Introductory Glyph, are date glyphs 9.18.5.0.0, which give the monument's date, A.D. 795.

Illustration 398.   Zoomorph P (M 16), Quiriguá,
south side.

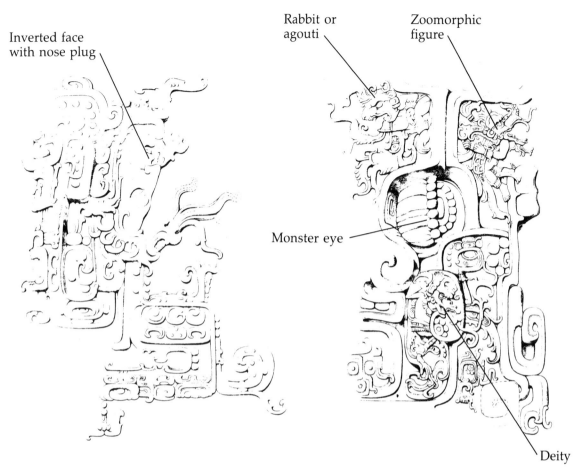

Inverted face with nose plug

Rabbit or agouti

Zoomorphic figure

Monster eye

Deity

Illustration 399.   Detail, Zoomorph P, west side.
Drawing by Maudslay, *Biologia Centrali-Americana*,
vol. 2, plates 60, 61.

Zoomorph P (West Face)

The west face is similar to the east face, with the
inverted serpent and inverted human face. Above
the eye is the Jog (rabbit or agouti) and a bearded
dragon.

Illustration 400.　Zoomorph P (M 16), Quiriguá,
west side.

Illustration 401. Zoomorph P, Altar (M 24), Quiriguá.

Altar of Zoomorph P (M 24)

The Altar of Zoomorph P is a large, flat disc of brown sandstone, which was dedicated on the same date as Zoomorph P, 9.18.5.0.0 4 Ahau, 13 Ceh (A.D. 795).

Illustration 401 shows the altar from south to north. If one looks at the picture upside-down, the face of the zoomorph can be seen on the north edge of the altar in the center. The mask is formed by the head of an anthropromorphic figure whose knees, legs, and feet can be seen in a semicross-legged position, surrounded on the south side by glyph blocks. The monster, on whose back the figure lies, has turtlelike claws.

This altar was found buried north of Zoomorph P by Morris and Strömsvik in 1934.

346

Illustration 402.   Zoomorph O (M 15) and altar (M 23), Quiriguá.

Zoomorph O (M 15)

Zoomorph O, dated 9.18.0.0.0 (A.D. 790), was carved during the reign of Sky Xul, who became king in A.D. 784 following the death of Cauac Sky. This monument is located in the ball court plaza, just east of the great Zoomorph P.

The Initial Series, in easily read bar and dot notations, is located in a single row across the bottom of the face. The lower jaw divides the numbers into two parts, 9.18. and 0.0.0.

The mask on the south portrays the fat-nosed Sun God. Originally a figure may have been at the north end, but it has been destroyed.

Illustration 403.   Zoomorph O (M 15), Quiriguá.

Illustration 404. Zoomorph O Altar (M 23), Quiriguá.

Altar of Zoomorph O (M 23)

The altar is dated 9.18.0.0.0 (A.D. 790), the same as Zoomorph O.

Although Zoomorph O is carved more crudely than the other Quiriguá monuments, its altar (M 23) is beautifully executed. The altar, carved from brown sandstone, depicts a masked dancing figure enmeshed in coils, perhaps of a serpent, or of smoke, mist, or water. The head points to the south and the feet point to the north. In his right hand, he holds an eccentric flint with an attached mask; a mask is also attached to his left hand, which extends over his head.

The head has a simian appearance with two fangs and an overhanging brow. His headdress, wristlets, and anklets are made of three-knot bloodletting symbols. The figure is portrayed with the attributes of GI of the Palenque Triad of Gods, especially the shell earplug.

The figure covers approximately one-third of the altar, and the other two-thirds present an elaborately arranged glyph panel. The inscrip-tion opens with full-figure glyphs, which Morley felt were so intricate that he was unable to decipher them.

The figure is probably the same personage as that on the Altar of Zoomorph P.

349

Illustration 405.   Altar M (M 13), Quiriguá.

Altar M (M 13) and Altar N (M 14)

Altar M dated 9.15.0.0.0 (A.D. 731), is the earliest monument in place in the Quiriguá Park. Maudslay called it the "Alligator Head." Morley considered it to be a jaguar.

It was erected at the first katun ending after the accession of Cauac Sky as ruler of Quiriguá and bears the Quiriguá emblem glyph. The Quiriguá emblem glyph, which includes Glyph T560 "Kankin Horizontal" of Thompson's *Catalog of Maya Hieroglyphs* (1962: 173), makes its earliest appearance at Quiriguá on Altar M.

Altar N is a double-headed monster. On one end is a human head, with a monster head on the other. It bears no inscription, but its style is such that it is probably one of the earliest monuments at Quiriguá.

Illustration 406.   Glyph T 560.

350

Illustration 407.   Altar N (M 14), Quiriguá.

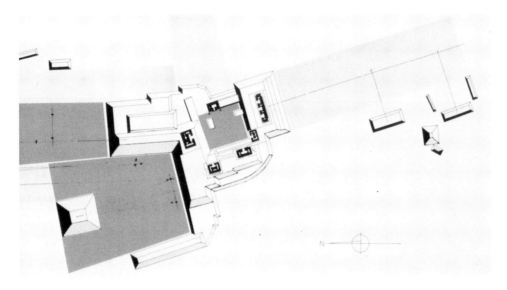

Illustration 408. Quiriguá Acropolis. From
Andrews, *Maya Cities*, Fig. 145.

Acropolis

Illustrations 388 and 409 show two aerial views
of the Quiriguá acropolis from the northeast and
east.

To the right is the massive east-west stairway
leading from the ball court plaza to the acropolis.
The great Zoomorphs P and O with their altars
are visible at the base of the stairway. This sandstone stairway was constructed by Jade Sky as
part of the final great construction at Quiriguá—
probably in celebration of the beginning of the
tenth baktun (10.0.0.0.0) in A.D. 830. Quiriguá
remained an active center for years after other
Classic Maya sites were either abandoned or in
sharp decline, and continued well into the ninth
century.

The structure in the middle foreground in Illustration 388 is 1B-5, which faces the acropolis
court. It was part of the final (Stage 1) construction period, after A.D. 810, and was constructed
of marble and rhyolite.

In the center is a covered area which protects
a wall (1B-Sub 1) where three Sun God (Kinich
Ahau) masks were found, none of which are
now in place. This wall was found between
Structures 1B-3 on the south and 1B-4 on the
north end of the restored stairway, which bounds
the west side of the acropolis court.

The stairway on the west side of the plaza
leading to Structures 1B-3 and 1B-4 was part of
the latest construction that covered the Kinich
Ahua wall. See Illustrations 344 and 411.

In the southwest corner of the court is Palace
1B-2, which was constructed by Cauac Sky early
in his reign—before A.D. 740—during Construction Stage 3. This was probably Cauac Sky's residence and remained basically unaltered for a
hundred years, until Quiriguá was abandoned.

At the south end of the acropolis plaza is
Structure 1 (1B-1), a residential palace, built by
the last-known ruler of Quiriguá, Jade Sky, who
became king in 9.18.15.0.0 (A.D. 805). The palace
bears the date 9.19.0.0.0 (A.D. 810).

The acropolis was a residential complex for
the rulers. It had a variety of uses, but its principal function was residential-administrative for
a series of rulers. The first identified ruler is
Cauac Sky, whose rule began in A.D. 724; the
last is Jade Sky, who ascended the throne in A.D.
805. The other elite of Quiriguá lived in the area
surrounding the site core.

Illustration 409.   Acropolis from the northeast.
Palace 1B-5 in the foreground with the West
Acropolis to the right and Palaces of Jade Sky and
Cauac Sky to the left.

Illustration 410.   Jade Sky's Palace to the left and
Cauac Sky's Palace to the right.

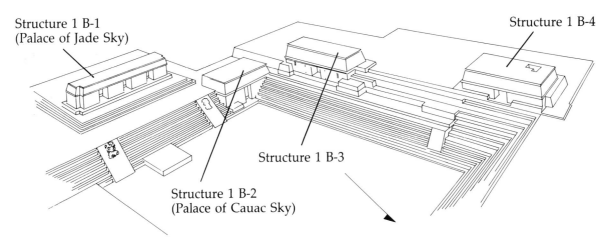

Structure 1 B-1
(Palace of Jade Sky)

Structure 1 B-4

Structure 1 B-3

Structure 1 B-2
(Palace of Cauac Sky)

Illustration 411.   Quiriguá Acropolis Court
showing Palaces of Jade Sky (1B-1), Cauac Sky (1B-2), and residential structures (1B-3 and 1B-4).
Drawing by M. Remmert (after Morley, Andrews,
and Sharer).

Palaces of Jade Sky and Cauac Sky (1B-1, 1B-2)

Jade Sky constructed a palace at the south end of the acropolis plaza. Along the molding was a Long Count date 9.19.0.0.0 9 Ahau 18 Mol (A.D. 810). Next to it, in the southwest corner of the plaza, is a palace constructed sixty or seventy years earlier by Cauac Sky. These were residential structures utilized by the rulers and their retinue. Sharer says, "The large masonry structures of the Acropolis are considered to be primarily residential because they have multiple rooms and usually possess benches, windows, and 'curtain holders' (notches in doorways, presumably to hold textile curtains)" (Sharer 1978: 60).

Further evidence that the acropolis was an elite residential area comes from a service building found on the east side of the acropolis. The building contained pottery vessels for kitchen storage.

Jade Sky's Palace (1B-1), 105 feet long by 18 feet wide, had three principal rooms $14^{1}/_{2}$ feet long by $4^{1}/_{2}$ feet wide, which opened onto the plaza to the north. The eastern and western rooms have smaller doorways on each end, which gave access to smaller chambers. There were stone heads fastened to the wall about $5 {}^{1}/_{2}$ feet from the floor in the middle and west chambers.

Cauac Sky's Palace (1B-2) was $44^{1}/_{2}$ feet long, 27 feet wide, and 17 feet high. A single doorway opens onto the plaza at ground level. The construction by later rulers almost completely buried this palace, but it was retained—most likely in tribute to the greatness of Cauac Sky. The principal doorway leads into a room oriented east and west, from which a door opened onto L-shaped interior rooms. In the west room is a stone bench $7^{1}/_{2}$ feet long and $3^{1}/_{2}$ feet wide, built against the northwest corner. The bench had an interior opening about $2^{1}/_{2}$ feet by $2^{1}/_{2}$ feet running its entire length at the back. At the time of excavation, a number of blackened river rocks were discovered under the bench, which Morley assumed were stones that had been heated many times to produce a steam bath.

Illustration 412.   West Acropolis.

West Acropolis Residential Structures (1B-3,1B-4)

During Construction Stage 2 (A.D. 740-810), the entire west side of the acropolis was reconstructed. The north-south ball court, which had been built before A.D. 740 in the Copán style, was buried. The new platform was the foundation for the Kinich Ahau wall containing three masks of Kinich Ahau, the Sun God. This wall was the focal point of the stairway that led up from the acropolis plaza on the east.

Toward the end of this period, after the death of Cauac Sky, the west side was again rebuilt. The Ahau wall was covered. The new stairway now visible was constructed along with Palaces 1B-4 on the north (right) and 1B-3 on the south (left).

Morley excavated 1B-3 in May 1919, and found that it contained a large central chamber and two lateral rooms. A sweat bath similar to the one found in Cauac Sky's palace is located against the north and west walls of the north chamber. The sweat bath is entered by an opening one foot ten inches wide and two feet six inches high, and extends westward about eleven feet, where it makes a turn to the left (south) for another two feet. At that point, it opens into a small

vaulted chamber some four feet long, two feet eight inches wide and about five feet high. This small chamber was the sweathouse.

House 1B-4 is located on the north side of the west terrace, just to the right of the protective metal roof, which now covers the Ahau wall.

At the west end of the east-west chamber of 1B-4 is a narrow stairway, which rises to a small landing in the northwest corner of the building, where a flight of five steps to the south reached the roof. As Morley says, "While by no means unique, interior stairways are sufficiently rare in Maya architecture to merit attention when found, and the one in Structure 4 is of especial interest since it seems to be preserved practically to its original height of 12 feet, i.e., nine or ten steps" (Morley 1935: 145).

355

Illustration 413.   Palace 1B-5.

Palace 1B-5

Palace 5 is a Late Classic construction, built during Construction Stage 1 early in the ninth century. It is the largest (sixty-two feet by forty-two feet) building at Quiriguá, and was built with block masonry of rhyolite and marble. Marble was not local to Quiriguá and its importation and use in Palace 5 demonstrates the affluence of the city at the beginning of the ninth century.

At one time, Palace 1B-5 was decorated with stucco, which has disappeared. It opened with a single door south onto the acropolis plaza. The door is exceptionally wide—ten feet six inches—for Maya architecture.

On the west end of the first room is a doorway opening into a long room, which takes up the entire west end of the building. On the east end of the first room, another doorway leads to a small interior room with a bench on three sides.

Conclusion

Were the Classic Maya a civilization?

We have seen who they were, how they lived, what they built, and the kind of art they produced. But were they civilized? Did their culture constitute a "civilization"? In twentieth-century terms of complex technology and political systems, they were not, but if we measure the manifold accomplishments of the Maya by a broader objective yardstick, the answer seems to be that they were. In anthropology, civilization is not measured in terms of individual freedom or man's humanity to man, but rather by the collective accomplishments of the society.

The Maya were a sanguinary people who practiced torture and human sacrifice, but can we fault them when in our age warfare, terrorism, and repression are commonplace?

From the anthropologists' viewpoint, several tests may be applied to a social system to determine whether it can be considered a civilization. These tests do not consider human compassion.

1. Did they have a governing class?

Were they egalitarian or did they have a hierarchy of classes? Certainly, the Maya were elitists. The kings and nobles were far removed from the commoner. The noble families seemed to have controlled every aspect of Maya life—religion, trade, food production, and building. The real question here is whether established authority existed. The Maya had strong leaders who aggrandized themselves in stone and ceramics for public display for almost a thousand years. The kings were at the pinnacle of authority. Maya society was the epitomy of a hierarchical system with nobles, ecclesiastics, militarists, merchants, artisans, and peasants.

2. Did the culture have elements of specialization?

The depictions of Maya court life on the painted ceramics show kings, nobles, warriors, servants, and scribes, and the massive architecture devoted to adulation of the gods points to a priest class. The evidence of trade and highly developed raised-field agriculture demonstrates the existence of a specialized merchant and agricultural class. The Maya artisans were craftsmen in ceramics, obsidian, and jade carving. They were also stone masons, plasterers, and architects.

3. Did they have a standardization of crafts?

The great similarity of architecture and iconography throughout the lowland Maya area demonstrates standardization. Although each area manifested different characteristics, the overall technology was much the same. The same deities are found in almost every Maya site, and the writing and number system indicate that the language was standardized.

The art and architecture were similar at any given period from city to city. The layout of cities, monuments, pyramids, temples, and stelae were similar. Even the dress of the rulers depicted on the vases was nearly the same.

4. Were they literate?

As far as we know, the written language of the Maya was not refined enough to express every idea. Nevertheless, it enabled the Maya to record events, dates, places, names, and lineages. And they were able to compute and record time with amazing accuracy and detail.

The Maya were the only prehistoric people in the Western Hemisphere to have any written language. They were accomplished scientists, especially in astronomy, mathematics, and calendrics.

5. Did the Maya produce significant art?

The pictures in this book leave little doubt that the Maya created monumental architecture—perhaps as massive, impressive, and enduring as any building before modern times. The Maya stone stelae, sculpture, ceramics, wood carvings, and mural painting are testament to the artistic achievements of the Ancient Maya.

6. Did they build cities?

Anthropologists consider urbanization one of the tests of civilization. Our investigation of Tikal, Copán, and Quiriguá leaves no doubt that they were cities, which compared with or far surpassed those of Europe between the fall of Rome and A.D. 800.

7. Were they creators of public works?

The existence of public works is another test of civilization. As people congregate, urban problems arise. The urban dweller is no longer able to provide for all of his own needs. He must become a specialist of sorts, doing for others what he does best and depending on others for many of his needs.

The close proximity of living and specialization of work create social problems of many kinds, which require some authority to make laws and settle disputes. Organized authority and continuing leadership are evident in the existence of public buildings, roads, waterworks, and sewers. The Maya built them all, and by their public works they demonstrated a degree of civilization.

8. Were they workers in metal?

Here, and only here, do the Maya fall short of the anthropologists' criteria for determining civilization. They were neolithic, Stone Age people, who did not discover and utilize metals as did their predecessors and contemporaries elsewhere in Europe, Asia, and the Middle East.

On balance, after examining these elements of civilization, we can say that the Classic Maya were the most advanced Precolumbian people and that their culture compared favorably with other cultures in Europe during the Middle Ages. Their recognition as one of the world's great cultures has been delayed by two factors: The first is that their civilization waned and died some seven hundred years before historic times in North America, which has made our acquisition of knowledge about the Maya culture so painfully slow. The second and probably the most significant factor is that the Maya Indian civilization was not a part of what we call Western civilization—it did not contribute directly to the European culture upon which twentieth-century North American civilization is founded.

The Classic Maya were a civilization that should be ranked with the world's great ancient cultures.

Glossary

Abaj Takalik: A Precolumbian site on the south-western slope of the Guatemalan mountains with evidence of a pre-Maya culture.

Altar de Sacrificios: An Early Preclassic site in the Petén area of the Maya lowlands. Evidence of the Xe culture found here.

Alux (pl. *aluxob*): A forest spirit of the Maya lowlands, which appears to be analogous to a leprechaun or dwarflike figure.

Apron moldings: Outward-sloping walls over inset vertical panels.

Autonomous stelae: Freestanding stone shafts (stelae) located independent of pyramid-temples.

Baktun: A period of 400 tuns of 360 days each; a pseudo-Maya term.

Basal platform: A raised, horizontal flat surface that acts as an architectural base.

Batter: The sloping face of a wall when viewed in cross section. A wall with inverted taper, thicker at the top than at the bottom, has negative batter.

Bearing wall: A material layer, usually of masonry construction, which encloses space and carries the thrust of the roof load to the ground or substructure.

Becan: A Preclassic lowlands site located in Campeche, Mexico. The site was surrounded by a moat.

Calendar Round: The 52-year period which must pass before a day of the 260-day cycle will recur on the same day of the month.

Capital: The uppermost member of a column; it serves as a transition from the shaft to the lintel.

Capstone: A capping stone.

Cerros: A recently excavated Preclassic and Protoclassic Maya site located in northern Belize.

Chaac (Chac): Maya god of rain.

Chichén Itzá: A Maya and Mexicanized Maya site located in Yucatán, east of the modern city of Mérida.

Classic period: Maya history from A.D. 250 to 900.

Copán River: A river which begins in northern Honduras and flows northward and joins the Montagua River in Guatemala.

Corbel: A projecting wall member used as support for an element of the superstructure.

Corbel (Corbeled) vault: A masonry projection supported by corbels and frequently connected to form a vault.

Cornice: A projection that crowns a building or wall.

Cross vault: A vault formed by the intersection of two or more simple vaults.

Cuello: A recently excavated Preclassic and Classic Maya site located in northern Belize. Excavations show continuous occupation from 2500 B.C.

Cycle: (a) An older term for what is now usually called a baktun; (b) any of the many reentering series of Maya calendrical-religious phenomena, particularly the 52-year period.

Dresden Codex: One of the three surviving Maya codices.

Dzibilchaltún: A Preclassic Maya site located north of Mérida in Yucatán, Mexico.

El Baul: A site on the Pacific littoral of Guatemala. Stela I (A.D. 36) at El Baul is the earliest dated monument in the Maya area proper. A Long Count of 7.19.15.7.12.

Emblem glyph: A glyph that is typical for a particular place and represents some local phenomenon, perhaps a place name.

Engaged pilasters: Partly embedded or bonded upright rectangular piers.

Facade: Usually the front of a building; also the other sides when they are emphasized architecturally.

Facade mask: A carved head or face used as ornament on the front of a building.

Frieze: A sculptured or ornamental band.

Full-figure variant: An elaborately carved glyphic representation of a number, god, or animal.

Glyph: A carved figure or character, incised or in relief; a hieroglyph.

Glyph block: A physical division of an inscription, usually containing one or two main signs and one or more affixes; a column of glyphs.

God K: Also known as GII of the Palenque Triad of Gods. He is associated with rulership. A principal identifying feature is a flare in his forehead.

GMT (Goodman-Martinez/Hernandez-Thompson correlation): A system of correlating the Maya calendar with the Gregorian calendar. It is also referred to as the "11.16" correlation in which A = 584,283.

Group E Complex: An architectural assemblage, which takes its name from Group E at Uaxactún, designed for celebration of solstices and of other astronomical events.

Haab: A Maya term for "year," applied normally to the period of 365 days, but also sometimes to the "year" of 360 days.

Head variant: A glyph that shows the head of an animal or deity; an elaborate form of a simpler glyph.

Hero Twins: Hunahpú and Xbalanqué, who overcome the lords of the underworld in the *Popul Vuh.*

Hieroglyph: A picture writing character.

Hunahpú: One of the Hero Twins of the *Popol Vuh* who overcame the lords of death in the underworld, Xibalba.

Ideograph: A written symbol for a word that conveys the idea intended, rather than the sound.

Initial Series: A Classic Maya method (also called Long Count) for dating events by the day-count from a starting point. Identified by its initial position in longer inscriptions. Each digit is vigesimal rather than decimal: in a date transcribed 9.6.10.0.0, the first digit states 9 cycles of 400 years (each having 20 periods of 20 years) have elapsed, followed by 6 20-year periods or katuns, 10 tuns or years of 360 days each, 0 uinals or months of 20 days each, and 0 kins or days. The total enumerates the days which have elapsed since the starting point; the Maya equivalent of August 11, 3114 B.C.

Initial Series Introducing Glyph: A large compound glyph, often written across two glyph columns, containing a variable central element, which is apparently the name of the deity presiding over the month in which the Initial Series date fell.

Izapa: A Precolumbian site located near Tapachula, Mexico; a pre-Maya culture.

Kaminaljuyú: A Precolumbian site, the ruins of which are found in the suburbs of Guatemala City; a Late Preclassic culture.

Katun: A period of twenty tuns.

Kin: A day.

Lintel: A beam used to span an opening.

Loltun cave: A site in the Puuc hills south of Mérida, Yucatán, Mexico, with pottery dating back to 2000 B.C.

Long Count: An interval which may be expressed in days elapsed from the base date of the Maya era, August 11, 3114 B.C.

Madrid Codex: One of the four surviving Maya books.

Maya era: The count of time elapsed from a base date 4 Ahau 8 Cumku, about 3,600 years in the past, when Maya inscriptions became common.

The Maya occasionally counted from other base dates, but this is by far the most common base.

Maya highlands: Generally the Pacific Slope and the mountain chain of Guatemala, northern Honduras, and northern El Salvador.

Maya lowlands: An area consisting of Yucatán, Campeche, Quintana Roo, Tabasco, and Chiapas in Mexico; Belize; and Petén in Guatemala.

Mayapán: A Postclassic Maya site in Yucatán.

Medial moldings: An architectural term referring to a middle molding or break in the facade of a building.

Mesoamerica: The area where civilizations arose in Mexico and Central America. The culture area of Mesoamerica is defined geographically by the presence or absence of a series of culture traits, which are specifically characteristic of Mesoamerican cultures. Generally, it is the area from the Valley of Mexico to Honduras.

Milpa: A small burned clearing planted and abandoned after a few seasons.

Molding: A continuous narrow surface, either projecting or recessed, plain or ornamented, whose purpose is to break up a surface, to accent, or to decorate by means of the light and dark it produces; as in cornice molding, which is the topmost molding; and medial molding, which is the second or middle molding that marks the roof edge.

Motagua River: A river in Guatemala beginning in the mountains near Guatemala City and flowing northeastward to the Gulf of Honduras.

Ocós: An early Preclassic (about 1500 B.C.) site located on the Pacific littoral of Guatemala; probably not Maya-speaking. A ceramic horizon or phase.

Olmec: The earliest Precolumbian civilization, which was located in the present Mexican state of Veracruz at San Lorenzo and La Venta between 1200 and 400 B.C. Best known for the huge stone heads.

Oratory: Place of worship, especially a small room set apart for private devotions.

Palenque: A Classic Maya site located in Chiapas, Mexico, southeast of Villahermosa.

Paris Codex: A surviving Maya book.

Petén: An area of lowlands in northeast Guatemala.

Pier: A vertical, unattached masonry support.

Plinth: The lowest member of a base; also, a block serving as a base.

Popol Vuh: Sixteenth-century Quiché Maya book of Maya myths.

Post-and-lintel construction: Architectural technique based upon vertical pillars or posts spanned by horizontal lintels.

Postclassic period: The era of Maya culture that followed the Classic period, the evidence of which is found primarily in the Yucatán area. Maya history from A.D. 900 to 1540.

Preclassic period: Maya history from 2500 B.C. to A.D. 250.

Quetzal: Central American bird of brilliant plumage.

Río de la Pasión: A river in the western Petén of Guatemala which flows northwestward into the Usamacinta River.

Roof comb: A structure placed on the roof of a building, which resembles the comb of a cock, very often of open work.

Rubble: Rough, broken stones used in filling courses of walls.

Sacbe (pl. sacbeob): Maya raised artificial road.

Seibal: An early Preclassic site in the Petén area of the Maya lowlands.

Short Count: The series of thirteen different katun endings by which the later Yucatec Maya dated events within a range of 260 tuns.

Standard ceremonial assemblage: A central temple-pyramid facing south, flanked by two temple-pyramids, one on each side, constructed on a platform with an entrance on the south.

Stela (pl. stelae): A freestanding stone monument, usually sculpted.

Substructure: Undercarriage; groundwork.

Talud-tablero: A Classic Teotihuacán architectural feature composed of a rectangular panel (tablero) cantilevered over a sloping wall (talud).

Teotihuacán: Nahautl, meaning "The City of the Gods," a Precolumbian city located in the Valley of Mexico some thirty-three miles north of modern Mexico City. It was the center of Mexican culture, beginning about 400 B.C. From early in the Christian era to A.D. 650 when it was destroyed, Teotihuacán was the largest and most important Precolumbian city in central Mexico.

Terrace: A raised, open platform usually with steeply sloping sides.

Tun: Maya term for "year," usually applied to the period of 360 days, but sometimes applied to the period of 365 days.

Tzolkin: 260-day cycle.

Uaxactún: A Maya Petén site located north of Tikal.

Uinal: The Maya "month" of twenty days.

Usumacinta River: A river which flows generally northwestward and marks the western boundary of the Petén in Guatemala and Chiapas in Mexico.

Variant glyph: Usually a more complicated version of a simpler glyph.

Vault: An arched structure of masonry, usually forming a ceiling or roof.

Vaulted portal: Opening or doorway leading into a vaulted or arched passageway.

Xbalanqué: One of the Hero Twins of the *Popol Vuh* who overcame the lords of death in the underworld, Xibalba.

Xibalba: Maya underworld.

Appendix 1
Key to Pronunciation

Maya pronunciation of vowels as in Spanish:*
a, between that of *rat* and *rather*; *e*, between that in *pet* and *prey*, but short; *i* as *ee* in greed; *o* as in *on*; *u* like our *oo* in *boo*, but pronounced as *w* before another vowel.

Consonants as in English except that *c* is always hard; *x* as *sh*, so *uix* is pronounced *weesh*. *Qu* is pronounced like *k* before *e* and *i*; consonants followed by an apostrophe are pronounced with a quick closing of the glottis, somewhat as in military commands—*shun* for *attention*. Final *e* is always pronounced.

Examples	
Ahau	Å-how
Uo	Wō
Pax	Pŏsh
Xoc	Shōk
Cauac	Kå wák
Xbalenqué	Sh balan-kay
Hunahpú	Hoón åh póo

---

*From J. Eric S. Thompson, *The Rise and Fall of Maya Civilization* (Norman, 1954, 1966), xv. Printed by permission of the University of Oklahoma Press.

Appendix 2
Tikal Chronology

Gregorian Date	Maya Long Count	Period	Ceramic Complex	Ceramic Horizon	Event
August 11 3114 B.C.	13.0.0.0.0 4 Ahau 8 Cumku				Mythical date the Maya established for computation of time
2000 B.C.		Early Preclassic			Beginning of the Maya Preclassic Period
1000 B.C.		Middle Preclassic		Mamon	Developed ceramics, neckless jars and curved vessels. Early trade in obsidian and quartzite
600 B.C.			Eb		Beginnings of Tikal architecture on ridges between swamps. Flint tools. Possible sub-structure of Lost World Pyramid

continued

Gregorian Date	Maya Long Count	Period	Ceramic Complex	Ceramic Horizon	Event
500 B.C.			Tzec		Buildings and platforms constructed. Substantial population at Tikal. Pits in bedrock on North Acropolis
300 B.C.		Late Preclassic		Chicanel	
200 B.C.			Chuen		Ceremonial architecture. North Acropolis construction begun. Corbeled vault developed
100 B.C.			Cauac		North Acropolis was a 75-by-90-foot platform with a stairway entrance. At Tikal there were platforms and temples with stuccoed facades and masks. Vaulted tombs, apron moldings, and construction in the Plaza of Seven Temples
50 B.C.		Proto Classic			Large temples and tombs. Polychrome stucco. Plaza of Seven Temples raised 12 feet. Lost World Pyramid constructed with stairways and masks.
A.D. 1					
A.D. 150			Cimi		Polychrome pottery made and traded
A.D. 250		Early Classic	Manik	Tzakol	Beginning of the Classic Period. Vaulted temple architecture.
A.D. 292	8.12.14.8.15 13 Men 2 Zip				Stela 29. Earliest known Tikal stela (Tikal Museum)
A.D. 320	8.14.3.1.12				Leiden Plaque. Possible accession date of Jaguar Paw
A.D. 379	8.17.2.16.17				Accession date of Curl Nose. Replaced the Jaguar Paw family dynasty. May have been non-Mayan. (Stelae 4 and 18) Appearance of Teotihuacán motif

Gregorian Date	Maya Long Count	Period	Ceramic Complex	Ceramic Horizon	Event
A.D. 426	8.19.10.0.0				Accession of Stormy Sky, great early king of Tikal (Stelae 1, 2, 28, 31)
December 10 A.D. 435	9.0.0.0.0				Beginning of ninth Baktun
A.D. 455	9.0.10.0.0				Date of Stela 31 (Tikal Museum)
A.D. 457	9.1.1.10.10				Death of Stormy Sky
A.D. 475		Middle Classic		Tepeu	Reign of Kan Chitam. End of Early Classic (Stelae 9, 13)
A.D. 488					Reign of Jaguar Paw Skull (Stelae 3, 7)
A.D. 497					Reign of Bird Claw (Stela 8)?
A.D. 528					Reign of Curl Head (Stelae 10, 12)
A.D. 593	9.8.0.0.0		Ik		
		Late Classic			End of Middle Classic
A.D. 682	9.12.9.17.16		Imix		Accession of Ah Cacaw (Ruler A). Construction of Temple I and Temple II. Beginning of the Late Classic period and the final period of prosperity and population expansion (Stela 16)
A.D. 734	9.15.3.6.8				Accession of Ruler B, son of Ah Cacaw, builder of Temple IV and Temple of the Inscriptions (Stelae 5, 20, 21)
A.D. 768	9.16.17.16.4				Accession of Chitam (Ruler C), son of Ruler B. Constructed the roof combs on the Temple of the Inscriptions (Stela 19, 22)
A.D. 810	9.19.0.0.0				Stela 24 erected in front of Temple III, Last Temple constructed
A.D. 830	10.0.0.0.0				Beginning of tenth Baktun. End of 4,000 year calendar

continued

Gregorian Date	Maya Long Count	Period	Ceramic Complex	Ceramic Horizon	Event
A.D. 869	10.2.0.0.0		Eznab		Stela 11 (Great Plaza), last known stela erected
A.D. 900		Postclassic			End of Classic period
A.D. 928	10.5.0.0.0				Tikal probably abandoned
			Caban		

Appendix 3
Cameras, Film, and Aerial Photographs

This volume contains approximately 275 color photographs selected from some 3,200 pictures taken by the authors at Tikal, Copán, and Quiriguá.

In taking these photographs we used three cameras, a Nikon F-2 with MD-2 motor drive, a Nikkormat, and a Hasselblad 2000 FC with an HC-4 Prism eye-level viewfinder. On the Nikon F-2, we used a Nikkor-S Auto 35mm f/2.8 lens, a Zoom Nikkor Auto 43—86mm f/3.5 lens, and a Nikkor Q Auto 135mm f/2.8 lens; on the Nikkormat, a Zoom Nikkor 43—86mm f/3.5 lens; and on the Hasselblad, a Zeis Planar 80mm f/2.8 lens. Since haze is almost always a problem in the tropics, we used a haze filter on all shots. The filters used were Vivitar Skylight (1A), Rolev M.G. UV, and a Nikor L37 haze filter with the Nikkor lenses, and a haze filter with the Hasselblad.

For film, we used primarily Kodacolor II with an ASA rating of 100. We chose this film because its color fidelity is quite good, and it is very tolerant of higher temperatures. On many occasions, and for extended periods of time, we had no facilities to maintain our film at proper temperature. We did use other film also. The photographs of the interior of the Five-Story Palace and Lintel 2 on Temple III at Tikal, for example, were made with Kodacolor 400, with an ASA 400 rating.

We recognize that some people feel they achieve better results with transparencies than with color negative film. In our opinion, however, the color negative film was more suitable for our objective of obtaining photographs in which the colors were rendered as naturally and as faithfully as possible.

All of the color photographs in this book were

printed by Color Central of Wichita, Kansas, who, we believe, achieved an excellent color balance to portray the subject realistically. Some manipulation in the printing process was necessary to bring out the detail of the stone carvings on buildings and stelae. We had some success in using flash to produce "artificial sunlight" on the shady side of a stela, while still retaining a properly exposed background; however, at times, both the sun and the flash seemed perversely determined to wash out the detail on the stone. By using "burning" and "dodging" during printmaking, Color Central was able to bring out details of iconography and glyphs that otherwise would have been lost.

All of our exposed film was sent to Eastman Kodak for processing of negatives and printing of their standard 120 film 3S print (approx. $3^{1}/_{4}$ × $3^{1}/_{4}$ inches) and 35mm film 3R print (approx. $3^{1}/_{2}$ × 5 inches). We used these standard prints as proofs. We identified and catalogued each print with its negative, and filed the negatives and prints in albums. For our first book, *Maya Ruins of Mexico in Color* (1977), we used contact prints for the initial sorting. This system was good for picture organization, but identification of the subject and the quality of each shot was more difficult to ascertain, since each roll of 35mm film was printed on one sheet, producing negative-size prints. Using that system, we wasted a greater number of enlargements than we did when working with the "tourist-size" prints.

Since we traveled exclusively in relatively small single-engine aircraft, both space and weight were at a premium, and tripods were left at home. Therefore, all the pictures were taken with the cameras hand-held, with the not unexpected result that some of the shots showed some fuzziness from camera movement, particularly when enlarged to a satisfactory size. Camera movement seemed to have appeared more often with the Hasselblad than with the Nikons, possibly because it is a heavier camera. We salve our consciences with the thought that with a small and lightweight tripod, the camera movement would probably have been just as bad, if not worse.

To obtain photographs of the proper aspects of the various structures and monuments at the several sites, it was necessary to visit each site several times and at different times of the year. Copán, for instance, has an entirely different appearance in winter when it is dry than it does in the summer when vegetation is lush and green. The seasons are important for another reason. As the sun moves from solstice to solstice, the light on the monuments changes radically; there is an optimal time of year for photographing each stela and each facade. The Maya built summer and winter temples with the sun position in mind. One must also make use of both morning and afternoon light.

Photographing these sites from the air provides another useful and pleasing viewpoint. Before setting out to take aerial photographs, we secured permission from the governments of Guatemala and Honduras. Producing sharp aerial photographs with a handheld camera is difficult. Good sunshine is an absolute must, yet a clear day is unusual in Guatemala and Honduras. Generally clouds are scattered or in broken layers. On the ground, clouds are no problem; the wait until the sun breaks out is usually short. But in the air, clouds can be a real problem. Just as the plane is brought into position to shoot, a cloud may cover a portion of the ruins, making it necessary to fly around and make a new approach when the sun is out again.

We used two airplanes, a Beechcraft Bonanza S35, and a Cessna 185A. The Bonanza was modified to provide a vent opening in the glass on the passenger side, so that we could shoot from both the pilot seat and the passenger seat. The Cessna is easier to photograph from, as it is a highwing plane, and the wind will hold the vent windows open when the stops have been removed. These openings are necessary because it is impossible to shoot a usable aerial photo through the glass.

We also made another modification, providing auxiliary fuel tanks on both airplanes to give us at least seven hours of maximum power cruise. This extra time is necessary for two reasons. Sometimes there is no fuel available at a scheduled refueling point—you never know until you land there. And in Guatemala, so far as we were able to determine, the only fuel available is at

Guatemala City, so it is necessary to carry enough fuel to make the aerial tour and return to Guatemala City without refueling.

There are some points to remember in taking aerial photographs. Since all shots are made at infinity, depth of field is no problem, so a relatively large lens opening with the camera set at the highest shutter speed available is suggested. We set the Nikkormat at 1/1000 of a second and the Nikon and Hasselblad at 1/2000 or 1/1500 of a second and opened the aperture to accommodate that setting. The light is bright in the tropics, so generally an f/3.5 or smaller lens opening is adequate. The fast shutter speed is necessary to counteract the vibration and movement of the airplane.

We took oblique aerial views. We tried to place the airplane in a position that would correspond to a tower of sufficient height and in the proper location to photograph the area or a particular building. We regulate what is to be included in the picture by a variation in the altitude of the plane, not by using a telescopic lens. We are both pilots, so that on one run the photographs were taken from the passenger's side and on the next from the pilot's side. At first, we would slow the plane down to just above a stall—with the Bonanza we lowered the wheels and put down the flaps—but we later found that this was no advantage. Even at ordinary airspeeds, the Nikon with the motor drive set for single exposures can expose fifteen to twenty frames in a single pass. In fact, the planes at low airspeed seem to vibrate more, so the slower speeds were counterproductive.

Appendix 4
Chronological Table

Dates	Periods	Maya Long Count (approximate)
A.D. 1530		11.15.10.0.0
	Postclassic	
A.D. 900		10.3.10.0.0
	Late Classic	
A.D. 680		9.12.10.0.0
	Middle Classic	
A.D. 475		9.2.0.0.0
	Early Classic	
A.D. 250		8.10.10.0.0.
	Protoclassic	
A.D. 50		8.0.10.0.0
A.D./B.C.		
	Late Preclassic	
300 B.C.		
	Middle Preclassic	
1000 B.C.		
	Early Preclassic	
2500 B.C.		

Bibliography

Adams, R. E. W.
1977a *The Origins of Maya Civilization* (ed.). Albuquerque: University of New Mexico Press.
1977b *Prehistoric America*. Boston: Little Brown and Company.
1980 "Swamps, Canals, and the Location of Ancient Maya Cities," *American Antiquity* 54: 206

1982 "Ancient Maya Canals: Grids and Lattices in the Maya Jungle." *Archaeology* 35 (6): 28-35.

Adams, R. E. W., W. E. Brown, Jr., and T. Patrick Culbert
1981 *Radar Mapping, Archaeology, and Ancient Land Use in the Maya Lowlands*. Pasadena: California Institute of Technology.

Adams, R. E. W., and W. D. Smith
1981 "Feudal Models for Classic Maya Civilization." In *Lowland Maya Settlement Patterns*, edited by Wendy Ashmore. Albuquerque: University of New Mexico Press.

Adams, R. E. W., and T. Patrick Culbert
1977 "The Origins of Civilization in the Maya Lowlands." In *The Origins of Maya Civilization*, edited by R. E. W. Adams. Albuquerque: University of New Mexico Press.

Andrews, George F.
1975 *Maya Cities: Placemaking and Urbanization*. Norman: University of Oklahoma Press.

Ashmore, Wendy, and Robert J. Sharer
1978 "Excavations at Quiriguá, Guatemala: The Ascent of an Elite Maya Center." *Archaeology* 31 (6): 10-19.

Baudez, Claude F.
1980 Unpublished report on recent archaeological work at Copán.
1983 "The Sun Kings of Copan and Quirigua," paper presented at the Quinta Mesa Redonda de Palenque, Palenque, Mexico.

Bove, Frederick J.
1981 "Trend Surface Analysis and the Lowland Classic Maya Collapse." *American Antiquity* 46: 93–112.

Carr, Robert F., and James E. Hazard
1961 Tikal Report No. 11: Map of the Ruins of Tikal, Guatemala. University Museum Monographs, Philadelphia: University of Pennsylvania.

Chase, Diane Z.
1981 "The Maya Postclassic at Santa Rita Corozal." *Archaeology* 34 (1): 25–33.

Childe, V. Gordon
1950 "The Urban Revolution." *Town Planning Review* 21: 3–17.

Clancy, Flora
n.d. Unpublished Ph.D. thesis. Yale University.

Coe, Michael D.
1968 *America's First Civilization*. New York: American Heritage.
1973 *The Maya Scribe and His World*. New York: Grolier Club.
1975 *Classic Maya Pottery at Dumbarton Oaks*, Washington, D. C.: Dumbarton Oaks.
1977 "Olmec and Maya: A Study in Relationships." In *The Origins of Maya Civilization*, edited by R. E. W. Adams. Albuquerque: University of New Mexico Press.
1978 *Lords of the Underworld: Masterpieces of Classic Maya Ceramics*. Princeton, N. J.: Princeton University Press.
1980 *The Maya*. London: Thames and Hudson.
1982 *Old Gods and Young Heroes*. Jerusalem: Israel Museum.

Coe, William R.
1965 "Tikal: Ten Years of Study of a Maya Ruin in the Lowlands of Guatemala." *Expedition* 8 (1): 5–56.
1967 *Tikal, A Handbook of the Ancient Maya Ruins*. Philadelphia: University Museum of the University of Pennsylvania.

Coggins, Clemency
1975 "Painting and Drawing Styles at Tikal." Ph.D. diss., Harvard University.
1976 "Pattern and Process in the Maya Middle Classic Period," paper presented at the Seventy-fifth Annual Meeting of the American Anthropological Association, Washington, D.C.
1979a "A New Order and the Rule of the Calendar: Some Characteristics of the Middle Classic Period at Tikal." In *Maya Archaeology and Ethnohistory*, edited by Norman Hammond and Gordon R. Willey. Austin: University of Texas Press.
1979b "Teotihuacán at Tikal in the Early Classic Period." *Actes du XLIIe Congres International des Americanistes* (Paris 1976) 8: 251-69.

1980 "The Shape of Time: Some Political Implications of a Four-Part Figure," *American Antiquity* 45: 727.

Cohodas, Marvin
1978 "Some Unusual Aspects of Cross Group Symbolism." In *Tercera Mesa Redonda de Palenque*, vol. 4, edited by Merle Green Robertson and D. C. Jeffers. Monterey, Calif.: Herald Printers.
1980 Public Architecture of the Maya Lowlands.

Culbert, T. Patrick
1974 *The Lost Civilization: The Story of the Classic Maya*. New York: Harper and Row.
1977 "Early Maya Development at Tikal, Guatemala." In *The Origins of Maya Civilization*, edited by R. E. W. Adams. Albuquerque: University of New Mexico Press.

Dütting, Dieter
1978 "Birth, Inauguration and Death in the Inscriptions of Palenque, Chiapas, Mexico." In *Tercera Mesa Redonda de Palenque*, vol. 4, edited by Merle Green Robertson and D. C. Jeffers. Monterey, Calif.: Herald Printers.

Edmonson, Munro S.
1971 *The Book of Counsel: The Popol Vuh of the Quiché Maya of Guatemala*. Middle American Research Institute Publication 35. New Orleans: Tulane University.

Ferguson, William M., and John Q. Royce
1977 *Maya Ruins of Mexico in Color*. Norman: University of Oklahoma Press.

Freidel, David A.
1979 "Culture Areas and Interaction Spheres: Contrasting Approaches to the Emergence of Civilization in the Maya Lowlands." *American Antiquity* 44(1).
1981 "The Political Economics of Residential Dispersion Among the Lowland Maya." In *Lowland Maya Settlement Patterns*, edited by Wendy Ashmore. Albuquerque: University of New Mexico Press.

Freidel, David, Robin Robertson, and Maynard B. Cliff
1982 "The Maya City of Cerros." *Archaeology* 35 (4): 12–21.

Freidel, David A., and Linda Schele
1982 "Symbol and Power: A History of the Lowland Maya Cosmograph," paper presented at the Conference on the Origins and Evolution of Classic Maya Iconography, Princeton, New Jersey.

Furst, Peter T., and Michael D. Coe
1977 "Ritual Enemas." *Natural History* 86 (3): 88–91.

378

Gendrop, Paul
1974 "Consideraciones Sobre la Arquitectura de Palenque." In *Primera Mesa Redonda de Palenque*, Part 2, edited by Merle Greene Robertson. Pebble Beach, Calif.: Robert Louis Stevenson School.

Graham, John A. (ed.)
1981 *Ancient Mesocamerica*. Palo Alto: Peek Publications.

Greene, Merle, Robert L. Rands, and John A. Graham
1972 *Maya Sculpture from the Southern Lowlands, the Highlands and Pacific Piedmont, Guatemala, Mexico, Honduras*, Berkeley, Calif.: Lederer, Street and Zeus.

Hamblin, Robert L., and Brian L. Pitcher
1980 "The Classic Maya, Collapse: Testing Class Conflict Hypotheses." *American Antiquity* 45: 246.

Hammond, Norman
1977a "The Earliest Maya." *Scientific American* 236 (3). 116–33.
1977b "Ex Oriente Lux: A View from Belize." In *The Origins of Maya Civilization*, edited by R. E. W. Adams. Albuquerque: University of New Mexico Press.
1982a *Ancient Maya Civilization*. New Brunswick: Rutgers University Press.
1982b "Unearthing the Oldest Known Maya." *National Geographic* 162 (1): 126–40.

Harrison, Peter D.
1970 "Central Acropolis, Tikal, Guatemala. A Preliminary Study of Its Structural Components During the Late Classic Period." Ph.D. diss., University of Pennsylvania.

Hatch, Marion Popenoe
19?? "A Study of Hieroglyphic Texts at the Classic Maya Site of Quiriguá, Guatemala." Ph.D. diss., University of California, Berkeley.

Hellmuth, Nicholas
1976 *Tikal Copán Travel Guide*. Saint Louis: Foundation for Latin American Anthropological Research.
1981 Unpublished manuscript

Heyden, Doris, and Paul Gendrop
1975 *Pre-Colombian Architecture of Mesoamerica*. Translated by Judith Stanton. New York: Harry N. Abrams.

Jones, Christopher
1969 "The Twin-Pyramid Group Pattern: A Classic Maya Architectural Assemblage at Tikal, Guatemala." Ph.D. diss., University of Pennsylvania.
1977 "Inauguration Dates of Three Late Classic Rulers of Tikal, Guatemala." *American Antiquity* 42 (1): 28–60.

Jones, Christopher, and Linton Satterthwaite
1982 "The Monuments and Inscriptions of Tikal: The Carved Monuments," *Tikal Report* No. 33, Part A. Philadelphia: University Museum, University of Pennsylvania.

Joralemon, David
1974 "Ritual Blood-Sacrifice among the Ancient Maya, Part 1." In *Primera Mesa Redonda de Palenque*, vol. 2, edited by Merle Green Robertson. Pebble Beach, Calif.: Robert Louis Stevenson School.

Kelley, David H.
1962 "Glyphic Evidence for a Dynastic Sequence at Quiriguá, Guatemala." *American Antiquity* 27: 323–35.
1976 *Deciphering the Maya Script*. Austin: University of Texas Press.
1980 *Astronomical Identities of Mesoamerican Gods*. Contributions of Mesoamerican Anthropology, Publication 2. Miami: Institute of Maya Studies.

Kubler, George
1975 *The Art and Architecture of Ancient America*. Bungay, England: Chaucer Press.

Leventhal, Richard M.
1981 "Settlement Patterns in the Southeast Maya Area." In *Lowland Maya Settlement Patterns*, edited by Wendy Ashmore. Albuquerque: University of New Mexico Press.

Lowe, Gareth W.
1977 "The Mixe-Zoque as Competing Neighbors of the Early Lowland Maya." In *The Origins of Maya Civilization*, edited by R. E. W. Adams. Albuquerque: University of New Mexico Press.

MacNeish, Richard S., Jeffrey K. Wilkerson, and Antoinette Nelken-Turner
1980 *First Annual Report of the Belize Archaic Archaeological Reconnaissance*. Andover, Mass.: Robert S. Peabody Foundation for Archaeology.

Mathews, Peter
1983 "Palenque's 'Mid-Life' Crises," paper presented at the Quinta Mesa Redonda de Palenque, Palenque, Mexico.

Maudslay, Alfred P.
1889–1902 *Biologia Centrali-Americana*, 5 vols. London: Porter.

Morley, Sylvanus G.
1920 *Inscriptions at Copán*. Carnegie Institution of Washington Publication 219, Washington, D. C.
1935 *Guide Book to the Ruins of Quiriguá*. Carnegie Institution of Washington. Supplementary Publication 16, Washington, D. C.
1956 *The Ancient Maya*, 3rd ed., rev. by George W. Brainerd. Stanford: Stanford University Press.

1975 *An Introduction to the Study of Maya Hieroglyphics.* New York: Dover.

Nuñez Chinchilla, Jesus
1975 *Copán Ruins: Complete Guide of the Great Mayan City.* Translated by Tina Bendana, Elena Isabel Nuñez V., Jerry and Samuel Dickerman. Tegucigalpa:

Pahl, Gary
1976 Film 15,188. Precolumbian Studies Library, University of Texas, Austin Pasztory, Esther 1974 *The Iconography of the Teotihuacán Tlaloc.* Studies in Pre-Columbian Art and Archaeology, No. 15. Dumbarton Oaks, Washington, D. C..

Proskouriakoff, Tatiana
1950 *A Study of Classic Maya Sculpture.* Carnegie Institution of Washington Publication 593, Washington, D. C.
1960 "Historical Implications of a Pattern of Dates at Piedras Negras, Guatemala." *American Antiquity* 25: 454–75.
1963 *An Album of Maya Architecture.* Norman: University of Oklahoma Press.
1968 "The Jog and Jaguar Signs in Maya Writing." *American Antiquity* 33 (2): 247–51.

Quirarte, Jacinto
1977 "Early Art Styles of Mesoamerica and Early Classic Maya Art." In *The Origins of Maya Civilization,* edited by R. E. W. Adams. Albuquerque: University of New Mexico Press.

Recinos, Adrian
1950 *Popol Vuh: The Sacred Book of the Ancient Quiché Maya.* English version by Delia Goetz and S. G. Morley from the translation of Adrian Recinos. Norman: University of Oklahoma Press.

Rice, Don S., and Dennis E. Puleston
1981 "Settlement Patterns in the Petén." In *Lowland Maya Settlement Patterns,* edited by Wendy Ashmore. Albuquerque: University of New Mexico Press.

Robicsek, Francis
1972 *Copán: Home of the Mayan Gods,* New York: Museum of the American Indian, Heye Foundation.

Robiscek, Francis, and Donald M. Hales
1981 *The Maya Book of the Dead: The Ceramic Codex.* Charlottesville: University of Virginia Art Museum.
1982 *Maya Ceramic Vases from the Classic Period: The November Collection of Maya Ceramics.* Charlotte: Maya Publishing Company.

Roys, Ralph L.
1933 *The Book of Chilam Balam of Chumayel.* Carnegie Institution of Washington Publication 438, Washington, D. C.

Sahagún, Bernadin
1956 *General History of the Things of New Spain.* Monographs of the School of American Research, No. 14, Part 9, Santa Fe, N.M.

Schele, Linda
1976 "Accession Iconography of Chan-Bahlum in the Group of the Cross at Palenque." In *The Art, Iconography and Dynastic History of the Segunda Mesa Redonda de Palenque,* part 3, *Proceedings of the Segunda Mesa Redonda de Palenque,* edited by Merle Greene Robertson. Pebble Beach, Calif.: Robert Louis Stevenson School.
1978 "Geneological Documentation on the Tri-figure Panels at Palenque." In *Tercera Mesa Redonda de Palenque,* vol. 4, edited by Merle Greene Robertson and D. C. Jeffers. Monterey, Calif.: Herald Printers.
1983 *The Mirror, the Rabbit and the Bundle: "Accession" Expressions from the Classic Maya Inscriptions.* Studies in Pre-Columbian Art and Architecture, No. 25. Washington, D.C.: Dumbarton Oaks.

Sharer, Robert J.
1978 "Archaeology and History at Quiriguá, Guatemala." *Journal of Field Archaeology* 5 (1): 51– 70.

Spinden, H.
1913 *A Study of Maya Art.* Memoirs of the Peabody Museum, vol. 6. Cambridge, Mass.: Harvard University.

Stephens, John Lloyd
1969 *Incidents of Travel in Central America, Chiapas and Yucatán.* (Unabridged republication of 1841 original edition.) New York: Dover.

Stone, Andrea
1983 "The Cosmological Monster Theme at Quiregua, Guatemala," paper presented at the Quinta Mesa Redonda de Palenque, Palenque, Mexico.

Tate, Carolyn
1980 "The Maya Cauac Monster: Formal Development and Dynastic Context," paper presented at the Cuarto Mesa Redonda de Palenque, Palenque, Mexico.

Thompson, J. Eric S.
1954 *The Rise and Fall of Maya Civilization.* Norman: University of Oklahoma Press.
1962 *A Catalog of Maya Hieroglyphics.* Norman: University of Oklahoma Press.
1970 *Maya History and Religion.* Norman: University of Oklahoma Press.
1972 *A Commentary on the Dresden Codex.* Philadelphia: American Philosophical Society.

Tozzer, Alfred M.
1941 *Landa's Relacion de las Cosas de Yucatán.* Papers of the Peabody Museum of American Archaeology and Ethnology, vol. 18, Cambridge, Mass.: Harvard University.

Turner, B. L., II
1978 "Ancient Agricultural Land Use in the Central Maya Lowlands." In *Pre-Hispanic Maya Agriculture,* edited by Peter D. Harrison and B. L. Turner, II. Albuquerque: University of New Mexico Press.

Willey, Gordon R.
1974 "The Classic Maya Hiatus: A "Rehearsal for the Collapse?" In *Mesoamerican Archaeology: New Approaches,* edited by Norman Hammond. Austin: University of Texas Press.
1977 "The Rise of Maya Civilization: A Summary View." In *The Origins of Maya Civilization,* edited by R. E. W. Adams. Albuquerque. University of New Mexico Press.
1981 "Maya Lowland Settlement Patterns: A Summary View." In *Lowland Maya Settlement Patterns,* edited by Wendy Ashmore. Albuquerque: University of New Mexico Press.

Willey, Gordon R., and Richard M. Leventhal
1979 "Prehistoric Settlement at Copán." In *Maya Archaeology and Ethnohistory,* edited by Norman Hammond and Gordon R. Willey. Austin: University of Texas Press.

Willey, Gordon R., Richard M. Leventhal, and W. L. Fash, Jr.
1978 "Maya Settlement in the Copán Valley." *Archaeology* 31 (4): 32–43.

Willey, Gordon R., and Dimitri Shimkin
1973 "The Classic Maya Collapse: A Summary View." In *The Classic Maya Collapse,* edited by T. Patrick Culbert. Albuquerque: University of New Mexico Press.

Index

Maya Ruins in Central America in Color

Designed by Barbara Jellow
Composed by
the University of New Mexico Printing Plant
in VIP Palatino
Printed by Kingsport Press, Kingsport, Tennessee
on Sterling Litho Dull
Bound by Kingsport Press
in Lexotone and stamped in gold